Reginald Lord Brabazon

Prosperity or pauperism?

Physical, Industrial, and Technical Training

Reginald Lord Brabazon

Prosperity or pauperism?
Physical, Industrial, and Technical Training

ISBN/EAN: 9783743465053

Manufactured in Europe, USA, Canada, Australia, Japa

Cover: Foto ©Lupo / pixelio.de

Manufactured and distributed by brebook publishing software (www.brebook.com)

Reginald Lord Brabazon

Prosperity or pauperism?

PROSPERITY or PAUPERISM?

PHYSICAL, INDUSTRIAL, AND

TECHNICAL TRAINING.

EDITED BY

THE EARL OF MEATH,

(LORD BRABAZON.)

LONDON:
LONGMANS, GREEN, AND CO.
AND NEW YORK: 15 EAST 16th STREET.
1888.

All rights reserved.

PREFACE.

As I believe that many of our social evils would, in a great measure, be removed, if an improvement were to be effected in our national system of education by the inclusion in the Government Code of physical, technical, and industrial training, I have thought that I might, perhaps, in some small degree hasten this much-to-be-desired reform by republishing in a cheap and popular shape some of the more recent expressions of opinion in support of this view. Hence the appearance of this book. I trust it may somewhat assist towards the formation of a public opinion which, within no distant period, shall insist upon alterations being made in the national code of education, so that our young men and maidens may start in life with healthy bodies, with a knowledge of *things* as well as of books, with the power of using their *hands* as well as their heads, and of making the most of small resources.

If some such reforms, as are advocated in these pages, were effected, the future generation, furnished with the means of leading industrious, prosperous, and happy lives, would find itself in a much superior position to the present, which, being nourished mainly on intellectual food, finds its body starved and its hands paralysed.

MEATH.

83 LANCASTER GATE. W : *January*, 1888.

CONTENTS.

I. PHYSICAL AND INDUSTRIAL TRAINING.

	PAGE
HEALTH AND PHYSIQUE OF OUR CITY POPULATIONS. By the Earl of Meath	1
OPEN SPACES AND PHYSICAL EDUCATION. By the Earl of Meath	13
THE HALF-TIME SYSTEM OF PHYSICAL AND INDUSTRIAL TRAINING. By Edwin Chadwick	23
PHYSICAL TRAINING IN ELEMENTARY SCHOOLS. By Charles F. Bearsley	27
GYMNASTIC INSTRUCTION IN BOARD SCHOOL PLAYGROUNDS. By W. Bousfield	32
MANUAL INSTRUCTION. By Sir John Lubbock	35
NOTES ON THE COST OF MANUAL TRAINING IN THE PUBLIC ELEMENTARY SCHOOLS OF LONDON. By Edric Bayley	47
ARE WE DECAYING? Article from the 'Scotsman'	52
PHYSICAL TRAINING. Address by the Earl of Meath	56

II. INDUSTRIAL AND TECHNICAL TRAINING.

THE INDUSTRIAL TRAINING OF DESTITUTE CHILDREN. By Samuel Smith, M.P.	63
THE NEED OF TRADE SCHOOLS. By Richard T. Auchmuty	78
MANUAL TRAINING IN SCHOOL EDUCATION. By Sir Philip Magnus	92

CONTENTS

	PAGE
TECHNICAL EDUCATION. *By H. Cunynghame*	105
EDUCATIONAL REFORMS. *Article from the 'Times'*	116
EDUCATION AS IT IS AND AS IT OUGHT TO BE. *W. Fowler's Letter to 'Times'*	120
TECHNICAL AND TRADE INSTRUCTION. *Speech by the Marquis of Hartington*	121
THE ORGANISATION OF INDUSTRIAL EDUCATION. *By Professor Huxley*	125
TECHNICAL AND COMMERCIAL EDUCATION. DEPUTATION TO GOVERNMENT ON	128
SLÖJD. *By Evelyn Chapman*	131
INDUSTRIAL TRAINING IN ELEMENTARY SCHOOLS. *Letter to 'Times' (Earl of Meath)*	143
FOR LACK OF KNOWLEDGE. *Letter to 'Daily News' (Lady Leigh)*	147
A PLEA FOR INDUSTRIAL TRAINING FOR GIRLS. *By R. L.*	149
INDUSTRIAL TRAINING FOR GIRLS. *By Miss Headdon*	157
COOKERY IN ELEMENTARY SCHOOLS. *By Miss F. L. Calder*	161
TECHNICAL INSTRUCTION. *By Samuel Smith*	171
A NATIONAL NECESSITY. *By Edward J. Watherston*	179
TECHNICAL EDUCATION IN ELEMENTARY SCHOOLS: THE FORM IT SHOULD TAKE. *By Edward J. Watherston*	198
TECHNICAL EDUCATION (REPORT OF ROYAL COMMISSION). *By F. C. Montague, with Preface by Sir Bernhard Samuelson, Bart., M.P.*	210
INDUSTRIAL ART IN SCHOOLS. *By Charles G. Leland*	277
EDUCATION, EMIGRATION, AND COLONISATION. *By John Bellows*	318
EDUCATION IN GERMANY. *Letter to 'Times' (Samuel Smith)*	328
EVENING SCHOOLS UNDER HEALTHY CONDITIONS. *By the Rev. J. B. Paton, D.D.*	333

PHYSICAL, INDUSTRIAL, AND TECHNICAL TRAINING.

I. PHYSICAL AND INDUSTRIAL TRAINING.

HEALTH AND PHYSIQUE OF OUR CITY POPULATIONS.[1]

BY THE EARL OF MEATH.

THE self-complacency of John Bull is proverbial; it is extremely difficult to persuade him that there is any quality in which he is inferior to those born on other soils than that of Britain, and if there is one quality more than another upon which he prides himself, it is his physical superiority to the men of other nations. Has he not over and over again, it is said, given proofs of such superior excellence, from Cressy and Agincourt to Waterloo and Inkermann? Did not the strong right arms and unerring aim of British bowmen scatter the chivalry of France in those victories of the fourteenth and fifteenth centuries? and has not the same story been repeated under different forms throughout successive ages? Were not the finest cuirassiers of France driven like chaff before the wind when they came in contact with the superior weight and strength of the Life Guards at Waterloo? and is it not acknowledged that at Inkermann our little handful of men, overwhelmed by numbers, must have been swept into the sea had it not been for the individual dogged courage and physical strength of the British soldiery, who, with their usual obstinacy, knew not when they were beaten, and snatched a victory, when by all the recognised rules of war they ought to have been annihilated?

[1] Reprinted, by permission, from the *Nineteenth Century*, July 1881.

National pride within certain limits is useful. It produces self-confidence, which is as indispensable to a nation as it is to an army. A people which has lost faith in itself is doomed, but wise men, whilst fostering a healthy national self-respect, will see that it is founded on solid foundations; that the reputed superiority is real; that it is not a dream of the past, nor the vain imaginings of dwellers in a fool's paradise. It is well that all matters should be brought to the test of truth, the question of 'physique' not less than others of apparently greater importance, and indeed this is a question not unworthy of serious consideration. Let it not be thought that it is a matter of indifference whether the average breadth of chest or height of Englishmen varies an inch or so one way or the other. National physique depends upon national health, and health is as necessary to the happiness and prosperity of a nation as it is to an individual. *Mens sana in corpore sano* may be said of the aggregate as of the unit.

Is it then a fact that we English are physically stronger than our neighbours? and if so, are the conditions of life of the mass of our population such as will conduce to the maintenance of this superiority?

Injured patriotism will assuredly ask whether the records of athletic sports do not plainly show that not only is the Anglo-Saxon race pre-eminent in the achievement of feats of agility and strength, but that even our own ancestors were unable to reach the pitch of perfection in athletic sports which has been since attained by their sons. It will be asked whether it was not left to the men and even to the women of the nineteenth century, and mainly to those of English race, to overcome the difficulties of ice and snow, crag and precipice, and to scale those virgin mountain heights previously untrodden by the foot of man. We shall be told that to raise such a question when a Whymper has but just returned from his victorious campaigns amongst the giants of the Andes, a man to whom it was but an ordinary morning's task 'to wipe off,' as he himself most unreverentially expresses it, some mountain Titan which never before, since the foundation of the world, had been forced to acknowledge the supremacy of man; at such a moment of all others to come forward and express a doubt on the physical capabilities of Englishmen, argues an ignorance of facts which, to say the least, is unpardonable. The sailor might with justice take up the parable and point to the glorious victories of British pluck and endurance in the icy regions of the North, where cold, darkness, hunger, and disease are the daily portions of those adventurous spirits who, for the sake of carrying the British flag further north than that of any other nation, have cheerfully undergone these hardships, and consider it an honour to be allowed the privilege of partaking in them. Are these men, it may be argued, in any way inferior to their predecessors? Would not Drake, Anson, or Nelson be proud to command such men? and would they not consider them quite equal, if not superior, to those brave sea-dogs who, in their days, caused the name of England to be feared throughout the four quarters of the globe? Nor need the traveller be silent. The names of Livingstone, Burton, Speke, Cameron, Stuart, Warburton, and many others, speak to the enterprise and daring of men of English blood. They have performed feats of endurance under tropical skies which ofttimes have proved beyond the physical powers of their native followers, men born and bred in the countries they traversed, inured to their climates, and who had never been exposed to the alleged deleterious influences of civilisation and of city life. All this is indeed true, and many more instances of strength of body and of undaunted courage may be brought forward to controvert any rash theory of national physical deterioration. Almost all Englishmen are naturally fond of country pursuits and of athletic sports. The number of the well-to-do has vastly increased since the commencement of this century; means of rapid locomotion permit of large classes living in the country which formerly were forced to reside permanently in towns; and thus it happens that athletic pursuits engage the attention of a much larger number of well-to-do persons amongst the mercantile and commercial classes than used formerly to be the case. Never were there so many packs of hounds and so well attended as there are at present. So much so is this the case, that the railway companies find it worth their while to run, for the convenience of members of the mercantile and professional classes residing in our largest towns, special trains during the hunting season, to and from the principal meets of foxhounds. It is hardly possible to take a stroll of a Saturday afternoon in the well-to-do outskirts of a populous town without seeing a game, and it may be several games, of football in winter, and of cricket in summer, being engaged in by a large number of young men who, during the rest of the week, have been occupied in business pursuits. Our rivers are crowded with craft manned by the young men of our commercial classes. During the autumn the mountainous parts of our own island and that country which is called 'the playground of Europe' teem with visitors whose means would formerly not have permitted them to enjoy this healthy exercise and relaxation of mind. These greater facilities for getting into the country have certainly improved the physique of our better-class townsmen. The effeminate shop-clerk, against whom *Punch*, at the time of the Crimean war, used never to be weary of levelling the shafts of his ridicule, has developed into the stalwart volunteer, the oarsman, or the bicyclist. It is, indeed, unnecessary to multiply instances to prove the presence amongst us of large numbers endowed with physical powers, and inspired by a lion-hearted courage, worthy of the best days of our ancestors. Perhaps it would be impossible for any country to produce as fine a body of young athletes belonging to the well-to-do classes as are to be found at our Public Schools and Universities. Nay, more; taking into consideration the increase of comfort and of population, the England of to-day could probably, under a system of universal military conscription, produce a greater number of fine regiments as regards height and breadth of chest than the England of 1800. But does this admission, or do all these instances of a high standard of physical strength and courage amongst certain classes of the population, prove that other classes, even now the most numerous, and which under the present order of civilisation must inevitably increase, and that at no slight rate; do these instances, I say, in any way prove that these less favoured classes are even now not degenerating in health and strength? As cities increase, will not the physical powers of their inhabitants assuredly decrease, unless steps are taken, and that soon, to counteract the evil effects of the crowding together of masses of human beings within extremely limited areas? Is it not a fact that the population of these islands is annually becoming more and more a town one, crowded together without light, without air, without the means of obtaining proper exercise, and in the case of many without wholesome, or even necessary food, warmth, and clothing? If we do not as yet discover signs of national deterioration in health, may it not be because the average is maintained by the high state of the physical condition of more favoured portions of the community? Do our athletes, our sportsmen, our travellers, our mountaineers, issue from the crowded lanes of overgrown cities? Are not their homes to be found rather amongst the pleasant places of the earth, in rural manor-houses, in retired parsonages, in country villas, or in the healthy portions of well-to-do towns, in the midst of comfort and of plenty, with every means of exercising the healthy bodies which they have inherited from healthy and well-to-do progenitors? Are not our navvies, our merchant seamen, our ironworkers, our gamekeepers, our gillies, and all who require physical strength in the exercise of their employment, obtained as a rule from the country and small town population? It may be said that our soldiers are recruited in towns. Although it is true that the mass of our recruits are enlisted in towns, it does not follow that they have been brought up in them, though no doubt many and perhaps the majority are. Many a country-bred lad walks into the neighbouring large town for the purpose of enlisting. We have no record of the number of town-bred recruits rejected by the inspecting surgeon for physical defects. None but those likely to develop under the influences of good food and healthy exercise are accepted. Even these we do not see in the ranks until they have been withdrawn for some months from hurtful influences, and have been carefully trained with a view to the increase of their physical powers under conditions of life most favourable to their development.

What are the conclusions to which we are naturally led by the above considerations? That the robust and athletic are to be found amongst the well-fed, the well-clothed, the well-housed; that good food and clothing, fresh air and exercise, are necessary to the healthy development of the human frame; and that, where these health-requirements are wanting, physical qualities may be expected to degenerate.

The police records attest that the finest men physically and intellectually come as a rule from the small country towns, and it is precisely in the small country towns that life amongst the lower class presents its easiest aspect.

Now that almost all who have any pretension to the name of well-to-do can get away, for at all events some short portion of the year, from the smoky and grimy city, there is a real danger lest the health-requirements of those left behind, and they the least influential of the community, should be neglected. Formerly it was the interest of the rich as well as of the poor citizen to secure open spaces and means of recreation, but if even the superior artisan can now afford to live away in a healthy suburb, who is left whose interest will induce him to raise his voice on behalf of the poor against the constant invasions of brick and mortar? Let the reader walk through the wretched streets of one of our large manufacturing towns, or through those of the eastern and southern districts of London. If he returns satisfied with the results of his investigations, he must indeed be gifted with a very sanguine temperament. Should he be of average height, he will find himself a head taller than those around him; he will see on all sides pale faces, stunted figures, debilitated forms, narrow chests, and all the outward signs of a low vital power. Surely this ought not to be. We are not Turks, to cry out 'Kismet!' and then turn on the other side, satisfied that what is is good, and cannot be avoided. If the exigencies of civilisation and the limited size of our island home require that millions shall pass their lives under the unnatural conditions consequent on city life, it is surely incumbent on the nation to see that every assistance is given these unfortunates to enable them to bring up their children in as high a degree of health as the unfavourable circumstances of their lives will admit. Cities must exist, and will continue to increase. We should therefore turn our attention seriously to the question how to bring health within the reach of our poorer city populations. Had Victor Hugo passed his life within reach of the noxious vapours of a Widnes, in the heart of a Newcastle, on the banks of the odoriferous Clyde, or within the purlieus of a Whitechapel court, it may be doubted whether, as on a certain recent occasion, he would have been eloquent in the praise of cities, and have styled them 'divine.' Places which at the beginning of this century were small hamlets are now large manufacturing towns, teeming with people huddled together under conditions adverse to health and to the development of a robust population. What similarity to their present appearance did Glasgow, Dundee, Newcastle, Liverpool, Manchester, Birmingham, Leeds, Sheffield, Bradford, and a hundred other places, present at the commencement of this century? How long will it take before the manufacturing towns and villages with which Lancashire is studded shall have joined one another, and that county become one vast hive of human industry? When will the modern Babylon cease to add town to town, and what will be the limit of its extension? Can we look with complacency on the fact that the population of these islands is annually becoming more and more a town one; that annually more and more human beings are engulfed by the advancing tide of buildings, and become absorbed in endless streets and courts and alleys; that fresh air and the means of wholesome exercise are daily being withdrawn from larger and larger numbers of people; that crowded streets and ill-ventilated dwellings produce vitiated air; that the want of a proper supply of oxygen and of means of obtaining healthy exercise weakens the human system; and that daily and hourly a larger number of men and women, conscious of impaired vitality, resort to the spendthrift habit of drawing upon capital to replace income by permanently injuring their constitutions for the sake of the transitory stimulus which is obtained through the use of alcoholic liquors? Vain are the efforts of temperance societies and reformers as long as they leave untouched the condition of things which engenders the mad craving for drink. Are men and women brought up under such circumstances likely to be the parents of healthy children? Nature is stern—she has no compassion—as men sow, in like manner shall they reap. Certain well-known laws have been laid down by Providence for the guidance of man, and if he in his obstinate blindness deliberately chooses to violate them, he must abide the consequences. Wholesome and sufficient food, warm clothing, fresh air and exercise, are necessary, at all events in childhood, to the healthy development of the human frame. How many of these requisites ordinarily fall to the lot of the children of the poorer classes in our large towns? Let those who go in and out amongst them answer. Ask the Board school teachers in the poorer districts of London whether children are not sometimes sent to school without having tasted food; whether they do not occasionally fall off the benches from sheer physical exhaustion; whether the teachers, from motives of humanity which do them credit, do not often supply out of their own slender resources the more pressing necessities of these wretched starvelings. Let the district visitors answer whether the children, with just sufficient clothing on their half-starved frames to satisfy the demands of decency, but not sufficient to promote warmth, do not often in the depth of winter return to homes where it is the exception rather than the rule to find a fire burning on the hearth. Ask the medical officer what is the sanitary condition of these houses, and whether it is possible for these children ever to breathe air which is not more or less contaminated. Ask the police constable how far off is the nearest public park or open space where the children now rolling in the neighbouring gutter might enjoy their games free from the dirt and contamination of the present scene of their sports. It is much to be feared he would stare in astonishment at the remark, and would answer that such a paradise was not within the reach of such as these. The truth is that our eyes are blinded to the evil effects of overcrowding by reason of the continued stream of fresh blood which is ever flowing from the more healthy districts into our towns, thus hindering and delaying the natural physical decay of the constitutions of the inhabitants of the latter, which would otherwise be more rapid and consequently more apparent. If we could establish a thoroughly efficient blockade of our large cities, and allow no further immigration into them from the country, it would not be many years before the mortality in our centres of population, as compared with that in healthier districts, would be so marked, and the physical deterioration in our city populations would become so apparent, that we should be forced to take immediate steps to prevent their utter annihilation. But it may be said, 'This is an old story, and may have been true before public attention had been called to the overcrowded state of the back slums of our large cities, but since the passing of the Artisans' Dwellings Act, and the establishment of working men's dwellings companies, all this has been altered, and the working classes are now housed as well as their incomes will permit.' Would that this were the case! Alas! the efforts of these companies, great as they have been, are but as a drop in the ocean, and the difficulties which are met with in working Mr. (now Lord) Cross's Act have sadly limited its operation. What then can be done? If Acts of Parliament and companies whose capital is counted by millions avail but little, what hope is there of a better future? Probably neither private efforts nor indeed public measures, unless of a much more arbitrary character than in the present state of public opinion are likely to be adopted, would altogether avert the deleterious influences of prolonged existence for several generations in crowded cities; but surely something might be done, if not for the adults, at all events for the children, of our city populations, to strengthen their growing frames, and thus give them some chance of contending with success against the hurtful influences which surround them. We said that wholesome and sufficient food, warm clothing, fresh air and exercise, were necessary to the healthy development of the human body in time of youth. Is it quite impossible for this rich country to see that the children educated at its Board schools shall be provided at all events with some of these requisites? Amongst not the least of the benefits which the children of the poor have derived from the Education Act of 1870, there are two not to be overlooked : firstly, that if a child be ill-clad or starved, the fact must in time be known to the teachers, and through them to the outside world; and, secondly, that during a considerable portion of the day, that child, instead of shivering in a cold garret, must of necessity be seated in a warm room. Here we have, therefore, warmth provided by the School Board, not a bad substitute for warm clothing. Would it greatly shock the nerves of our political economists if we were to suggest that the School Board, having provided warmth for the children attending their schools, might still further benefit them by furnishing two classes of dinners, to be cooked, if possible, by the scholars themselves—the first composed of the cheapest food which could be provided, such dinners to be supplied gratis to the most destitute children attending the school; the second, a more attractive and substantial meal, to be sold to the more well-to-do scholars, and consumed by them on the spot? By good management it might be possible to make the latter class of dinners pay for the former; and if the dinners were well cooked, it is probable that the parents might find it worth their while to purchase for themselves the meals which their own children had cooked. A profit might thus accrue to the school, whilst the children would have practical experience in the class of cookery which would be of most use to them in after life. We have already said that many School Board teachers are in the habit of providing meals for the more destitute scholars at their own expense. It is not right that a class who as a rule are not too highly paid, or over-favoured by fortune, should be called upon either to shut their eyes and harden their hearts, if they can, against the sight of children suffering from the effects of hunger, or else to draw upon their own scanty incomes for the means of affording them relief. If the pill above suggested should be too large a one for the contracted gullets of our economists (though it may, *en passant*, be mentioned that dinners at nominal prices are provided for the children in the national schools of Germany), philanthropists might surely be invited to look upon the subject as one not unworthy of their consideration. Money might be worse spent than in providing cheap dinners, at all events during the winter months, for the destitute children attending our Board schools. If this were done, not only would the School Board officers find the list of truant children rapidly diminish, and the school gain favour with the most obdurate of parents, but we should be sure that every child in a Board school (which ought to mean every child in a large city) was provided with at all events one good meal a day, and that its body was warmed for a certain number of hours during the twenty-four. Now as to fresh air and exercise, the other requisites for health. The Rev. S. A. Barnett, Vicar of Whitechapel, has for some time been in the habit of boarding out during the summer months the children of his poorer parishioners in the country and at the seaside. The Leicester Charity Organisation Society has also been instrumental in carrying out a similar scheme, and the London Charity Organisation Society, encouraged by the success which has attended these efforts, has referred the question of boarding out to a special committee, which has reported favourably on the subject. It is to be hoped, therefore, that before long some general organisation will be established, by means of which city-bred children, whether convalescent or not, may from time to time be enabled to breathe true country air, refresh their minds and eyes and ears by the sights and sounds of country life, and lay in a stock of health against the hour of their return to town. Most Board schools possess a small yard attached to the school, within which the children are allowed to amuse themselves, and sometimes have the opportunity given them of exercising their limbs in running round a 'giant's stride.' This is good as far as it goes, but it is a poor substitute for the games which country children enjoy. Would it not be possible, in the absence of a park or open space, to encourage children to do something better than loiter about, or bully one another, or 'talk bad,' as it is called, when congregated in knots? Might not the 'giant's stride' be supplemented by a couple of fives courts, a cat's gallows, or a circular running path? Prizes might be given to successful competitors in these healthy exercises in the open air, and provision might be made for proper exercise on wet days by suspending a few ropes, rope-ladders, and a trapeze or two to the ceiling of the schoolroom. These might be so arranged as to be drawn up to the ceiling by means of a pulley during the lesson hours, and thus not interfere with the ordinary work of tuition. The above plan, in the absence of a proper gymnasium, has been most successfully carried out in a school with which the writer is acquainted. In Germany and Switzerland gymnastics are made as much a part of the system of education as reading and writing. If Germans and Swiss, who mostly live in country districts or in small towns, where ample means of exercise are to be found, consider it essential for the maintenance of national health that their children should be taught gymnastics, surely it is of some importance that our city-bred English children, who never have any opportunity of using their limbs, should be supplied with these artificial means of strengthening their bodies and of fortifying their nerves. There is no reason why a certain knowledge of gymnastics should not be required of every School Board master, so that he might be able to superintend these exercises during the hours which are now nominally given up to play, but which are really often passed in a manner neither conducive to morality nor to health. The teachers, who perhaps suffer from want of exercise more than the scholars, would welcome the establishment of good gymnasia and fives courts, and would find themselves clearer in head and brighter in mind after an hour's bout at the one or the other, whilst their scholars might possibly perceive in them a greater equanimity of temper. Each School Board district in London is provided with a spacious room, now used for meetings of managers, and for other similar purposes connected with the business of the schools. These might with very small expense be easily fitted up as gymnasia, without in the least interfering with the objects for which they were built, and here might be held advanced classes in gymnastics under properly qualified instructors. In addition to these classes, is there any reason why these rooms should not be thrown open, under proper supervision, on week-day evenings, subject to a small annual payment or entrance fee, to former School Board scholars, or, indeed, to any young lads between the ages of thirteen and twenty, who chose to spend their evenings in healthy exercise, rather than in the dissipation of the gin palace, the music hall, or the cheap gaff? Prison statistics inform us that men rarely take to a life of crime after twenty-one years of age, and that the criminal classes are as a rule recruited from young men between the ages of fifteen and twenty, who not infrequently are induced to desert honest industry, and to enter upon a life of crime, by associating of an evening with bad characters in low places of resort. A young man after hard work or close confinement all day must have society and recreation of some sort. Where at present can he find this out of the gin palace or music hall? English towns, as compared with Continental ones, are lamentably deficient in places where of an evening a young man can find innocent and wholesome recreation. Surely the establishment of gymnasia for the use of the youth of our towns would not be foreign to the educational purposes for which School Boards exist. Physical and intellectual education should go hand in hand. The London School Board has so far acknowledged this principle as to allow prizes to be given to their scholars for swimming and drilling, and have encouraged them to become proficients in both exercises. If gymnasia were fitted up, and occasionally thrown open, as suggested, and made attractive to the young men of the neighbourhood, no doubt these establishments would shortly become a source of income to the Board.

The object of this paper will have been fulfilled if it induces some School Board authorities to devote greater attention to the question of improving and of promoting the physique of the city-bred children assigned to their care. The ideas thrown out do not profess to meet all the difficulties of the question of the health of our city populations. The writer is well aware that he has but touched the fringe of the subject; that a radical reform can never be effected until much bolder and more important measures than he has proposed, or would venture to suggest, have approved themselves to our parliamentary and municipal authorities. He has therefore confined himself to considering the best means of improving the health of our city children, leaving to abler hands the wider question of how to deal with the adults. If some improvement, even though slight, may reasonably be expected to accrue to the health of the rising generation in cities by the adoption of the above suggestions, surely it would be worth an effort to endeavour to bring them into practice. *Salus populi suprema est lex.*

OPEN SPACES AND PHYSICAL EDUCATION.[1]

BY THE EARL OF MEATH.

OF late years a marked increase has taken place in the number of urban parks, gardens, and playgrounds of the United Kingdom which are accessible to the public. This activity on the part of municipal authorities, and of philanthropic societies and individuals, is largely owing to the growth of a public opinion favourable to the creation of pleasant oases, refreshing to the mind and body, wherever the undue extension of bricks and mortar has banished man from the humanising influences of nature, and has

[1] Reprinted, by permission, from the *National Review*, December 1886.

turned the soil into a stony wilderness. The credit of giving the impulse which set this public opinion in motion is due, in a great measure, to Miss Octavia Hill. She it was who, in season and out of season, was never weary of preaching, often to deaf ears, the importance of preserving open spaces for the benefit of the poor, and especially of their children. She it was who first put into practice the principles she preached, and turned a fetid London court into an 'open-air drawing-room.' Her example has been largely followed. Within the short space of three years the Metropolitan Public Gardens Association, through the generosity of the public, has alone been enabled to throw open to the people of London four playgrounds and seventeen gardens, and, of these, one of the former and one of the latter have been permanently transferred to the care of the local municipal authorities. This transference of open spaces from the care of an association supported by voluntary subscriptions to that of a public body like a local vestry or district board, means, of course, an increase (though an infinitesimal increase) of the rates, and there are those who, from not thoroughly appreciating the important issues involved in the matter, question the justice or the propriety of a public authority increasing the burdens of the people, for what they consider to be a luxury rather than a necessity. Such a doctrine will find no support at my hands, even supposing these open spaces could be regarded as luxuries. I believe that there are luxuries of a public character, such as museums, art galleries, &c., which the Government of a rich and prosperous nation is justified in providing for the benefit, refinement, and enjoyment of the people committed to its charge; but the question will arise, Can parks, gardens, and playgrounds, means for the preservation of the public health, be considered luxuries? Should they not much more justly be ranked amongst public necessities? Health is one of the first of these, and in my opinion no expense should be spared, and no opportunity neglected, to increase the average standard of the nation's health and strength. If a people's average standard of vitality be lowered, that people will assuredly be handicapped in the race of nations by as much as that standard has been lessened. The health of the mind is largely dependent on the health of the body, and although, occasionally, a powerful and healthy brain may be found in a diseased body, as a rule the mind and the body act and react one upon the other, so that a nation (and it should be remembered that a nation is nothing more than the aggregate of the men and women composing it) will only have as much muscular power and brain force as may be the sum total of these qualities possessed by the men and women of which it is formed. A simple reference to the last census returns will show that this country is increasing at the rate of 340,000 a year, and that these 340,000 are not added to the country population, but are absorbed by the large overgrown cities of Great Britain and Ireland. Now it is a well-known and universally recognised axiom of hygienic science, that, other things being equal, the health of a population is in inverse ratio to its density; in other words, that the more the people are congregated together, the more unhealthy do they become. This being the case, it will be readily seen that *unless steps are taken to counteract the operation of this natural law, the inhabitants of our towns must degenerate in health*, which is as much as to say that this is the destined fate of two-thirds of our population; for at this moment there are in Great Britain two men living in towns for every one living in the country.

Now what are the most obvious steps to be taken to counteract this natural tendency of disease to dog the steps of men when crowded together? Why, to open out the population as much as possible, or, if this cannot be done, at all events to break up these dense masses of humanity by intersecting them, wherever and whenever possible, with open spaces. If this be the first remedy, then surely it is the duty of those who are the guardians of the public health to provide such open spaces; for individuals cannot be expected to buy them for the general good, and in no way, in my opinion, could public money be more legitimately spent than in thus preserving and improving the health of the community. I trust that I have clearly shown that the providing of public gardens and open spaces in large towns is no question of ornamental luxury, but one very closely connected with the health of the people, and as such should be considered a most legitimate object for the expenditure of public money.

If it be right that the people inhabiting our large towns

should be provided at the public expense with parks, gardens, and playgrounds, for similar reasons I think many will agree with me that, where possible, gymnasia should be attached to elementary schools, and that systematic instruction should be given to the children in gymnastics and calisthenics. The body should be trained as well as the brain. At present our system is entirely a one-sided one. We starve the body and overwork the brain, and the former takes its revenge on us by refusing to nourish the latter; the brain, unable to bear a strain, which would be no strain if the body were properly cared for, frequently breaks down, and broken health ensues, followed sometimes by insanity, and even death. Germany, Switzerland, as well as Norway and Sweden, have for long been alive to the necessity of caring for the body in order to get the best work out of the brain: and although the inhabitants of these states, being mostly country bred, are not in such urgent need of physical training as are the populations of our crowded towns, the sums expended by the Governments of these nations on the compulsory gymnastic training of the young would appear incredible to the educational authorities of this country. Whilst I have been writing, the physical aspect of the education of women has occupied the attention of the British Medical Association, and its President, Dr. Withers Moore, has been giving the following strong expression to a belief that women are suffering through over-pressure in brain-work whilst at school and college :—

'From the eagerness of woman's nature,' says Dr. Withers Moore, 'competitive brain-work among gifted girls can hardly but be excessive, especially if the competition be against the superior brain-weight and brain-strength of man. They require,' he asserts, 'to be protected from their own willingness to study.' And how, we may add, can they be better protected than by being encouraged to turn some of their energies towards the improvement of their physical natures by means of calisthenic and gymnastic exercises, or by healthy open-air games suitable to their sex? In a pamphlet which has lately appeared, Mr. Alexander, Director of the Liverpool Gymnasium, discusses the provision in England for physical education, points out its inadequacy in every respect, and states what are the nature and extent of the required reforms. He maintains that there are many teachers in charge of existing gymnasia who would be glad to have their services utilised in the daytime; that the obstacle to physical training is the eagerness with which result fees are looked after, so that the teachers cannot spare the school children during the day. Surely the remedy for this is to include gymnastics in the school course, and to grant fees for successful physical as well as mental training, say, in accordance with the school-average width of chest.

Mr. Alexander says:

'Let there be a central training-school where certificates will be granted to those who pass an examination of proficiency; let there be a code of exercises decided upon of a light, recreative, and popular character, with plenty of mental stimulus about them, as there should be about all exercises. Let the exercises be useful, such as swimming drill, by which children can be thoroughly practised in the movements before they enter the water, thus facilitating their swimming lesson. If the Education Department will not give the necessary half-hour per diem for this, then at least give it directly after school hours, and watch the beneficial result that will surely take place. One or two professional instructors could visit the schools in each town in order to keep up the standard of efficiency, and inspections could take place at convenient periods. *The experiment, to have a fair chance, should share in the result fees.*'

To show that it would be an easy matter to calculate the result fees to be given for average increase in circumference of chest in consequence of gymnastic training, I annex a form prepared by Dr. W. P. Brookes, of Much Wenlock, who for many years has taken a deep interest in the question of physical training, and by which it will be seen that from statistics taken in the Much Wenlock National school for six months, from August 21, 1871, to February 21, 1872, in the case of six boys who went through a course of drill and gymnastic training consisting of the use of Indian clubs, the vaulting-horse, horizontal and parallel bars, the average increase in chest circumference was $1\frac{4}{8}$ inch; whilst in the case of six other boys who went through a course of instruction in drill alone, it was but $\frac{11}{24}$ of an inch. I shall produce one more witness to the necessity for physical training, namely, Dr. George Fletcher, who has had large experience as a medical officer. In a paper on 'The Management of Athletics in Public Schools,' read before the medical officers of schools in January last, Dr. Fletcher insists that a large amount of exercise in pure air is required to keep lads in bodily health, and he contends that all games and physical exercises in schools should be regulated, and be under supervision. The experience I have gained as Chairman of the Metropolitan Public Gardens Association has shown me the wisdom of this remark. Ordinary town lads are unacquainted with the games in which English school-boys of a higher social grade delight. Their ways are rough, they are unaccustomed to discipline, and, if turned loose into a playground without supervision, are unable to avail themselves of the advantages offered them. Their sport degenerates into bullying or horseplay, with no good physical result. Gymnastic apparatus, under these circumstances, becomes a positive danger, and broken heads, arms, and legs are certain to be the result if the lads are allowed to use them without supervision or instruction; but under a good teacher they soon learn discipline, enjoy themselves, and become as keen followers of organised games as any school-boy at Eton or Harrow. Dr. Fletcher's words are:—

'It should be remembered that, as regards compulsion in games, bodily exercise should be as carefully supervised by the masters as mental exercise; for it is not wise that boys should be left to manage these physical matters entirely by themselves, thinking that you can trust nature, and all will come right, and that the boy for whom exercise is desirable will be prompted by nature to take just the amount required for his health. No such thing. In the general routine of lessons a boy is compelled to conform to certain rules for the education of his mind; this is not here left to nature nor to the boy's disposition, for, if it were, there would, in most instances, be a miserable deficiency of brain exercises, or, in a few rare cases, a mischievous excess. If a boy does not like his Virgil or his Euclid his masters do not leave him to take what he likes of those subjects; he is compelled to enter into them, and to get through a certain amount, and often will soon excel in some branch of study from judicious compulsion; so with games—do not allow the boy to play only when he chooses; at any rate, you are improving his bodily vigour, and he has had every chance of excelling in some branch of athletics. Let it be fairly instilled into the minds of parents by masters, that the education of the *body* is not far behind the education of the *mind* in importance, and the *amount* and *kind* of exercise both of mind and body should be always considered together.'

Englishmen, as a rule, do not look to the Government to introduce reforms unless these reforms are first demanded by a large section of the community. This characteristic of the national temperament has its strong and also its weak side. If, on the one hand, it makes the people self-reliant, on the other it is a distinct discouragement to the spirit of amendment in governing bodies, who, instead of being continually on the alert to discover and put into practice improvements in the management of their different departments, as a rule consider it rather the duty of an official to throw cold water on all suggested innovations which threaten to alter the orthodox routine of work. The result of this customary apathy on the part of our officials makes it necessary for reformers to acquire popular support before bringing the question of any reform to the notice of governing bodies, and in order to obtain this support the public must be educated, and urged to action, by the subject requiring reform being constantly presented to their attention. Bearing these facts in mind, those of us who believe that in order to preserve the national health and physique at the proper standard, reforms in our system of education and in the management of our towns are imperatively demanded, should not be disheartened because so little apparent progress would appear to be made in the popularisation of national hygiene and of physical training, but should lose no opportunity of promulgating their views, on the platform, through the press, and by all those means of spreading information and of influencing public opinion which modern civilisation affords. Action has already been taken in this direction by the Manchester Open Spaces Committee and by the Metropolitan Public Gardens Association. The former has obtained the signatures of the following influential and eminent persons to a petition urging the appointment of a Royal Commission to consider the question of physical training:—H.R.H. the Princess Louise, H.R.H. the Duke of Cambridge, His Grace the Lord Archbishop of York, His Grace the Duke of Westminster, the Rt. Rev. Bishop of Bedford, Bishop Suffragan for East London, the Very Rev. the Dean of St. Paul's, London, the Very Rev. the Dean of Manchester, the Ven. Archdeacon Farrar, the Rt. Hon. the Earl of Carnarvon, the Rt. Hon. the Earl of Meath, the Rt. Hon. Lord Wolseley, the Rt. Hon. Lord Aberdare, the Rt. Hon. Lord Tennyson, His Honour Judge Hughes, Maj.-Gen. E. G. Bulwer, C.B., Edwin Chadwick, C.B., Sir Andrew Clark, Bart., M.D., Sir T. S. Wells, Bart., F.R.C.S., Sir James Paget, Bart., Sir Henry E. Roscoe, LL.D., M.P., Sir William Roberts, M.D., Sir Henry Thompson, F.R.C.S., Rev. E. A. Abbott, D.D., City of London School, Rev. E. C. Wickham, M.A., Head Master of Wellington College, Rev. J. M. Wilson, M.A., Head Master of Clifton College, Bristol, Rev. Samuel A. Barnett, St. Jude's, Whitechapel, Rev. C. H. Spurgeon, Matthew Arnold, M.A., LL.D., D.C.L., Robert Browning, D.C.L., Professor Tyndall, Professor Huxley, Professor J. G. Greenwood, Principal of Owens College, Manchester, Rt. Hon. A. J. Balfour, M.P., William Abraham, M.P., Joseph Arch, M.P., Thomas Burt, M.P., F. N. Buxton, M.P., William Crawford, M.P., B. W. Foster, M.P., Albert Grey, M.P., W. H. Houldsworth, M.P., George Howell, M.P., S. Morley, M.P., John Wilson, M.P., J. E. Morgan, M.D., Professor of Medicine, Victoria University, Manchester, Jno. Tatham, B.A., M.B., Medical Officer of Health, Salford, Ernest Hart, Esq., F.R.C.S., Charles Roberts, Esq., F.R.C.S., Walter Besant, Esq., John Ruskin, Esq. Sympathy and general approval, without signature of the form sent, have been expressed by: The Rt. Hon. the Earl of Derby, the Rt. Hon. G. J. Goschen, M.P., Sir John Lubbock, Bart., John Tomlinson Hibbert, M.P.

The Metropolitan Public Gardens Association has sent the following Memorial on the subject to the Education Commission, and a somewhat similar one to the School Board of London:—

To the Rt. Hon. Sir RICHARD ASSHETON CROSS, M.P., G.C.B. (Chairman), and the Members of the Royal Commission on Education.

 The Memorial of the members of the Metropolitan Public Garden Association, respectfully showeth,—

That your memorialists are of opinion that increased facilities for the physical training of the young of both sexes, and further provision for their wholesome recreation, are much needed in all the larger towns of the United Kingdom; and feeling that this is a subject which is within the lawful scope of the inquiry of the members of the Royal Commission on Education, they humbly beg to urge its consideration.

They base their belief upon the following grounds :—

1. That physical training is not at present one of the obligatory subjects for the ensurance of a Government grant in elementary schools.

2. That several teachers in Board or Voluntary schools are unable to give instruction in gymnastics or calisthenics either in the playgrounds or the rooms of the schools.

3. That there is a want of some fund from which the maintenance, out of school hours, of existing playgrounds can be defrayed.

4. That there is great difficulty in obtaining, in densely populated districts, adequate open spaces for public recreation.

5. That there is a marked difference in bodily health and vigour, and in a predisposition to disease and immorality between the young in the country and those in towns.

They believe that these difficulties might be overcome in the following ways :—

1. By the alteration of the Code of Education, so that physical training should be included among the obligatory subjects, and in this way necessarily introduced into each department of every elementary school.

2. By assistance given towards the introduction of instruction in physical training into the curriculum of all training colleges.

3. By the enforcement of a regulation that all playgrounds in connection with public elementary schools should be kept open, *under supervision*, for the use of the children and young people of the neighbourhood between and after school hours.

4. By a grant of further powers to local public bodies for the

purchase of land for opened or covered gymnasia, and for suitable recreation grounds for the use of the general public.

They believe that if these suggestions were carried out, the following results would ensue to the rising generation :—

1. A decrease in juvenile mortality, a better physical development, and a greater amount of bodily health.
2. An increase in the mental powers.
3. A decrease in crime, drunkenness, and immorality.

It is therefore the earnest desire of your memorialists that the members of the Royal Commission on Education should take this matter into their serious consideration, and consent to hear evidence upon the need of better means for physical training and increased facilities for wholesome recreation in all towns.

And your memorialists will ever pray, &c.

A National Physical Recreation Society has lately been established for the promotion of the physical education of the working classes, under the presidency of Mr. Herbert Gladstone, M.P., supported by the Hon. A. F. Kinnaird, Colonel G. M. Onslow (Inspector of Military Gymnasia), Lord Charles Beresford, M.P., the Hon. T. H. W. Pelham, and Mr. T. C. Edwardes-Moss, M.P., of athletic fame, with Mr. A. Alexander, F.R.G.S. (Director of the Liverpool Gymnasium), as Honorary Secretary. An association with such influential leaders should be able to work wonders in the improvement of the physical education of the people, and in the confident hope that at no distant period the bodies of the poorer children of this country will be as well cared for as their brains, I ask those who read this paper to assist in forming a public opinion favourable to the maintenance, by municipal authorities, of open spaces, playgrounds, and gymnasia in towns, and to such alterations in the Education Code as will bring up a generation of English men and women, physically capable of bearing the burden of the high civilisation and extended empire they have inherited from their forefathers. *Civium vires, civitatis vis.*

APPENDIX.

Statistics of the Drill and Gymnastic Training given to Twelve Boys in the Much Wenlock National School, from Aug. 21, 1871, to Feb. 21, 1872.

DRILL AND GYMNASTICS.

Increase, after Six months, in the Circumference—

Boy	Of Chest	Of Upper Arm	Of Fore Arm
	Inches Inches		
1	From $27\frac{1}{2}$ to $28\frac{3}{4} = 1\frac{1}{4}$ inch	$\frac{1}{4}$ inch	Nil
2	" 28 " $29\frac{3}{4} = 1\frac{3}{4}$ "	$\frac{1}{2}$ "	$\frac{1}{4}$ inch
3	" 30 " $31\frac{3}{4} = 1\frac{3}{4}$ "	$\frac{1}{2}$ "	Nii
4	" $27\frac{1}{2}$ " $29 = 1\frac{1}{2}$ "	$\frac{1}{2}$ "	Nil
5	" $28\frac{1}{4}$ " $30\frac{1}{4} = 2$ inches	$\frac{1}{2}$ "	Nil
6	" $27\frac{1}{2}$ " $30\frac{1}{4} = 2\frac{3}{4}$ "	$\frac{3}{4}$ "	$\frac{1}{2}$ inch

Average increase in circumference of chest $= 1\frac{5}{8}$ inch, *i.e.* nearly 2 inches.
Exercises :—Indian Club, Vaulting Horse, Horizontal and Parallel Bars.

DRILL ALONE.

Increase, after Six Months, in the Circumference—

Boy	Of Chest	Of Upper Arm	Of Fore Arm
	Inches Inches		
7	From $24\frac{1}{2}$ to $24\frac{3}{4} = \frac{1}{4}$ inch	$\frac{1}{4}$ inch	Nil
8	" $27\frac{1}{4}$ " $27\frac{3}{4} = \frac{1}{2}$ "	$\frac{3}{4}$ "	$\frac{1}{2}$ inch
9	" $29\frac{1}{2}$ " $30 = \frac{1}{2}$ "	$\frac{1}{4}$ "	$\frac{1}{4}$ "
10	" $26\frac{1}{4}$ " $26\frac{3}{4} = \frac{1}{2}$ "	$\frac{1}{4}$ "	Nil
11	" $25\frac{1}{2}$ " $26 = \frac{1}{2}$ "	$\frac{1}{4}$ "	$\frac{1}{4}$ inch
12	" $25\frac{1}{4}$ " $25\frac{3}{4} = \frac{1}{2}$ "	$\frac{1}{4}$ "	Nil

Average increase in circumference of chest $= \frac{11}{24}$ inch, *i.e.* nearly $\frac{1}{2}$ inch.

W. P. BROOKES, *Trustee.*
EDWARD STROUD, *Schoolmaster.*

National Review, December, 1880.

THE HALF-TIME SYSTEM OF PHYSICAL AND INDUSTRIAL TRAINING.

BY EDWIN CHADWICK, ESQ., C.B.

Reprinted by permission.

SIR PHILIP MAGNUS, in an article on manual training in school education in the *Contemporary Review* for October, quotes Mr. Swire Smith, a member of the late Commission on Technical Instruction, who states that 'the half-time children of the town of

Keighley, numbering from 1,500 to 2,000, although they receive less than fourteen hours of instruction per week, and are required to attend the factory for twenty-eight hours in addition, yet obtain at the examinations a higher percentage of passes than the average of children throughout the whole country receiving double the amount of schooling.' Similar experiences may be cited from Ireland. In the district schools, where they receive orphans who have been trained in the Board schools, they always find their mental training below that of the half-time children. Sir Philip presents the experience as new—as it doubtless is to him—but he might have found that the like experiences had been developed at the Central District school of the City of London itself a quarter of a century ago, and was displayed in evidence before the Commission of Elementary Education in 1861, and in repeated demonstrations that the long-time system and the omission of physical training are in violation of the laws of physiology. The recently awakened attention to the subject may, however, be welcomed.[1]

[1] Complaints are made, by head teachers of the half-time schools, that the subject of physical and industrial training and the interests of the poor in it have been excluded from the recently appointed Commission of Inquiry into elementary teaching, and that this has been done apparently in the interests of the Educational Department, in the maintenance of its Code, and of its long-time system. The question of the extension of physical and industrial training upon the half-time system will, however, require very distinct examination and treatment, especially in its economical aspect. As to the long-time system under the Code, the great body of the school teachers are very unanimous in its condemnation. Mr. W. J. Pope, President of the Metropolitan Board Teachers' Association, at a crowded meeting of that body held the other day, said :—' I contend that not one-half the real educational work is being done that might be done. I contend that, as one of your former presidents said, we ought not to be engaged for 75 per cent. of our time in urging on, worrying, and overpressing 10 per cent. of our scholars. I contend that teachers are not happy in their work, and I make bold to say that the British taxpayer does not get full value, nor anything like it, for his money. . . . Summing up against our present system, I charge against the Education Code that it cramps—in fact, prevents—education. I charge against it that it is responsible for the fact that only 4 per cent. of those who leave our schools continue their education in night schools. I charge against it that in crushing out the individuality of the teacher it is responsible for one-half the truancy which goes on. I charge against it that owing to it one-half of the education vote is practically wasted ; and, far above all, I charge against it that it tempts the teacher to do wrong. To some of us it is known that, under its percentage and reporting influence, many of our weaker brethren often fall.

THE HALF-TIME SYSTEM

This system was introduced by myself and my colleagues under our Commission of 1833 on the Employment of Young Persons in Factories, to prevent over-work and also to prevent under-education, by requiring three hours' attendance in school. It was devised chiefly for the protection of children against over bodily work, and also to serve for protection against over, as well as under, mental work, in which it has been, when properly administered, eminently successful, as well as in maintaining juvenile earnings. It is now made the basis of the education in the Army and Navy schools, and in district poor-law schools, and industrial and reformatory schools, comprising upwards of fifty thousand schools in which there is physical training. It is in the course of extension in France and in Germany. In his recent report on the elementary education on the Continent, Mr. Matthew Arnold states that 'there are now 2,989 half-day schools in Prussia in which all the children have but half a day's schooling.' 'It is found that the rural population greatly preferred the half-day school, as it is called, for all the children, because they had thus the elder children at their disposal for half the day,' *i.e.* for remunerative employments. But Mr. Arnold appears not to have been informed that, notwithstanding the excellence of the long-time elementary teaching there, it fails to reduce the amount of crime, which is much greater in Germany and Berlin than in this country, and the same fails also here;—but that the physical and industrial training here, which augments the capability of the immediate earning of good

The Code makes it to their advantage to refuse admission to the backward, to work out those who become backward, and to do a hundred and one other things which the uninitiated know not of. The Code, in fact, is a temptation to do evil, and through it the honest teacher is placed at a great disadvantage.' Turning to the subject of discipline, Mr. Pope remarked : ' To such a pass was juvenile rowdyism then come—four years ago—that, as your President, I felt compelled to say that the time was fast coming when the discipline of schools would concern other than teachers. . . . Since then, the London rough has had his amusement with the West-end shops and clubs, and the " Board Teacher" has shown that the majority of the rowdies had been brought up under the sentimental influence of the Code and School Boards. Obedience to the law,' continued Mr. Pope, ' lies at the foundation of all good character and all true prosperity, and if it be not required in the schoolroom we cannot expect our children to become good citizens. I am of opinion that the majority of our scholars may be guided by love and reason.' This address was received by the meeting with loud acclamations of approval.

wages, reduces crime everywhere effectively, and is the only system of elementary training of which I have heard that does so. An arrangement may be made for the same method of teaching for the Roman Catholic children of Ireland as they have in England. The results obtained in the reformatory and industrial schools in Ireland, as reported by Sir John Lentaigne, are in satisfactory analogy with those obtained in some institutions in England. The educational change required may be admired solely on the grounds of the economy of the work. In the organisation of schools on a large scale there is a gain of educational power from better classification for some simultaneous class teaching, with a better paid and more highly qualified staff, and more speedy results at a lower cost. In the average small school of 100, with a master and mistress at 100*l*. per annum, the instruction can only be given at an annual cost of 1*l*. 10*s*. per head, or at a total cost for six years of 9*l*. per head; whilst in a larger school of 700, with a staff of teachers and a female teacher at 240*l*., the cost of the teaching power is reduced to 1*l*. per head, and the work is accomplished in from three to four years at a total cost of 4*l*. per head. In the large half-time schools the same buildings, with the same staff, may be made to accommodate double sets of half-timers on the same day. In the larger district schools the cost of the physical and industrial training, as well as the mental training power, is from 1*l*. 5*s*. to 1*l*. 10*s*. per head of the pupils as against 2*l*. 5*s*. per head of the common long-time Board schools. It is the opinion of the most experienced of the teachers in these schools that the half-time principle must become generally prevalent. Sir John Lentaigne, in his report for 1842, declares that the statistics for those of Ireland 'show how completely the character of a *nation* can be changed by judicious legislation applied to the proper training and treatment of the young.' This independent opinion is in accordance with my conclusions enunciated some years ago from the independent experience of England of the power of mixed physical and mental training for early changing the character of a nation.

PHYSICAL TRAINING IN ELEMENTARY SCHOOLS.[1]

BY CHARLES F. BEARSLEY, M.A.

No one who has visited one of the newest and most efficient of our Board schools can fail to have been impressed by the thoroughness of the arrangements and the completeness of the educational machinery, so far as it goes. At the same time, it would not be strange if one came away with the feeling that there is a onesidedness about the whole system. This imposing building, with its ingenious apparatus and skilled staff, is devoted entirely to the training of the mental faculties. As a rule, the physical development of the scholars is left to take care of itself. Reading, writing, arithmetic, history, geography, grammar, in some cases the elements of science, even languages, as well as drawing, sewing, and cookery, are taught after the most approved methods. In nearly every time-table systematic physical training is conspicuous only by its absence.

But the high pressure caused by this multitude of subjects, while it increases the danger of physical education being neglected, at the same time makes it all the more necessary.

In higher class schools the need is not so clamant. Taking as their model the two great English Universities, which the Frenchman with unconscious satire described as great schools where the English youth resort to learn rowing, our secondary schools cannot be broadly accused of neglecting physical exercise. Even in such schools, however, the boys who most need developing on the physical side often derive least benefit from athletics. Usually it is the naturally robust who are the greatest devotees of cricket, football, and boating. During some years' experience in a better-class boarding-school, I noticed some cases of boys who, though constitutionally weak and awkward, braved the ridicule of their schoolfellows, and became more or less of experts; but in too many cases the weakly or diffident avoided altogether the exercises in which they were unable to excel. So that something more than the mere opportunity is required. And what of our girls' schools? How few of them make adequate provision for regular exercise!

[1] Reprinted, by permission, from the *Sanitary Record*, December 15, 1886.

It is in elementary schools, though, that the need is greatest. In large towns the children of the Board school have little chance of indulging in the invigorating games in which their more fortunate fellows revel. The playground is necessarily of very limited area, generally enclosed by buildings, and frequently paved or asphalted. Though serving well enough as a drill-ground, it is neither large enough nor suitable otherwise for miscellaneous games. In some schools with playgrounds of this sort the boys learn military drill, and the girls are taught calisthenics, with very good results. This is in the right direction; but what is wanted is something more general and, if possible, more systematic. Instead of being regarded as an extra, physical training should have a place in the ordinary daily routine.

It has little chance of becoming more general and systematic till it is officially recognised in grant-earning schools as a part of the curriculum, and is paid for as such. I have no desire to see a further extension of the payment-by-results system, and I certainly do not advocate individual examination in athletics. I should regret if the annual inspection were to add to the doubts and fears that already beset our youngsters as the annual ordeal approaches. Ought little Polly, who is queen of her class in arithmetic, to have her days made dismal by the thought that, after all, she is rather a poor hand with the 'stirrups'? Or should poor Tommy, whose reading is good and whose spelling is faultless, be disturbed in his slumbers by dreaming that he has 'failed' on the trapeze? By no means. But, if physical exercise is really of importance, why not teach it and pay for it as a 'class subject'? The recognised class subjects in the English Code are English, drawing, geography, elementary science, history, and (for girls) needlework. Each of these may earn a grant of two shillings for every scholar in average attendance; and, important as these are, it is surely not too much to seek to place physical training on the same level. It is useless to ignore the fact that, under our present commercial system of national education, which assesses a half-knowledge of arithmetic at three shillings, and rewards a passable smattering of French with four, the likelihood of a subject being taught depends almost entirely on how much money can be earned in a given amount of time devoted to it per day or per week. The subject that brings in no money, or that is unfairly handicapped in the race for grants, will be nowhere. At present the only encouragement given by the Code to physical training is the permission to teach military drill during school hours; but, although this usually entails extra expense for an instructor, not a halfpenny of grant is paid for the time so spent. If physical exercise is to be generally introduced into our elementary schools, it must be put on an equal footing with other subjects. Then teachers may devote a fair amount of time and attention to it without being harassed by the thought that for the time thus employed they will be able to show no pecuniary result.

If physical training were to be thus endowed as a source of school revenue, it might be considered necessary to have, as a guarantee that some definite work would be done therefor, a syllabus of exercises for each year. A suitable scheme could easily be arranged. Probably much might be learned from a study of the German and Swedish systems of gymnastics. It might, however, be better at first to leave the scheme of exercises to be arranged by the teachers, subject to the approval of the school inspector. I do not at present propose to offer many detailed suggestions, but shall confine myself to a few general principles that should be kept in view.

In the first place the exercises, while tending to the healthy development of all the bodily organs, should be, as much as possible, of a recreative character. In the younger classes they must be very largely so, just as the Kindergarten system seeks to educate the senses and the intellect by attractive exercises in form, colour, and number. Some actual pastimes might be occasionally introduced, and the charm of combined rhythmic movement should not be forgotten. It is generally understood that exercise taken for its own sake is not so beneficial as when it is incidental to some pleasant occupation or the attainment of some engaging end. Of course there must be a good deal of routine work in any practicable scheme. Even though it were found unavoidable that the course should consist entirely of gymnastic drill, it might still be expected to be attended with solid benefit. A great part of the intellectual training of children has to be conducted on the 'drill' principle. Drill there must be; but the regular change from mental to physical drill would do much to refresh the jaded powers of both scholar and teacher. I say 'teacher' advisedly, for the teachers should share in all the exercises and in all the sports of the children. It is in fact almost as much in the interests of the teachers as of the scholars that I desire to see physical training made a regular part of our school system.

On this account I would strongly recommend that the exercises be taught not by visiting teachers but by the ordinary staff. There is another reason for this, well known to practical educationists. Visiting teachers are generally regarded as a kind of necessary evil. They have not the same hold of the children as those who have them constantly in hand; often, though perhaps eminent specialists, they are unskilful in teaching and dealing with children; and the arrangements necessary for them to meet the scholars in suitable detachments often interfere seriously with the organisation of a school. A system of physical training which necessitates such aid is bound to break down. To insure its success it must be workable by the ordinary staff. Gymnastics and calisthenics, which are not at present entirely neglected in our training colleges, would then become subjects in which proficiency would be desirable; and there is no question that in a short time teachers thoroughly qualified for the work would be turned out.

In the next place, when a new subject is introduced into a curriculum, the standard set up should not be too high. The new drawing schedule for elementary schools is a case in point. Instead of giving a stimulus throughout the country to the teaching of drawing, this schedule, through its being pitched rather above the present capabilities of elementary schools, is likely, in many districts, to fairly stamp out art-teaching in school. Too ambitious a programme of physical training would be equally unsuccessful. In fact, the grant should be paid rather for the time spent in the exercises, and for the hearty enjoyment and smooth discipline with which the children go through them, than for the performance of actual gymnastic feats. Some aptitude for the latter may fairly be looked for; but, if the inspector is satisfied that reasonable time is devoted to physical training, that it is taught in accordance with sound physiological and hygienic principles, and that it is benefiting the children, payment of the grant should be recommended. There should, moreover, be only one scale of payment. Were there, as in the case of the present class subjects, a higher and a lower grant, according to the degree of excellence, a loophole might be left for 'over-pressure' to creep in. For the same reason physical exercise should not be additional to the three class subjects which are at present allowable in any one school, but alternative to them. Would it be too much to make it an imperative subject?

With respect to time, some minimum, perhaps two hours per week, as in the case of drawing, should be required to be devoted to physical training. This time should be judiciously distributed between the lessons. This is very important. An hour a day would not seem too much; but that would necessitate a higher grant. About 1l. per head is a good annual school grant; and about twenty-five hours is the average school week, exclusive of religious teaching, which earns no grant. We may, therefore, say roughly that every two hours and a half per week should earn about two shillings per head of annual grant. This is the full grant for a class subject. If, therefore, five hours a week were required, it would probably be necessary to pay a grant of four shillings. This might be too much to hope for. Merely to make physical training an alternative to the present class subjects would not, it should be observed, entail any addition to the education estimates. On the other hand, to demand for it much more time than for the other class subjects, and at the same time to pay no higher grant, would be to kill the scheme at its birth.

Lastly, as to apparatus, rooms, &c. A good many invigorating exercises require no apparatus. For a good many others apparatus could easily be fitted up in the ordinary class-rooms. Many exercises on the parallel and horizontal bars, as well as vaulting and leaping, could be performed by a class in rapid succession. On a row of rings or stirrups, suspended along the free space of a class-room, the pupils could exercise themselves in detachments. Any additional outlay on appliances of this sort should be regarded as a part of educational expenditure as necessary as the cost of a desk and seat for each scholar. A regular gymnasium would, no doubt, be a great acquisition to every school; but it is by no means indispensable. Even where there is one, part of the exercises should be performed in the class-rooms; and it would be desirable to have a considerable portion of the training given in the open air.

Of the feasibility of the scheme suggested I have, as a practical teacher, no doubt whatever. It is quite as workable as the present elaborate sewing schedule, and much more so than the teaching of cookery in elementary schools. The essential feature of the plan is its inclusion in the Code as a grant-earning subject, and this, I have shown, need cause no extra demand on the national purse. Combined with the general adoption of school dinners, it would go far to eradicate over-pressure, and to make our educational system complete. Besides the importance of mere muscular superiority as a factor of national greatness, how much does the power of excelling, both in intellectual effort and in industrial work, depend on sound physical stamina? It is admitted, too, that a tendency to intemperance is fostered by the depression due to a weakly organism; and thus physical education would be one practical remedy against our greatest national curse. In a word, if physical training were made general, our people would be more robust, society would be the gainer, Britain would be the stronger.

GYMNASTIC INSTRUCTION IN BOARD SCHOOL PLAYGROUNDS.[1]

TO THE EDITOR OF THE 'DAILY CHRONICLE.'

SIR,—The Metropolitan Public Gardens Association, of which I have the honour to be chairman, recently petitioned the School Board of London and the Royal Commission on Education to take into their most serious consideration the low physical condition of the children attending the Board schools of our large towns, and urged upon these bodies the necessity of paying attention to the improvement of the health and strength of the rising generation.

In most civilised countries the physical education of children

[1] From the *Daily Chronicle* of December 30, 1886.

is now as carefully considered as the mental. England stands almost alone in its neglect. In order to gauge the opinions of the school managers in London 1,142 letters have been addressed to them, asking them for suggestions in regard to the best way of utilising the playgrounds with a view to the increased health of the children. Amongst the numerous suggestions given, some have replied advocating the systematic instruction of the children in gymnastics, and lamenting that a Government grant is not given for training in gymnastics and calisthenics. The enclosed letter from Mr. W. Bousfield, the chairman of the Works Committee of the School Board of London, is, you will perceive, in support of this view, and I trust that its publication may lead not only to attention being paid to the important suggestions contained in his letter, but to the inclusion of physical and technical training in the list of subjects in the Education Code for which a Government grant can be obtained.

I am, Sir, yours faithfully,
BRABAZON,
Chairman of the Metropolitan Public Gardens Association.

December 29.

[COPY.]

33 Stanhope Gardens, Queen's Gate, W.: December 11.

DEAR LORD BRABAZON,—I have read the packet of letters from London School Board local managers on the use of playgrounds which you kindly lent me. I now return them, and am glad to see that nearly all of the writers are impressed with the importance of providing physical instruction for the children, and are willing to give such help as they can to promote it in their schools.

The School Board has already placed certain gymnastic appliances in its playgrounds, but there is at present no systematic instruction in their use, and the teachers do not generally take an interest in teaching their boys to take advantage of them, although there are exceptions to this rule. Some such instruction and even organisation of games of play appears necessary, as the poor children attending the schools have not the hereditary habit of amusing themselves healthily out of doors possessed by English boys of a higher class.

While I think the School Board would be glad to give facilities for physical training in the playgrounds, I believe there would be objections felt to incurring additional expense in providing teachers.

If, however, the Association of which you are chairman were able in certain schools to give gymnastic instruction, and made an application to the Board with that object, I believe the playgrounds would be put at your disposal on certain fixed times, such as Saturdays and on summer evenings, on the understanding that your Association would be completely responsible for providing proper supervision of the children during the time of their use.[1] The school-keepers, who are now responsible for this supervision, have their time so much engaged, that it would be undesirable to add to their labours in this matter, even if they were additionally paid for it. Probably the Board would be more willing to agree to such an arrangement if a trial were made first in a few schools only. I will send you a list of some playgrounds, which seem specially adapted to your purpose, when I have talked the matter over with the Board's architect. Very likely many teachers and managers would give their help to your Association in this work; but it would be unadvisable to rely entirely on voluntary supervision of the children, as any breakdown in the essential maintenance of order would necessarily lead to the discontinuance of the arrangement.

Since my conversation with you on Friday, I have read with much interest your article in the 'National Review' of this month, and entirely agree with the views you there express. To carry them out, public opinion must be educated and brought to bear on the action of the Education Department and of the Government. There can be no doubt that a recognition in the Educational Code of physical training, and a small additional payment of Government grant to schools where due attention is paid to the physical improvement of the children, would do more to make such training universal than anything else. I believe that in the first European war in which England is engaged our lamentable experience of the staying powers of many of our urban recruits will, of a certainty, oblige the nation to insist, as a simple matter of safety, on more careful attention being paid to the physical strength of the mass of the population. Why should we wait for bitter experience to force us to do what reason and public spirit sufficiently show now to be necessary?

This is a cognate subject, also vital to the interests of the

[1] The Metropolitan Public Gardens Association, of 83 Lancaster Gate, has undertaken to give gymnastic instruction and to maintain order on Saturdays in five Board School playgrounds, individual members having made themselves responsible for the annual cost of a playground, viz. 14*l*. Offers to maintain additional playgrounds, open for instruction on Saturdays, will be thankfully received.

country, on which it is urgently necessary that pressure should be put on the Education Department. A small tentative beginning of teaching the use of tools to boys in order to give them a liking for handicraft work, and to modify to some extent the unpractical and purely literary education given them and the consequent impulse towards sedentary and clerklike occupation, has recently been made by the School Board; but I regret to say that the Government auditor has surcharged the expenditure incurred, and the Board will therefore be prohibited in future, unless the Government veto be withdrawn in consequence of its remonstrances, from any further essays of the kind. You will feel what a blow this action is to those who are anxious that vast sums of public money now spent on our elementary education should be made fruitful to the nation to the utmost extent.

If your Association should think fit to approach the Government and urge recognition of the national importance of physical and technical training in our elementary schools, I would suggest that the School Board should be asked by deputation to concur in your petition.

I cannot, of course, say with any certainty what course the Board would take, but I believe it would sympathise with and support your efforts to increase our national strength by helping our London children to lead useful, happy, and healthy lives.

I am, dear Lord Brabazon, very truly yours,

(Signed) WILLIAM BOUSFIELD.

MANUAL INSTRUCTION.

BY SIR JOHN LUBBOCK, BART., M.P.

MR. MUNDELLA, in an interesting address which he delivered at the Polytechnic last year, took us Londoners somewhat severely to task because more is not done in the metropolis to provide for the intellectual wants of our people. Certainly, I must admit, as a Londoner, that we are far from being as advanced as we could wish. I would, however, point out two reasons. In the first place, the areas of government in London are for many purposes too small. I have no desire to speak disrespectfully of vestries or vestrymen. But take the case of free libraries: London is reproached for having so few, but would Birmingham have had its magnificent library if it was governed by the vestries of the separate parishes? One reason which has defeated the efforts to establish free libraries in London has been that the parishioners have been told that, while the expense would fall on them, readers could come in from other parishes. A bill should be proposed next session to remedy this by amending the Free Libraries Act in the metropolitan district by making the area that of the union instead of the parish. Again, why have we in our educational institutions so few members and students belonging to the great shopkeeping community? It is on account of the excessively long hours in London shops. This again is to a great extent owing to the difficulty in such immense communities of obtaining and securing common action. I hope that next session we may do something to mitigate this great evil. Free libraries and shorter hours in shops are two of the most pressing wants in London. Still, I cannot help thinking that Mr. Mundella was rather too severe on us. Can any provincial city show a nobler work than that carried on by Mr. Quentin Hogg at the old Polytechnic Institution? The members and students now, I understand, number nearly ten thousand, and not only does Mr. Quentin Hogg devote an immense amount of time to the work, but the annual cost to him cannot be much below 10,000*l*. a year. If it had been in one of our provincial cities we should probably have heard more of it. Londoners are, perhaps, too modest. Our London School Board has done its work efficiently, and is generally blamed for spending too much rather than too little. Again, the stimulus which has been recently given to the cause of technical education in England has no doubt been very greatly due to the City and Guilds of London Technical Institute, so ably directed by Sir Philip Magnus. The Commissioners on Technical Instruction, in their interesting report on technical education, have given endless cases showing the great importance of technical instruction, and I cannot help thinking that much more technical education might be introduced even into elementary schools. Something of the kind indeed is done in the case of girls by the instruction in needlework and cookery, which latter, I am happy to see, is showing satisfactory results. Why should not something of the same kind be done in the case of boys? There are some indeed who seem to think that our educational system is as good as possible, and that the only remaining points of importance are the number of schools and scholars, the question of fees, the relation of Voluntary and Board schools, &c. 'No doubt,' says Mr. Symonds, in his 'Sketches in Italy and Greece,' 'there are many who think that when we not only advocate education but discuss the best system, we are simply beating the air; that our population is as happy and cultivated as can be, and that no substantial advance is really possible. Mr. Galton, however, has expressed the opinion, and most of those who have written on the social condition of Athens seem to agree with him, that the population of Athens, taken as a whole, was as superior to us as we are to Australian savages.'

That there is some truth in this probably no student of Greek history will deny. Why, then, should this be so? I cannot but think that our system of education is partly responsible.

Technical teaching need not in any way interfere with instruction in other subjects. Though so much has been said about the importance of science and the value of technical instruction, or of hand-training, as I should prefer to call it, it is unfortunately true that in our system of education, from the highest school downwards, both of them are sadly neglected, and the study of language reigns supreme.

This is no new complaint. Ascham, in 'The Schoolmaster,' long ago lamented it, and Milton, in his letter to Mr. Samuel Hartlib, complained 'that our children are forced to stick unreasonably in these grammatick flats and shallows;' and observes that, 'Though a linguist should pride himself to have all the tongues Babel cleft the world into, yet, if he have not studied the solid things in them as well as the words and lexicons, he were nothing so much to be esteemed a learned man as any yeoman or tradesman competently wise in his mother dialect only;' and Locke said that 'Schools fit us for the university rather than for the world.' Commission after commission, committee after committee, have reiterated the same complaint. How then do we stand now?

I see it indeed constantly stated that, even if the improvement is not so rapid as could be desired, still we are making considerable progress in this direction. But what are the facts? Are we really making progress?

On the contrary, the present rules made by the Education Department are crushing out elementary science. There are two heads Elementary Science may be taken under, which are known as 'class subjects' or 'specific subjects.' Under the Code there are four so-called class subjects, only two of which may be taken. One of them must be English, which I am afraid in a great many cases practically means grammar. Consequently, if either history or geography were selected for the second, elementary science must be omitted. It has been pointed out over and over again that the tendency must be to shut out elementary science, because the great bulk of the schools are sure to take history or geography. The last report shows how grievously this has proved to be the case. The President and Vice-President of the Council, in the report just issued, say that elementary science ' does not appear to be taken advantage of to any great extent at present.' This is a very mild way of putting it. Mr. Colt Williams says, more correctly, that 'specific subjects are virtually dead.' Mr. Balmer observes that 'specific subjects have been knocked on the head.' In fact, out of the 4,500,000 children in our schools, less than 25,000 were examined last year in any branch of science as a specific subject. Take, for instance, the laws of health and animal physiology. Only 14,000 children were presented in this subject. Yet how important to our happiness and utility. Neither Mr. Bright nor Mr. Gladstone, I believe, ever learnt any English grammar, and as regards the latter it has been recently stated, by one who knows him intimately, that the splendid health he enjoys is greatly due to his having early learnt one simple physiological lesson.

Turning again to the class subjects, last year elementary science was only taken in 45 schools out of 20,000. This, however, was not because it was unpopular, but simply on account of the rules laid down in the Code. According to Mr. Williams, grammar—which, under compulsion, was taken in over 19,000 schools—was not a popular subject, and if only the Code permitted it, it would be dropped in half his schools. One of her Majesty's inspectors, in the last report, seemed to regard it as an advantage of grammar that 'its processes require no instruments, no museums, no laboratories.' This, on the contrary, is one of its drawbacks. It fails to bring the children into any contact with nature. Indeed, Helmholtz is probably correct in his view that the rules of grammar, followed as they are by long strings of exceptions, weaken the power of realising natural laws. Again, it is surely undesirable to attach so much importance to the minutiæ of spelling. Dr. Gladstone has shown that the irregularities of English spelling cause, on an average, the loss of more than one thousand hours in the school life of each child. 'A thousand hours in the most precious seed-time of life of millions of children spent in learning that i must follow e in "conceive" and precede it in "believe"; that two e's must, no one knew why, come together in "proceed" and "exceed," and be separated in "precede" and "accede"; that "uncle" must be spelt with a c but "ankle" with a k, and numberless other and equally profitless conventions! And this while lessons in health and thrift, sewing and cooking, which should make the life of the poor tolerable, and elementary singing and drawing, which should make it pleasant and push out lower and degrading amusements, are in many cases almost vainly trying to obtain admission.' At present we really seem to follow the example of Democritus, who is said to have put out his eyes in order that he might reason better. It was a truer instinct which identified the 'seer' and the 'prophet.' It seems very undesirable that our rules should be so stringent as to lay down 'a flattening iron' over schools, but if the choice of subjects were dictated at all, why, of all subjects in the world, should grammar, with its dry and bewildering technicalities, be especially favoured? I do not, however, wish to disparage grammar; all I desire is that it should not block the way; that elementary science should have a fair chance. The three objections which are sometimes heard, especially at School Board elections, are over-pressure, over-expense, and over-education. That there is really no general over-pressure Mr. Fitch and Mr. Sydney Buxton have satisfied most impartial judges. Still the relief afforded by a change from literature to science, from books to nature, from taxes on memory to the stimulus of observation, is no doubt of the most grateful character.

Mr. Matthew Arnold, in his recent 'Report on certain Points connected with Elementary Education in Germany, Switzerland, and France,' points out that in German elementary schools there is a 'fuller programme' and a 'higher state of instruction' than in ours. He takes Hamburg as a good typical case, and he tells us that 'the weekly number of hours for a Hamburg child between the ages of ten and fourteen is, as I have said, 32; with us, under the Code, for a child of that age, it is 20.' And then, or I should rather say, 'but then,' 'the Hamburg children have as the obligatory matters of their instruction, Religion, German, English, History, Geography, Natural History, Natural Philosophy, Arithmetic and Algebra, Geometry, Writing, Drawing, Singing, and Gymnastics, thirteen matters in all.' In one of our schools under the Code the obligatory subjects are 'three —English, Writing, and Arithmetic. Of the optional matters they generally take, in fact, four, Singing and Geography . . . and as specific subjects, say, Algebra and Physiology, or French and Physiology. This makes in all, for their school week of twenty hours, seven matters of instruction.' As a matter of fact I have shown that comparatively few children are presented in any specific subject. But even if two are taken, this would only bring up the subjects to half those included in the ordinary German course. Mr. Arnold 'often asked himself' why, with such long hours and so many subjects, the children had 'so little look of exhaustion or fatigue, and the answer I could not help making to myself was, that the cause lay in the children being taught less mechanically and more naturally than with us, and *being more interested.*'

I feel sure there is a great deal in this; variety in mental food is as important as in bodily food, and our children are often tired simply because they are bored.

As to expense, it is really ignorance and not education which is expensive.

But then we hear a great deal about over-education. We need not fear over-education; but I do think we suffer much from misdirected education. Our schoolmasters too often seem to act as if all children were going to be schoolmasters themselves.

It is true that more attention is now given to drawing in

some schools; and this is certainly a matter of very great importance, but some changes must be made in the Code before that development can be made which we should all wish to see. Manual work in boys' schools seems to be exactly parallel with, and in every way analogous to, that of needlework in girls' schools, and I am inclined to agree with Sir P. Magnus that the value of the one kind of teaching should be as fully recognised and assisted by the State as that of the other. Why could they not introduce carpentering or something of that sort which would exercise the hands of the boys as well as their heads? I have myself tried an experiment in a small way in the matter of cobblery, and although the boys did not make such progress as to be able to make their own boots, they no doubt learned enough to be able to mend them.

The introduction of manual work into our schools is important, not merely from the advantage which would result to health, not merely from the training of the hand as an instrument, but also from its effect on the mind itself.

I do not indeed suppose that, except in some special districts, we can introduce what is known as the 'half-time' system, in the sense that the children will do ordinary work for wages, though Mr. Arnold tells us in his 'Report on certain Points connected with Elementary Education in Germany, Switzerland, and France,' that in Prussia 'the rural population greatly prefer the half-day school, as it is called, for all the children, because they have the elder children at their disposal for half the day.'

I do not, I confess, see why a system so popular in Germany should be impossible in England; but what seems more immediately feasible is that our boys should be trained to use their hands as well as their heads. The absence of any such instruction is one of the great defects in our present system.

Such teaching need not in any way interfere with instruction in other subjects. Mr. Chadwick has given strong reasons for his opinion, 'That the general result of the combined mental and bodily training on the half-school time principle is to give to two of such children the efficiency of the three on the long school time principle for productive occupations.'

Again, the Commissioners on Technical Instruction, speaking of schools in the Keighley district, say, 'The most remarkable fact connected with these schools is the success of the half-timers. The Keighley district is essentially a factory district, there being a thousand factory half-timers attending the schools. Although these children receive less than fourteen hours of instruction per week, and are required to attend the factory for twenty-eight hours in addition, their percentage of passes at the examination is higher than the average of passes of children receiving double the amount of schooling throughout the country.'

In our infant schools we have generally object lessons or some more or less imperfect substitute of that kind for the very young children. But after this, with some rare exceptions, our teaching is all book-learning, the boy has no 'handwork' whatever. He sits some hours at a desk, his muscles have insufficient exercise, he loses the love and habit of work. Hence to some extent our school system really tends to unfit boys for the occupations of after life, instead of training the hand and the eye to work together; far from invigorating the child in what M. Sluys well terms, 'le bain refraichissant du travail manuel,' it tends to tear his associations from all industrial occupations, which, on the other hand, subsequently revenge themselves, when their turn comes, by finally distracting the man from all the associations and interests of school life.

This principle of manual instruction has been elaborately worked out in Sweden, where it is known as the 'Slöjd' system, by Mr. Abrahamson and Mr. Solomon, and has been already adopted in over six hundred schools. It has recently been the subject of a very interesting memoir by M. Sluys,[1] who was deputed by the Belgian Minister of Education to visit Mr. Abrahamson and report upon it. The importance of manual practice as an integral part of all education was long ago realised by the genius of Rousseau, and first worked out practically and as regards young children by Froebel. Basedon indeed, in 1774, introduced manual instruction as a counterpoise to mental work; but Finland seems to be the country where the value of manual instruction as an integral part of education was first realised, when, thanks to the efforts of Uno Cygnæus, the Government

[1] *L'Enseignement des Travaux Manuels dans les Ecoles primaires de garçons en Suède.* Rapport prés. à M. Le Min. de l'Inst. Publique par M. A Sluys, et conclusion de MM. A. Sluys et H. Vankalken. Bruxelles, 1884.

enacted in 1866 that it should be an obligatory subject in all primary and normal schools. The system of Basedon appears to have been less successful than might have been expected, probably in great measure because the instruction was confided to artisans, whereas it seems to be of great importance not to separate the direction of the manual from that of the mental training.

There have been indeed two very different points of view from which manual instruction has been recommended. The first looks at the problem from a specially economical point of view. The school is arranged so as to elicit the special aptitudes of the pupils; to prepare and develop the children as quickly and as completely as possible for some definite trade or handicraft, so as to, if possible, assure them, when leaving school, the material requisite of existence. In this way it is maintained that the wealth and comfort of the nation can be best promoted.

The second theory regards the manual instruction as a form of education; the object is to give to the hand, not so much a special as a general aptitude, suitable to the varied circumstances of practical life, and calculated to develop a healthy love of labour, to exercise the faculties of attention, perception, and intuition. The one treats the school as subordinate to the workshop, the other takes the workshop and makes it a part of the school. The one seeks to make a workman, the other to train up a man. In short, the Swedish system is no preparation for a particular occupation, but is intended as a means of general development. The time devoted to manual instruction is there from four to six hours a week.

Of all handiworks carpentering has been found most suitable. The work of the smith strengthens the arm, but it does not train the hand—tends rather indeed to make it too heavy. Moreover, the work is rather hard for children. In basket-work the fingers alone are exercised; few tools are required or mastered, the younger children cannot finish off a basket, and it is an additional disadvantage that the work is done sitting. Bookbinding is too limited and too difficult, moreover it does not afford sufficient opportunities of progressive difficulty. Work with cardboard is in many respects very suitable, but it trains the fingers rather than the hand, and does not sufficiently develop the bodily vigour. On the whole, then, working in wood is recommended, and it is remarkable that it was long ago suggested by Rousseau.

Tout bien considéré, le métier que j'aimerais le mieux qui fût du goût de mon élève est celui de menuisier. Il est propre, il est utile, il peut s'exercer dans la maison, il tient suffisamment le corps en haleine ; il exige dans l'ouvrier de l'adresse et de l'industrie, et dans la forme des ouvrages que l'utilité détermine, l'élégance et le goût ne sont pas exclus.

Abrahamson has prepared a hundred models, which the children are successively taught to make, commencing with a very easy form, and passing on to others more and more difficult. The series begins with a simple wooden peg, and the series includes a paper-knife, spoon, shovel, axe-handle, flower-stand, mallet, bootjack, a cubic décimètre, a mason's level, chair, butter-mould, and ends with a milkpail.

When the model is finished it is inspected. If unsatisfactory, it is destroyed; yet if it passes muster the child is allowed to take it home. It is all his own work; no one has helped. It is indeed found important that the children should make something which they can carry away, and much stress is laid on the condition that they should make it entirely themselves, from the beginning to the end. If one does one part and one another, if one begins and another finishes it, neither practically takes much interest in it.

The objects made are all useful. At first some were selected which were playthings, or merely ornamental, but the parents took little interest in articles of this character; they were regarded as mere waste of time, and have gradually been discarded.

The different objects must be gradually more difficult. When the child is able to make any model satisfactorily he passes on to the next. He must never be kept doing the same thing over and over again. Useless repetition is almost sure to disgust. The man has to do the same thing over and over again, but the child works to learn, not to live.

Lastly I may mention that the objects selected are such as not to require any expensive outlay in the matter of tools.

The result, we are assured, gives much satisfaction to the parents and great pleasure to the children.

A weak point in our present educational system is that it does not awaken interest sufficiently to enable children generally to continue their education after leaving school. Yet in addition to all other advantages a wise education ought greatly to brighten life. Browning speaks of the wild joy of living; but that is not the sense in which life is ordinarily spoken of by the poets. They generally allude to it in a very different sense, as when Pope spoke of it as 'Life's poor play,' observing in another passage—

> These build as fast as knowledge can destroy,
> In folly's cup still laughs the bubble joy;

while Lytton said—

> With each year's decay,
> Fades, year by year, the heart's young bloom away.

A well-known hymn lays it down as an incontrovertible proposition—

> Brief life is here our portion,
> Brief sorrow, short-lived care.

But this is to a great extent our own fault. Too often we fritter away life, and La Bruyère truly observes that many men employ much of their time in making the rest miserable. Few of us feel this as we ought, some not at all. We see so clearly, feel so keenly the misery and wretchedness around us that we fail to realise the blessings lavished upon us. Yet the path of life is paved with enjoyments. There is room for all at the great table of Nature. She provides without stint the main requisites of human happiness. To watch the corn grow, or the blossoms set; to draw hard breath over the ploughshare; or to read, to think, to love, to hope, to pray: 'these,' said Ruskin, 'were the things that made men happy.'

Some years ago I paid a visit to the principal lake villages of Switzerland in company with a distinguished archæologist, M. Morlot. To my surprise I found that his whole income was £100 a year, part of which, moreover, he spent in making a small museum. I asked him whether he contemplated accepting any post or office, but he said, Certainly not. He valued his leisure and opportunities as priceless possessions far more than silver or gold, and would not waste any of his time in making money. Just think of our advantage here in London. We have access to the whole literature of the world; we may see in our National Gallery the most beautiful productions of former generations, and in the Royal Academy and other galleries the works of the greatest living artists. Perhaps there is no one who has ever found time to see the British Museum thoroughly. Yet consider what it contains; or rather, what does it not contain? The most gigantic of living and extinct animals, the marvellous monsters of geological ages, the most beautiful birds, and shells, and minerals, the most interesting antiquities, curious and fantastic specimens illustrating different races of men; exquisite gems, coins, glass, and china; the Elgin marbles, the remains of the mausoleum of the temple of Diana of Ephesus; ancient monuments of Egypt and Assyria; the rude implements of our predecessors in England who were coeval with the hippopotamus and rhinoceros, the musk-ox, and the mammoth; and the most beautiful specimens of Greek and Roman art. In London we may unavoidably suffer, but no one has any excuse for being dull. And yet some people *are* dull. They talk of a better world to come, while whatever dullness there may be here is all their own. Sir Arthur Helps has well said, 'What! dull, when you do not know what gives its loveliness of form to the lily, its depth of colour to the violet, its fragrance to the rose; when you do not know in what consists the venom of the adder, any more than you can imitate the glad movements of the dove. What! dull, when earth, air, and water are all alike mysterious to you, and when as you stretch out your hand you do not touch anything the properties of which you have mastered; while all the time Nature is inviting you to talk earnestly with her, to understand her, to subdue her, and to be blessed by her! Go away, man; learn something, do something, understand something, and let me hear no more of your dullness.'

Not, of course, that happiness is the highest object of life, but if we endeavour to keep our bodies in health, our minds in use and in peace, and to promote the happiness of those around us, our own happiness will generally follow.

NOTES ON THE COST OF MANUAL TRAINING IN THE PUBLIC ELEMENTARY SCHOOLS OF LONDON.

BY EDRIC BAYLEY.

THERE were, for the nine months ended Lady Day, 1887, on the rolls of efficient elementary schools in London, 615,335 children.[1] Of this number, 405,972 were in the Board Schools, and of these, 95,922, or rather less than one-fourth, (23·6) were above the age of eleven years, and about the same proportion (24·8) were in, or above the fourth standard.[2]

It is desirable that some manual training should be given to children in the elementary schools, and probably the age of eleven, or the fourth standard, would be a proper time for its commencement.

The appropriate training, for boys alone, might be working in wood; for boys and girls, modelling in clay; and for girls alone, cookery and laundry work.

Fixing the age of eleven years, or the fourth standard, as the time for the commencement of manual training, we arrive at the number of 150,000 children to be provided for.

We have to consider the cost of accommodation, tools, materials, and teachers.

In very few cases could accommodation be found in existing buildings; sufficient sheds might probably be erected in the larger playgrounds at no great expense, but to justify a loan for the cost of erection, the workshops must be substantially built. The cost of erection may be put at £256, the average building cost of the present cookery centres.

Mr. Henry H. S. Cunynghame estimates that a workshop to accommodate thirty pupils could be fitted up with the requisite benches and tools at a cost of £70. He states that the wear and tear of tools would be small, and that a standard of deal of good quality, costing about £12, would probably be sufficient

---

[1] Report of Bye Laws Committee of the School Board for London for the nine months ended Lady Day, 1887.

[2] Report of School Management Committee for the year ended March 25, 1887

for 300 boys for a year, and he puts the salary of a competent instructor at £2 a week, and of an assistant at £1 a week.¹

Putting the yearly cost of repairs and painting of buildings at £5, the depreciation in benches and tools at £14, (or twenty per cent. on £70), the cost of materials at £9, and the cost of teachers at £3 a week for forty weeks, we arrive at a yearly cost of £148 for each workshop.

The cost of materials would probably be decreased by the sale to the boys of some of their own work.

Mr. Cunynghame estimates that the fitting up of a workshop of similar accommodation for modelling in clay would not cost more than £24. The yearly cost would be about £134.16s.

The cost of fitting up a cookery centre is about £53. The cost of materials is more than recouped by the sale of cooked food. The average price of teaching for each centre is £72. This added to £15.12s., for repairs, painting, and depreciation, comes to £87.12s. as the yearly cost.

The cost of fitting up a laundry centre ought not to be more than £50. The cost of material would be recouped by the price paid for articles washed. The teaching should not exceed £60 a year. The yearly cost may be put at £75.

The lessons in manual training should be of two hours' duration, and be given twice a week. To allow of the introduction of manual training, the school hours might properly be extended from twenty-seven and a half hours a week, as at present, to thirty hours a week. This would allow three classes a day, or fifteen classes a week of thirty each, or 450 a week ; but as the lesson must be repeated during the week, each classroom would only suffice for 225 children.

The present rateable value of the metropolis is £30,715,485. A rate of a penny in the pound, after an allowance of ten per cent. for loss on collection, will give £115,000.

To provide accommodation for 150,000 children, 664 centres would be required ; but, as sixty-six cookery centres already exist,

¹ *Technical Education.* Paper read before the International Congress at Bordeaux, Henry H. S. Cunynghame, Assistant Charity Commissioner.— *Uses, Objects, and Methods of Technical Education in Elementary Schools.* H. S. Cunynghame, *Journal of the Society of Arts*, Feb. 18, 1887.—Evidence of Mr. Cunynghame before the Special Committee of the School Board for London on the subjects and models of instruction in their schools.

only 598 new workshops need be erected, at a cost of £256 each, or £153,088, which would be equal to 1⅓ (1·330) of a penny in the pound. This sum of £153,088 could be borrowed from the Metropolitan Board of Works in the usual way, and payment of principal and interest be spread over a term of fifty years. The yearly payments on this account would be about £6,506, which, added to the estimated yearly cost of maintenance, £78,023, would bring the total yearly cost to £84,529, or rather over two-thirds (0·725) of a penny in the pound.

A Government grant of 4s. a head on 149,400 children would be £29,880. The yearly cost of the existing cookery centres after allowing for the Government grant is estimated at £2,650.

These sums of £29,880, and £2,650, together £32,530, taken from £84,529, leave £51,999, or less than a halfpenny (0·452) in the pound as the increased yearly charge to the metropolis for the maintenance of the centres.

The initial cost of establishment would be £153,088 for building, and £32,396 for fittings and tools, together £185,484, or rather less than 1⅔rds (1·612) of a penny in the pound; but as the first of these sums would be raised on loan, the actual payment in the first instance for these centres would be only £32,396, or less than a third (0·282) of a penny in the pound.

It must further be remembered that the supply of class-rooms for manual instruction will ease the pressure on the existing class-rooms, which could only have been relieved by more building; and that the additional teachers required for manual training will only be equivalent to the addition which would have been required to meet increased population.

The number of class-rooms, children under instruction, initial cost of buildings, fittings, and tools, and yearly cost of maintenance would be somewhat as follows :—

INITIAL COST.

200 Centres for Wood-working for 225 Boys (=45,000)—

	£	s.	£	s.
For Building	256	0		
For Fittings and Tools	70	0		
	326	0	=65,200	0

200 Centres for Modelling for 225 Boys and Girls (=45,000)—

	£	s.	£	s.
For Building	256	0		
For Fittings and Tools	24	0		
	280	0	=56,000	0

132 Centres for Cookery for 225 Girls (=29,700)—

	£	s.	£	s.
For Building	256	0		
For Fittings and Tools	53	0		
	309	0	=40,788	0

ANNUAL COST.

	£	s.	£	s.
Repairing and Painting of Buildings	5	0		
Depreciation on Fittings and Tools (20 per cent on £70)	14	0		
Materials	9	0		
One Teacher at £2 for 40 weeks	80	0		
One Assistant at £1	40	0		
	148	0	=29,600	0

	£	s.	£	s.
Repairing and Painting of Buildings	5	0		
Depreciation on Fittings and Tools (20 per cent on £24)	4	16		
Materials	5	0		
One Teacher at £2 for 40 weeks	80	0		
One Assistant at £1	40	0		
	134	16	=26,960	0

	£	s.	£	s.
Repairing and Painting of Buildings	5	0		
Depreciation on Fittings and Tools (20 per cent on £53)	10	12		
Materials				
Teachers	72	0		

132 Centres for Laundry for 225 Girls (=29,700)—
For Building 256 0 0
For Fittings and Tools . . . 50 0 0
                                 ─────────
                                 306 0 0 = 40,392 0 0

Repairing and Painting of Buildings 5 0 0
Depreciation on Fittings and Tools (20 per cent. on £50) . 10 0 0
Materials 60 0 0
Teachers . . . .
                                                    ─────────
                                                    75 0 0 = 9,900 0 0
                                                             ─────────
                                                             78,023 4 0

664 Centres   149,400 Children   202,380 0 0
66 existing Centres at £256 each =   16,896 0 0
                                     ─────────
                                     185,484 0 0 (1·612 of £1)

598 at £256 to be raised by Loan, repayment to be spread over 50 years .

Payment of Materials and Interest of Loan . . . . 153,088 0 0 (1·330 of £1)
                                                  32,396 0 0 (0·282 of £1)

Government Grant at 4s. per head on 149,400 Children   29,880 0 0
Present Cost of Cookery Centres   2,650 0 0
                                  ─────────
                                  32,530 0 0
                                  ─────────
                                  6,506 0 0
                                  ─────────
                                  84,529 4 0 (0·725 of £1)

                                  51,999 4 0 (0·452 of £1)

EDRIC BAYLEY.

ARE WE DECAYING?

From *The Scotsman* of September 24, 1887.

SOME years ago—so runs the tale—a party of Englishmen set to work to try on the old armour which formed part of the decorations of a nobleman's hall. The result was very striking. Not a man of them could get a suit of the armour on. Modern bone and muscle had evidently come to the front in the inevitable struggle for existence in which, the scientists tell us, high and low life alike engages. On some such groundwork as is formed by the incident just related, people have come to credit the belief that we of this nineteenth century are bigger and finer men than our forefathers of the twelfth or thirteenth. We shake hands with ourselves, and are contented to regard our race foremost in physique, as well as in science, art, and all the other things which make up the wondrously complex existence we live out to-day. Recently, however, those of us who read the medical and scientific journals have found reason to modify this sweeping assertion. Very plain hints have been given that our national physique is by no means all that could be desired. Scientists have been comparing figures, and statisticians have compiled tables; while social reformers, in their turn, have been bewailing the fact that, as regards the masses, their lives are tending towards degeneration and wholesale decay of the race. These are alarming statements enough. Let us see if the case of those who assert that we are degenerating as a race is built upon stable ground, and if, in the event of the tale proving true, there remains for us any hope of recovering the way we have lost in the healthy course of life's development. It was Mr. Cantlie, a London surgeon, who first sounded the note of alarm. The average Londoner, he told us, rarely exists for a generation-time. He comes of a short-lived stock to begin with; and the conditions under which he exists all tend towards shortening his days, by weakening his energies and enfeebling his physique. Man, it must be noted, is not exempt from the laws which proclaim the dependence of living things upon their surroundings. Want of fresh air and light, overcrowding, excess of work and worry, lack of proper food as regards quantity or quality, or both, are conditions which as surely affect men as they mould and conform lower animals and plants. Then comes into play the great law of heredity—the infallible axiom of life, that 'like begets like.' A race of feeble folk in one generation beget the opposite of giants in the next. Mr. Simon long ago remarked how the gain of even a little extra health in one decade is multiplied trebly for all decades to come. So is it with disease and weakness. The effects of lowered physique now mean not only feebleness in the next generation, but perpetuated weakness; and this last leads to that degeneration of body which is the prelude to early death and to race decay. Looking at the masses of our city populations, 'cabin'd, cribb'd, and confined' as they are, it was not wonderful that Mr. Cantlie should have followed the ordinary lines of scientific logic in his declaration that Londoners are a short-lived race, and that they tend to die out rather than to run onwards towards the making of old families, and of persistent stocks. Lord Brabazon for years back has been reiterating the same opinion as a strong and practical argument in favour of open spaces for the recreation of the masses. London increases by nearly 350,000 souls each year. Large numbers of well-built country units are added annually to the city population; but this healthy stock, subjected to the unhealthy conditions of city life, soon goes the way of all the rest. Lord Brabazon uttered only a truth—ghastly enough in its way, but all-familiar to physiologists—when he said that if the city could be isolated and all intermarriage with the country prevented, the deterioration of the physique which would ensue would be such as 'to horrify the public,' and 'arouse a sense of national danger.' It is high time, therefore, that as a nation we awoke to the real meanings of the Cassandra-like warnings which science and sociology are dinning into our ears. The whole question is one of health, of better conditions of physical life, of extended opportunities for a more wholesome existence, as represented chiefly by pure air, good food, temperance, cleanliness, and means of healthful recreation. Not by any magical process can we grow in strength. The means are of the simplest character. Unfortunately, in the crush and crowd of modern life, it is exactly these simple means of health which are hardest to procure.

The latest of the warnings which have reached the public ear comes from no less notable a source than the Director-General of the Army Medical Department himself. It recently fell to the lot of Sir Thomas Crawford, M.D., to deliver an address before the British Medical Association in conclave assembled in the Irish capital. In the course of that address the lecturer adduced certain very pertinent facts concerning the question of race decay. His figures were drawn from the records of army enlistment, and as these records originate in the skilled medical examination of recruits, the statistics he offers are of high value from their undoubted accuracy. In the period from 1860 to 1864 inclusive no fewer than 32,324 examinations of recruits were made by army surgeons. The number of men required averaged 6,465, this being a small one, and the fact therefore telling in favour of rigid tests being applied to ensure the efficiency of the material offered in the shape of fighting men. The rejections, from all causes, numbered 371·67 per 1,000. The next period, from 1882 to 1886, presents us with 132,563 men who offered themselves for enlistment. The rejections here amounted to 415·58 per 1,000. The increase in rejections was, therefore, of a most marked character. Sir Thomas Crawford can explain it in one way only. The masses from whom the army recruits are chiefly taken, he tells us, 'are of an inferior physique to what they were twenty-five years ago.' That is the plain unvarnished truth, and as such it is by no means of a palatable kind to those who regard the national welfare as a thing to be conserved and prized. Examined more closely, it is found that these statistics reveal certain additional facts of interest. Lord Brabazon and Sir Thomas Crawford are in complete agreement regarding the deteriorating effects of town life on the masses. Among city-bred lads the proportion of rejections is highest; while the exact causes of their dismissal are such as point to a plain inferiority of body in some of the most vital characters of the healthy man. The town-bred recruit is thus of lighter weight than his country neighbour. He has, in other words, not attained a full development of frame. Again, his chest is narrowed beyond natural limits, and with this item we must associate a diminished lung capacity and an inferior breathing power. Why is it, for instance, that consumption, as a rule, attacks the apices or tops of the lungs first of all, and why does that fell disorder find a natural starting-point in the upper region of the breathing organs? The answer is simple enough. Because these are the parts of the lungs which even in the ordinary chest are least used, and, according to the great law of use and disuse, disease always attacks inert organs before those which are naturally and healthily employed. Applying this fact to the narrow-chested person, we see how much more susceptible to the inroads of chest disease the lungs of such a person must be. The weakly chest, in truth, implies a body which is handicapped in the race for life, and which has lost its staying power in the contest for existence. Again, the town-bred recruit is undersized, just as he is light-weighted, when compared with the man from the fresh air and the fields. His teeth, too, are found to share the process of physical degeneracy; and this condition, in turn, militates against healthy digestion, which is the foundation of all physical strength and bodily weal. The eyesight suffers, too, among other phases of degenerate life. Overcrowding, bad air, and impure food affect the vision in a remarkable way. The rejections for defective sight and eye diseases amounted in Sir Thomas Crawford's experience to nearly 42 per 1,000; and this estimate does not include those cases whose defects of vision were of such obvious kind as to exclude them even from the recruiting sergeant's list. A peculiar form of ophthalmia or eye inflammation is found, as Sir Thomas Crawford remarks, wherever we discover bad ventilation and impure air. It is seen in the bazaars of Cairo; you meet with it in the cabins of Connemara; and it crops up in school and prison alike, where the fresh air of heaven is not made a free gift to man. Even animals exhibit this form of eye disease when their stables or pens are not properly ventilated. At the beginning of the century soldiers were witnessed, invalided on this account, groping their way, stick in hand, through the streets. Nowadays, with improved ventilation, this disease is unknown in the army. Yet in our courts and slums it is ever present, telling its own mournful story of the lack of at least one necessity of healthy life. The warnings which are thus being showered upon us from one quarter or another should surely fall upon ears ready to hear and to obey the dictates of the science which teaches men how to attain to length of days. If as a race we have started on the way of physical backsliding, it is not too late to apply the break to the vehicle, and to arrest its rapidly cumulative progress on the downward path. There are plenty of agencies already at work in the interests of national health, which means national wealth and prosperity both. But we require these agencies to be increased in number and in power a thousandfold before we may congratulate ourselves that the tide has turned towards better days and longer life for us all. The opening of free recreation-grounds and breathing spaces for the people; the encouragement of physical exercises in the schools, especially the teaching of the plain laws of health, frugality, and temperance; the abolition of slums and the better housing of the masses—these are the principal means of reforming the tendency to race decay. The great statesman whose cry was *omnia sanitas* perchance saw with prophetic vision the prospect of better things in the way of health for the people than had been attained in his day. It remains for his successors to carry out a policy of national health-aid which shall make the people healthy, and because healthy, prosperous and happy.

PHYSICAL TRAINING.

(ADDRESS GIVEN BY THE EARL OF MEATH AT THE LIVERPOOL GYMNASIUM, OCTOBER 12, 1887.)

IT may not be out of place on an occasion like this to point out how gymnastic training has confessedly exercised a not unimportant influence in the making of a nation; and I hope that I may be able to show, before I have finished my story, that it contains a moral which this country would do well in all seriousness to consider. The crushing defeat which the Prussians sustained in the battle of Jena at the hands of Napoleon in 1806 forced them to look to the causes of that defeat, and to take steps to re-establish their position in Europe. The world is aware how, under the leadership of Prince Bismarck, Germany has risen to the very first rank amongst the nations of the world, but it is not so well known that the soldiers who won the battles of Sadowa and Sedan owe their success not merely to the skill of their officers or to their own bravery, but to the ability, forethought, and patriotism of men, many of whom had been in their graves for years when these battles were fought. Amongst these may be mentioned Johann Jahn and Adolph Spiess. Jahn recognised that the defeat of Jena could be traced to more causes than that of superior generalship. He was dissatisfied with the material of which the Prussian army was then composed. He detected in it moral and physical defects, and he thought he saw in it a flabbiness both of muscle and of moral fibre. The young men who filled the regiments of his country were, to his mind, wanting in hardihood, in physical strength, in activity, and in love of country, and he determined to devote his life to the improvement of the raw material from which the armies of his dear Fatherland would have to be recruited. It was not long before his idea assumed a practical shape. In 1811 he began to form the 'Turner-Vereine,' or gymnastic associations, which have played such an important part in the development of the German race. These associations gradually grew in number until there was hardly a village which could not boast of its gymnastic corps and of its open-air practising-ground. As it was Jahn's desire to foster a spirit of patriotism among the youth of his country, as well as to develop their bodies, he framed a code of rules to be observed by the members of the association when assembled in the field of exercise, some of which did not escape criticism, and which brought him into no little trouble. The benefits conferred by these associations on the German youth, however, gradually became apparent to the nation, and in 1840 Adolph Spiess was instrumental in introducing into German elementary schools a system of compulsory physical training. In Jahn's voluntary gymnastic associations only those youths who had a taste for active exercise were brought under physical training, whilst the weaklings and those who in all probability most needed physical development were neglected; but when every German lad had to pass through a compulsory course of gymnastic training, the march to Paris may already be said to have commenced. Germany is not the only nation which has recognised the importance of training the body as well as the mind. Sweden and Switzerland have for some years laid great stress on gymnastic training, and France has lately followed in their footsteps. Although Sweden is a poor country, she spends large sums annually on the physical training of children of both sexes in her national schools. The German thinks that gymnastics makes a child 'frisch, frei, fröhlich, und fromm,' which may be freely translated as 'lively, lissom, light-hearted, and leal.' *We* do not seem to care much what the child is like in character or in body as long as we can stuff into its poor little brain a recognised quantity of mental food, which it does not assimilate, which is forgotten in a year or two after leaving school, and which from its unpractical character, even if remembered, is of little real advantage to it in after life.

It is of the first importance to every one to be possessed of a healthy and vigorous body. Why then do we neglect the training of the bodies of our children, as if it were a matter to be left to chance? If the mass of the children in Great Britain were country-bred there might be some excuse for such conduct, but the exact reverse is the case. There are two town-bred to every country-bred child in this country, and the proportion is annually growing in favour of the former. This is a very serious fact, for it means the certain degeneration of the race unless steps are taken to counteract the downward tendency.

From time to time notes of warning have been sounded in our ears. A quarter of a century ago Dr. Hayles Walsh delivered a lecture upon the degeneracy of town populations. Mr. Cantlie, a London surgeon, was one of the first to point out that the average Londoner rarely exists for a generation-time. From inquiries made at the London Hospital, out of 800 cockneys only four were to be found of the fourth generation. Sir Thomas Crawford, M.D., the Director-General of the Army Medical Department, lately told the British Medical Association that in twenty-five years the number of rejections for the army have increased from 371·67 per thousand for the years 1860-64 to 415·58 for the years 1882-86, showing an excess of 43·91 per thousand in favour of 1860-64. He says, 'There is evidence of perceptible deterioration or degeneration of type in the lower order of the people. . . . In seeking for an explanation of this apparent deterioration I have been forcibly impressed with the fact that the recruits drawn from town-bred populations give by far the largest proportion of rejections, while the causes of rejections usually indicate a decidedly inferior physique. The inferiority is shown by the difference in weight between town and country recruits, as well as by the greater frequency of rejections for want of sufficient capacity of chest, loss and decay of teeth, and diminutive stature.'

Dr. Fothergill, in a paper read before the Anthropological Section of the British Association at Manchester on September last, and which has been republished in this month's 'National Review,' says, 'It has long been recognised that town populations have a tendency to deteriorate ; . . . the facts have long been recognised and are notorious. Compare the people seen on market day at Carlisle, Wetherby, or Peterborough, with the population encountered at Shoreditch, Hammersmith Broadway, Marsh Lane. Leeds, and the towns of the great industrial hives of Lancashire and Yorkshire generally.'

Similar evidence has been given by Sir Crichton Brown in his report on the condition of children in some of the London Board schools. Mr. Charles Roberts, F.R.C.S., in an article published in this month's 'Fortnightly Review,' says that an examination of the statistics published by Sir Thomas Crawford in the report to which I have already alluded leads him (Mr. Roberts) to an exactly opposite conclusion to that arrived at by Sir Thomas. But Mr. Roberts himself acknowledges that the average stature of a native of London (a city which recruits its inhabitants from all parts of Great Britain and Ireland) is half an inch short of that of the whole kingdom ; that ' Bristol, with a fairly mixed but local population, shows similar relation to the counties of Somerset and Gloucester ; ' and that at Sheffield, where the industrial class is much in excess of other classes, the stature is about an inch less and the weight about 10 lbs. less than that of the West Riding of Yorkshire. Mr. Roberts, though sanguine as to the future of our national physique, is not so enamoured of the present condition of things as not to desire that it should be improved. He says ' physique . . . and its variations, are dependent on and controlled by food, exercise, and sanitary surroundings. . . The taste for athletic exercises, gymnastics, boating, skating, and cycling, so enthusiastically practised by the educated classes, is extending to the masses; while the agitation for the introduction of physical training, technical education, and handicrafts into elementary schools promises well for the future of their children. Much, very much remains to be done to rescue our still underfed and overcrowded town population from the insanitary conditions that environ them; but beyond what is already being done, the chief thing to do now is to impress on all persons having charge of the education and management of children, from the Vice-President of the Council to the youngest pupil-teacher, that physical activity is the law which regulates the growth and development of the body, and lays the foundation of both a good physique and an active, intelligent, and teachable mind; and to secure this more time and more skill in teaching physical exercises in schools, and more open spaces and playgrounds, are absolutely necessary.' As one who has worked for several years to obtain these objects, I welcome the expression of this opinion; and its force is enhanced when we remember that the above words are from the pen of no pessimist, but are those of one who views the physical condition of the masses from an optimistic point of view. Dr. Roberts seems to be of opinion that *some* time and *some* skill are expended in our national schools in the teaching of physical exercises. I fear that the amount of time and skill thus expended is infinitesimal in quantity.

In London, owing to the generosity of private individuals, and of the Metropolitan Public Garden Association, Swedish drill is taught to the girls in a few of the schools; but although the chairman and majority of the Board are favourably inclined to the introduction of physical exercises into the school curriculum for both sexes, they are unable to carry out their desires, as school boards are not permitted by law to expend money for this purpose, nor is any Government grant given for proficiency in physical exercises. Until such exercises are made compulsory in all national schools, until the Board schools are empowered to build gymnasia and expend money in the payment of teachers, and until Government grants are given for improved physique, it will be useless to expect any change in the health and strength of the children of our large towns.

Dr. Brookes, of Much Wenlock, who for years has advocated the introduction of physical exercises as a grant-bearing compulsory subject into the educational curriculum of our Board and national schools, has practically shown that by a system of chest and limb measurement it is possible to gauge progress in physical development made by a class of children, and to estimate the grant which should be given in accordance with a fixed scale of payment. The Government has promised to introduce next session into Parliament a Technical Education Bill. The friends of national physical education should endeavour to incorporate in that Bill a clause authorising Board schools to expend money on physical training, making it compulsory (except in cases where a medical certificate of exemption can be produced), and instructing the Education Department to include the subject amongst those mentioned in the code as capable of earning a Government grant. If this were done, and if Board school authorities were seriously to consider whether they could not with advantage follow the example set by some of the German and French national schools, where food is supplied to the scholars once a day at an exceedingly cheap rate, we should, I believe, within a few years notice a marked improvement in the physique of our city-bred young men and women. There are some persons who appear to think that strength of constitution and nerve are qualities of very little use in the nineteenth century. The very reverse is the case. Our ancestors lived quiet, peaceful, humdrum lives compared with ours. Time was of little consequence to them. It is the high pressure of life which tells upon the vital force of the present generation. We are always working against time. It is the man of strong constitution and of cast-iron digestive powers who will win in the long run. Look at our Parliamentary leaders; are they not all men with marvellous powers of withstanding fatigue? What sort of chance in the competition of life does a weakly barrister, solicitor, newspaper editor, physician, or a city clergyman possess? If in his youth he has not laid in a stock of health, and if from time to time he does not take care to replenish his store, he will be sure to break down, and be passed in the race by more physically capable competitors who may be mentally his inferiors. It is the same in the lower ranks of life. The compositor, the printer, the engine-driver, the railway porter, the omnibus conductor, the factory hand, both male and female, the dressmaker, the seamstress, and indeed all workers of both sexes in the social hive, require for success to be possessed of strong and healthy bodies. Health and strength are priceless possessions to the individual, and no less so to the nation. Woe to that country whose sons and daughters are incapable of bearing fatigue! she will be successful neither in peace nor in war. In peace she will be driven by stronger nations out of the markets of the world, and in war neither money nor science will avail to replace the sturdy arms and the steady nerves which should have been forthcoming to defend her.

II. INDUSTRIAL AND TECHNICAL TRAINING.

THE INDUSTRIAL TRAINING OF DESTITUTE CHILDREN.[1]

BY SAMUEL SMITH, ESQ., M.P.

I HAVE tried on various occasions to bring before the country the pressing need of Social Reform. I have urged that the great danger to our country lay in the growth of a poor, miserable, and degraded proletariat, living in close proximity to the wealthiest aristocracy the world has ever seen. I have tried to sketch the horrible condition in which vast numbers of our countrymen lived, especially in London and the great seaport towns, and have attempted to show that the real hope of the future lay in rescuing the young from the wretched career to which their parents too often consigned them.

Since that time a flood of lurid light has been thrown upon the condition of 'outcast London.' The evidence taken on the dwellings of the poor, the disclosures of the supineness of the London Vestries, the half-starved condition of the children in many of our Board Schools—these and many other revelations have produced a painful impression of the rottenness of our social fabric.

It is no doubt quite possible to exaggerate the magnitude of the evil. I gladly admit that the bulk of the nation has made wonderful progress both morally and materially in the last forty years. Yet I fear it must also be granted that there remains a large deposit of human misery in our midst, wholly untouched by the progress of the nation—just as poor, as corrupt, and as hopeless of improvement as at any previous period of our history. I do not feel at all sure that this deposit

[1] Reprinted, by permission, from the *Contemporary Review* of January 1885.

has not been increasing of late years: at all events, the difficulty of earning a living has been growing in the metropolis. I believe that a larger proportion of its population is now on the verge of starvation than was the case ten years ago. The trade of this country has for several years lost its former elasticity, and the rapid increase of population adds to the strain of life, and renders it more difficult for the poor unskilled labourer to hold up his head.

Admitting all that is proved in Mr. Giffen's valuable paper on the progress of the working classes during the past fifty years, I contend that this improvement does not touch the great floating element of casual unskilled labour which abounds in our large towns, and especially in the metropolis. Indeed, the very improvement in other sections of society makes it more intolerable that immense numbers of families should live in single rooms, as foul as pigsties, without the decencies or comforts of life, barely eking out a wretched subsistence on two or three days' casual labour per week, nearly half of which goes for the rent of the filthy dens they inhabit. Yet this is the condition in which multitudes of the people in London live, and the same holds good of Liverpool, Glasgow, and most of our large towns.

I am deeply convinced that the time is approaching when this seething mass of human misery will shake the social fabric, unless we grapple more earnestly with it than we have yet done, and my object in these remarks is to point out a new field in which the richest fruits may be reaped if we enter upon it with adequate courage.

In an article which I contributed to the 'Nineteenth Century' in 1883, I dealt with the care of the children by the State, and pointed out how inadequate were our safeguards against parental neglect, and how much more drastic was the legislation of America and other countries on this subject. I also advocated the emigration of pauper children to the Colonies, under proper guarantees, and showed how we might thereby drain away much of the hereditary pauperism of this country. I now wish to advocate a system of *industrial training for the children of our destitute classes conducted in night schools up to the age of sixteen.*

I am aware that at first sight this will appear to some a startling proposition, but I believe that a decade will not elapse before it is as commonly admitted to be wise and politic as national elementary education is now.

In order to bring this vividly before the reader, let me depict the life of a London schoolboy in the low parts of the city. He is compelled to attend school from five to twelve or thirteen years of age for five hours a day. Careful inquiry proves that in these poor districts 25 per cent. of the children come to school without breakfast, and have only a piece of dry bread, perhaps with some tea, for their dinner; their physical stamina is unequal to even a moderate intellectual effort, and probably half the school-time is passed in a sort of comatose state, in which they can learn absolutely nothing. They then go home to their miserable dens, where too often a drunken father or a profligate mother makes all happiness or morality impossible. They herd together in a single room, where all ages and both sexes sleep, eat, and dwell together. Hard as the school-life of such children is, it is much better than living entirely 'at home,' if such words can be used of their domestic surroundings, and it is no doubt true, as Sir Lyon Playfair has shown, that the mortality of children of school-going age has much decreased, owing to their being less constantly in the foul atmosphere of their fœtid slums. I thankfully admit that compulsory elementary education is the greatest factor yet known or tried for civilising the youth of 'outcast London.'

But it is a very imperfect agency; it comes far short of securing a fair prospect of a respectable after-life. Let me sketch still farther the process of youthful development. No children will stay in such filthy dwellings a minute longer than they possibly can; and so they spend their evenings on the streets, hearing and seeing all that is vile and debasing. Fancy what a picture of human life must be formed in the mind of a child who is familiar with the harlot and the drunkard from infancy upwards, and looks on these as the normal development of humanity! Yet so it is in many parts of our great cities. How little chance is there that short Bible lessons—excellent as these are—will counteract the 'object lessons' of human wickedness ever floating before their eyes! But the moment of supreme danger comes after leaving school. The little half-grown child of twelve or thirteen, stunted in all but its precocious knowledge of vice, is left free to wander at will by day and night on the streets. The parents of this class as a rule follow no regular trade; they pick up an uncertain livelihood from the innumerable precarious employments of a large city; they have no power to apprentice their children to an honest trade; many of them have no ambition; they have never known anything better than the uncertain livings of the streets, and they are contented that their children should be as themselves. A great proportion of them spend every farthing they can spare on drink, and have less concern for their offspring than the brute creation. Need one wonder that the children of this class—and it is a very large one—should reproduce the likeness of their parents? A few years spent on the streets in what is called 'hob-jobbing,' virtually settles their future lot; it stamps upon them indelibly the features of the tramp, the pauper, and the criminal; it feeds the horrible stream of fallen women which makes the streets of London hideous beyond those of any capital in Europe, and it prepares the way for a fresh crop of this baneful harvest in the next generation.[1]

For one of the gloomiest elements in the whole case is the extraordinary rapidity with which this degraded population multiplies; the birth-rate is far higher in these low slums than in the respectable neighbourhoods. Little girls frequently become mothers, and I am told that it is not uncommon for women of twenty to have three or four children.[2] The responsibility of bringing human beings into existence seems not to cross the minds of these sunken creatures; that they cannot feed or clothe their children is no hindrance to matrimonial or other alliances; and were it not for the vast infantile mortality, the numbers of the destitute classes would double or treble every

[1] 'Year by year, from seventy to eighty thousand London children pass out of elementary schools; of these, possibly the half obtain *bonâ-fide* occupation; as for the rest—the poorer part, inhabiting, too, the more densely populated quarters—there is nothing for them but the streets, and the almost certain life of a knave or a fool. It is probable that, every day, not less than seventy thousand boys and girls are actually "hob-jobbing about," utterly helpless, until they hob-job into gaols, penitentiaries, reformatories.'—Extract from *The Gaol Cradle, who rocks it?* By the Rev. Benjamin Waugh.

[2] The birth-rate in the prosperous district of Hampstead for the ten years 1871-80 was 24 per 1,000 annually; whereas in the poor and miserable district of Whitechapel it was 36 per 1,000, or just 50 per cent. higher.

twenty-five years. It may be truly said that nothing but starvation prevents this portentous increase.

Now, the sad thing is that no charitable outlay, however vast, could cure this terrible evil. Were we to suppose, as some socialists seem to think, that the thrifty and industrious classes should be made responsible for keeping the thriftless in comfort, this class would multiply far faster than has ever been known before. Parents relieved of all responsibility would neglect their offspring more than ever, and the millions of pauperised wretches would multiply into tens of millions in the not distant future. No wealth could long stand such a drain: the nation would sink into a Serbonian bog, in which all virtue and manliness would perish. No relief is to be found in any remedy which does not aim at producing individual virtue and independence: the proletariat may strangle us unless we teach it the same virtues which have elevated the other classes of society.

This leads me to describe more fully the scheme of reform I propose. It is, in short, an extension to all the destitute children of the land of the excellent system of industrial training which already obtains in the best of our district schools, in the Reformatory and Industrial schools, and in very many private institutions, such as Barnardo's admirable Homes in the east of London. It is to give to the thousands what is now given to the tens and twenties of our youthful population—to give it them, not as a reward for juvenile crime, nor as a badge of pauperism, but as a necessary part of education, quite as necessary as 'the three R's.' It is to make the training of the hands no less than the training of the head a part of national education; it is to conceive of 'education' as the fitting of a child for the duties of after-life, and, above all, for earning an honest livelihood.

Of course the *laissez-faire* school will say this is not the business of the State, just as they said fifty years ago that elementary education lay outside its province; but, if I am not mistaken, this objection will soon be brushed aside when the nation comes to see that we must either undertake this duty or risk anarchy in the future.

It is intolerable that millions of people should exist in our midst unable to live except on charity, because they have been taught in youth no means of livelihood. The little smattering of education got in our national schools by the children of this class is almost rubbed off them in the critical years that succeed school life; it only enables them to read the 'Police News,' the 'Newgate Calendar,' and such like rubbish, which is the chief literature that circulates in the slums. One sometimes wonders whether this so-called 'education' does not, in the case of many, only multiply their power for evil: the real education they most of all need is not given, viz. the habit of steady useful industry, the ability to turn their hands readily to any useful calling, and the power to fit themselves for a decent life, either at home or in the colonies. The critical period of child-life is from twelve to sixteen; it is then that the habits are formed which determine its future; at that vital stage the child-population of the slums are prowling about the streets, getting initiated into the arts of vice and crime.

The best career that is open to the boys afterwards is casual labour at the docks or warehouses—a field that is always glutted with hungry applicants; the best to which they can look forward in after-life is three days' work per week, affording on an average about 15s. per week of income, of which 5s. goes for rent, with a squalid, dirty wife and family usually on the brink of starvation. The career of the artisan, with his 35s. or 40s. per week, is forbidden to the common labourer, for he can get no early training; the great colonial field is closed against him, for he has no money to emigrate with, and, if despatched by charity to the shores of Canada or Australia, he is looked upon as a nuisance by the colonists; he cannot handle tools, he knows nothing of farm labour, he has no foresight, self-control, or independence; the life of the streets and slums of 'outcast London,' or 'squalid Liverpool,' has washed out of him every element that goes to make a successful colonist.

And so it happens that, while the flower of our population emigrate and build up prosperous fortunes at the Antipodes or across the Atlantic, the residuum remains behind, corrupting and being corrupted, like the sewage of the metropolis which remained floating at the mouth of the Thames last summer because there was not scour sufficient to propel it into the sea.

I can see no end to this vicious circle, unless the State provide for 'labour education' as well as mental education in our public school system.[1]

These ideas are rapidly being carried into effect on the Continent, under the name of technical training; prodigious efforts are being made, especially by France, Germany, and Switzerland, to cultivate the taste and talent of artisans, and they are extending them to a lower grade of schools, and in some places are requiring children to attend so-called 'Continuation Schools' at night up to the age of sixteen. But none of these countries needs the precise thing that we require in Great Britain; they have not nearly so many neglected children, nor so large a residuum of drunken and depraved parents. With us the case is far more urgent: we have terrible arrears of neglect to overtake; we were the last of the civilised States to enforce national compulsory education, and we shall have to do double work for many years to get abreast of the more advanced nations.

What I should like to see—were it possible of attainment—would be the adoption of *manual training* as a part of all school education in this country. I should recommend that Eton as well as Seven Dials should have industrial education. No country in the world produces so many helpless people among the middle

---

[1] 'A compulsory labour law, however undesirable in itself, is rendered absolutely necessary by varied and complicated causes, but by one chiefly—viz. the worthless character of many parents—necessary as a protection to the State. What do the selfish, animalised parents know of parental responsibilities, or care for the use or abuse of youth, the solemn duties of citizens, the basis of society, the weal of the State? Yet all these things are involved in their action towards their children. Themselves living from hand to mouth, they feel that it is right to turn out their children, regardless of all future consequences, on the chance of their somehow picking up a copper or two, and it is amazing to see how many a family can, and do, live thus on nothing to do. Did not *their* parents act thus? Were not they themselves turned out, and have not *they* got along? To the possibility of his children growing up to be sleepy labourers, beer-house loungers, idle paupers, what sleepy labourer, beer-house lounger, idle pauper, ever gives a thought? And if it could arise on his stolid imagination, why should he be shocked at the vision? Everything depends on the medium through which the prospect is seen His opinion—if opinion he has at all—is that everybody—husband, wife, and children—must "fend" for themselves, and take their chance.'—Extract from *The Gaol Cradle, who rocks it?* By the Rev. Benjamin Waugh.

and upper classes as England does. An unwholesome contempt for hand labour runs through all 'good society,' as it is falsely called; and so it is that when families are left destitute, as frequently happens among our improvident gentlefolk, it is found that none of them can earn their bread; neither sons nor daughters can emigrate, for there is nothing they can do that is of any use in the busy and practical communities of the New World. I believe that in far more cases than is generally supposed 'decayed' families in the upper and middle classes are supported by charity.

I much doubt, if an accurate census were taken of the self-supporting part of the population, whether it would not be found that as large a proportion of the people who wear broadcloth are in reality paupers as of those who wear fustian. There could not be a greater social boon conferred on this country than by engrafting on the educational system universally the teaching of some manual trade.

I am aware, however, that so sweeping a change as this is not within the scope of practical politics, and so I confine my suggestion to the children of what may be roughly called the destitute or semi-pauper class. It will at once occur as a difficulty, that the State cannot undertake the invidious task of discriminating them. Destitution has many shades: the deserving poor sink by imperceptible gradations into the profligate poor; the skilled artisan often falls through intemperance into the lower stratum; many members of the educated professions sink through their own vices into the slums; where are we to draw the line? I admit that a reply must be given to this objection. I propose that the general rule be to require all children, after leaving elementary schools (which is usually at twelve or thirteen), to attend night schools in the evening to receive manual training, *unless their parents or guardians can satisfy the inspector that they are usefully employed.* I would not propose that a child who is apprenticed to a trade, or even employed as an errand-boy in a shop, should be compelled to attend, and girls who were urgently needed for household work at home could also be excused, or only required to attend on one or two nights a week. The real object should be to make the meshes of the net fine enough to catch 'the street children,' those swarms of neglected juveniles whose parents can give no good account of them. It is impossible to estimate the number of this class, but I should not wonder if half a million, or one-tenth of the total number of school children, would be qualified for this wholesome discipline. And further, I have no doubt that as the immense advantages of this industrial training began to show themselves, many parents of a better class would be thankful to let their children share the benefit. It would only be needful to make provision in the first instance in considerable towns, say of over 10,000 population: the rural children do not need much training of this kind; they learn farm work in most cases, which is the best of all training. There would also be much less need of it in manufacturing towns, where children enter the mills as half-timers: the scheme would mainly apply to London and the great seaport towns, and need not impose a heavy burden on the State. We have a magnificent supply of Board Schools ready prepared, where most of the training could be cheaply given in the evening.

I would suggest that the boys should be taught carpentry, tailoring, shoemaking, printing, &c.; the girls sewing, cooking, washing, and domestic economy as far as possible. Some of these branches could easily be carried on in the existing school-rooms without injuring the furniture; others might require a shed or some cheap structure to be added for the coarse work. It would not be needful to occupy every school; certain centres might be fixed upon within easy reach of the children. The teaching of the boys might be given by skilled artisans, whose wages for two or three hours per evening would not be very high. I do not believe that the whole cost of training half a million children in this way need exceed half a million sterling per annum—say 1*l*. per head; whereas pauperism and crime cost the State fifteen millions a year, and mostly spring from the neglected children of this class.

I predict that within a generation, if we adopt these recommendations, we shall have reduced this heavy tax by one-half. A few years of such training would change the character of a boy's life. Physical labour, well directed and not overdone, is the truest recreation; there is nothing that boys are fonder of than learning handicrafts. When the taste is once formed, and the habit fixed, they may be left to take care of themselves. They will not often relapse into the indolent, hopeless life common to their class. A thousand avenues of useful employment will open up to them which are at present closed. They will find that they are welcome emigrants to every new country in the world.

Let those who doubt this pay a visit to Dr. Barnardo's Homes, where 700 boys, rescued from the worst of the slums, are trained to a cheerful, industrious life. He will see there a series of workshops, full of busy young life, and a diffused element of health and happiness which is wonderful, considering the horrible condition from which the boys were taken. The half-time system prevails there, as in the best pauper and industrial schools. It is found that children can do just as much head-work in the forenoon as if the whole of the day were so occupied; and the time given to manual work makes them far more healthy and happy.

I have no manner of doubt that in the poorer schools of the country the half-time system would answer far better than the existing one. The children of this class have but small mental capacity: three hours in the morning exhaust their little stock of nervous power, and the afternoon lessons are wearisome drudgery. The alternation of brisk physical work would make them far brighter and happier. I have carefully followed the discussion on over-pressure, and am convinced that great suffering is caused to a large class of ill-fed and weak children by the ridiculous attempt to force them into the same Procrustean bed with children of double their capacity. All this would disappear with the alternation of mental and physical exercise, and the school days of multitudes of children would become the happiest period of their lives.

I am aware that this suggestion goes beyond the scope of my previous remarks. My main object is to advocate *night labour schools*, after the period of school age is passed; and I do not suppose that the Government would so far change our present system as to adopt the half-time or alternative principle in existing schools. Yet I cannot forbear stating my opinion, that it would be much better for many of our poor children to have a couple of hours daily of simple manual instruction in our day schools. It would be capital preparation for the night labour schools which are to follow them.

The main point I wish to enforce is that the State should not let go its grasp of the child population without reasonable security against a relapse into pauperism, and indeed I may say in some cases into barbarism. I can imagine that on the part of many the objection will be raised that we shall create a great over-supply of skilled labour, that we shall flood the market with artisans and lower their wages. A similar objection was urged against the education of the masses fifteen years ago. It was said that the children of the poor would supplant the children of the gentlefolks in the educated professions. We did not listen to that ignoble argument; we did not close the portals of knowledge on the million, in order to keep a monopoly of the learned pursuits in the hands of a privileged class; and I am convinced we shall act in the same broad liberal spirit when it becomes a question of raising the lowest tier of our population. We wish to open to them the portals of industry, as we have already opened the portals of knowledge, and no selfish fears of other classes must stand in the way of it. At one time there was a great outcry against industrial training in prisons and reformatories, because it was expected to interfere with the labour market outside; but that has now passed away, and so in time will the dread that Society will suffer because all the members of which it is composed are more capable of earning their bread.

It is more than probable that work may not be found at home for all this population that we propose to train; but as Greater Britain contains sixty times the area of Great Britain, and only one-third of its population, there is ample room for them there, and this leads me to another branch of my argument.

The economical position of our country makes it imperative that we train our future citizens so that the surplus population may find homes in the thinly-peopled regions of the New World.

Lord Brabazon's article in the 'Nineteenth Century' on State-directed colonisation brought out this view most forcibly. He quoted from various writers, myself included, to show the tremendous problems we have to face owing to the rapid increase of our population. Permit me to recapitulate, in a few words, what I have written elsewhere on this subject, for it is at the root of the whole question.

This country, like all the settled and prosperous States of the world (France excepted), is confronted by a rapidly growing population; it has increased from $5\frac{1}{2}$ millions in the year 1700 to $10\frac{1}{2}$ millions in the year 1800, and is now (1884) 31 millions in Great Britain alone, and will apparently be 36 or 37 millions by the end of this century, and over 120 millions by the end of next, if the same rate of increase is maintained. It is also to be noted that the rate of increase is steadily becoming more rapid, owing to the great saving of life caused by improved sanitary arrangements, superior medical science, and abundant provision for nursing the sick and poor. Up to the beginning of the eighteenth century the rate of increase was extremely slow in all European countries, ours included. War, pestilence, and famine carried off a great portion of the people, and it is computed that the population of England only increased three millions in the 600 years after the Norman Conquest, or just about the increase of the last ten years. It has further to be added, that emigration was very small until the present century, and that the huge increase of this century, which will be three- to four-fold in Great Britain, is in spite of an emigration of several millions of our people. I see no reason why this process should be stayed in the next century, unless some national catastrophe occur. The death-rate is always falling, the birth-rate keeps up. Agencies for saving life are always increasing, and we ought, as prudent people, to provide against contingencies which are patent to the most careless observer.

We have, further, to face the fact that all this increase goes into our cities—the rural population is steadily decreasing: possibly this may be checked by changes in our land laws, but no changes in them can hinder arable land being turned into pasture where it pays better, nor can hinder labour-saving machinery being introduced. I believe that any relief that can be got from a more minute cultivation of the soil of this little island will not do much to change the course of events I have described. Our cities will keep growing larger and larger, and, I may add, more and more unmanageable. London has grown within this century from 1 to 5 millions of inhabitants, if we include the suburban area, and at the same rate of increase will reach twenty to thirty-five millions at the close of the next century. Let us remember that the world has never seen a city of more than two or three millions of people, except this gigantic metropolis of ours. Ancient Babylon and Rome never contained such multitudes as London already contains; and its growth is faster now than ever before in its history. In ten years another million will be added to 'Greater London'; and when or how is this process to stop?

Again, let me point out that the whole increase of our population for many years past has been fed with foreign food: we grow less than we did twenty or thirty years ago. One-half the population of Great Britain is now fed with foreign food; soon it will be three-fourths; possibly, by the end of next century, seven-eighths. This is not a cheerful prospect; the world is without any previous example of such a case: there have been great cities living by commerce, such as Tyre, Carthage, and Venice, but never a great nation except ourselves. It is hard to believe that we shall escape some fatal catastrophe unless we are wise in time and spread our population over the unoccupied parts of the globe. It may be said that, as long as we can manufacture for the world and import our food in exchange, we are as well off as if we grew it ourselves; but every man of business knows that it is becoming increasingly difficult to enlarge the outlets for our goods, as foreigners with one consent struggle to shut them out by high tariffs, while our colonies fast copy their example. I cannot believe that it is within the range of possibility that population can grow in this island as I have indicated without a desperate struggle for existence arising, in which our institutions and even civilisation itself might perish.

We ought to do as a captain does when he sees a storm approaching—reef our sails: we should prepare by fitting our people to use the wonderful safety-valve we possess in our vast colonial empire. We are indebted to Lord Brabazon for bringing before the public the question of State-directed colonisation; but I confess I see great difficulties in the way of its adoption. Granted that by an arrangement with the colonies we might secure farms at an outlay— including passage-money and temporary maintenance—of 100*l.* per family, and that we shall have good security for repayment; it would require a million sterling to transplant 10,000 families of 50,000 souls. This would give no perceptible relief. We should need to operate on a far larger scale. These islands could comfortably part with ten times that number of people annually, and most of them would depend upon the Government if it once undertook this duty. We might be called upon to spend ten millions a year in this way, and, as several years would elapse before repayment could be made, the State would soon incur an enormous pecuniary liability. But a greater difficulty remains. The demand for emigration would be made by the most useful and productive part of the population; at such time as this, when severe distress prevails, immense numbers of our best artisans would leave the country if tempted by such inviting proposals. We should encounter a scarcity of labour whenever trade revived, and the country would view with disfavour a depletion of its resources to be borne by those who remain behind. Besides, the Government would have to accept all able-bodied emigrants or reject all alike, for discrimination would be invidious and almost impossible. There would be a great risk, besides, of attracting immigrants from the Continent, in the hope of sharing these splendid facilities for settling abroad. The very class we wish to get rid of would remain behind, like the sediment at the bottom of a well. The wretched pauperised masses that swarm in our large towns are unfit for emigration. If the Government tried to shunt them off on America or Canada, they would meet with the same reception they did last year, when some Irish paupers were sent out. The unfortunate creatures would be returned on our hands, and we should only have raised a prejudice against all schemes of emigration. I do not wish to say that this plan may not have to be tried in some exceptional crisis—possibly we may be driven by dire necessity to adopt it; but I do say that it fails to relieve us of the crucial difficulty—how to rid ourselves of the useless and corrupting element in our cities.

Now, the plan I propose goes to the root of the matter; it undertakes to deodorise, so to speak, this foul humanity; it aims at turning into a productive and valuable commodity that which is now a wasteful and poisonous element in our social system. It does so at a very small cost, and by simply extending the educational lines we have already laid down. These boys and girls, well trained in industrial arts, would find their way without much difficulty into the colonies or the United States; or, if State aid had to be given, a very small amount would suffice; many of them would follow town occupations, and would not care to become farmers.

In conclusion, I wish to say a word or two about girls. Undoubtedly the difficulty is greater with them than with boys; they cannot be taught the numerous trades that boys naturally take up. It is not easy in night schools to find appliances for household work which girls most need to learn; besides, they are required from a very early age to help their mothers at home.

But the fact remains, that while a mass of girlhood is going to ruin in London and our large towns from absence of training and want of honest occupation, there is extreme difficulty in finding a supply of properly trained servants. Multitudes of poor women are pinching themselves to live on 5s. a week at slopwork, while mistresses cannot get cooks and housemaids at 20l. or 30l. per annum, with their food! It is a strange anomaly, yet so it is. I can only account for it by the want of any system for transforming the slatternly girl of the slums into the neat and tidy domestic servant. There is no way of bringing supply and demand together save a few benevolent institutions, which do not meet a tithe of the demand. Could not these night training schools do something to bridge over the chasm? Why could not cookery and housework form an essential part of a school girl's education? How much more important for the starving girlhood in the London slums to be fitted for domestic service than to know the heights of the Himalayas or the names of the Plantagenets! Surely there was some truth in the remark of the then Robert Lowe, when Rector of Edinburgh University, that British education was the worship of inutility! When shall we learn that the first necessity of a human being is to live, and only the second to have book-knowledge?

But another point remains to be noticed in respect of girls.

There is a great preponderance of females in this country; marriage is impossible for many of them on this account; while in the colonies and the Western States of America there is an equal preponderance of men, and no colonists are so welcomed as respectable women accustomed to household work. Surely this is an additional reason for trying to qualify these poor girls for a useful life in the colonies, in place of the wretched existence to which they are too often doomed at home.

Finally, I would say that our whole conception of education must be more practical than it has hitherto been. It is all very well to aim at high attainments, but there is such a thing as '*propter vitam vivendi perdere causas.*' We may buy even gold too dear. There are large classes of our population to whom the prime necessity of life is to learn to work, and so to live. This is well expressed in a letter I have from one who thoroughly understands this question: 'At present the unused manipulative power of the poor people is much what the unused brain-power was before the Education Act. Education was once voluntary, now labour is. Brains were once useless, now hands are.' What we want is to liberate that hand power which is going to waste, just as we have set free the brain power. There is a mine of potential wealth which lies beneath the surface. We must sink a shaft which will reach it; or, to change the metaphor, we must transmute this base metal into pure ore by the alchemy of wise and Christian statesmanship.

THE NEED OF TRADE SCHOOLS.[1]

BY RICHARD T. AUCHMUTY.

EDUCATION is in a transition state. Systems that have come down to us from past ages are found incapable of meeting the wants of the latter part of the nineteenth century. Especially is this the case in the way in which the young are taught how to work. Silently the old plan has passed away, and as yet no definite scheme has taken its place. Neither in this country (United States) nor in Europe can the apprenticeship system be said to exist. It became the custom in the Middle Ages to bind a lad who

[1] Reprinted, by permission, from *The Century* of November 1886.

wished to learn a trade by a written agreement to some master mechanic, for a specified number of years. In consideration of the lad's labour, the master was to care for him and teach him a handicraft. This custom continued until modern times. During the reign of Queen Elizabeth a law was passed forbidding any person to work at a trade without having first served an apprenticeship of seven years. Although this law was denounced by Adam Smith as tending to form labour monopolies, and the courts had decided it did not apply to any trade not practised at the time of its enactment, it was not repealed until the year 1814. The English and American apprentice laws still provide for indenturing a lad to a master mechanic, but such indentures are seldom made except by the overseers of the poor for pauper lads. An indenture between a master plumber of New York and three of his 'helpers' was recently published in trade journals as a curiosity. The old apprenticeship system perished, not because the indenture was looked upon as a species of slavery, nor because its results were unsatisfactory. It perished because the conditions of society under which it was possible no longer exist. The apprentice in former times lived with his master, sat at his table, and worked under his eye. For his conduct during his term of service and his skill when he became a journeyman his master was responsible. The modern apprentice is merely a hired boy, who, while making himself useful about a workshop, learns what he can by observation and practice. If he sees the interior of his master's house, it is to do some work in no way connected with his trade, and which may not increase the idea of the dignity of labour in the minds of such of his associates as are employed in stores or offices. In old times skill more than capital made the journeyman into a master. The master worked with his men. The more apprentices he could employ and the more thoroughly he could teach them, the greater his profit. The Act of Elizabeth was intended to secure the lad's labour to the employer, not to be a law, as it afterwards became, to limit the number of workers. The master now rarely works at his trade. His time is more profitably spent in seeking for customers, purchasing material, or managing his finances. The workshop is put in charge of a foreman, whose reputation and wages depend on the amount of satisfactory work that can be produced at the least cost. The foreman has no time to teach lads, and, as there is but little profit in their untrained labour, does not usually want them. There still survives from the old apprentice system of former days the idea that a lad employed in a workshop shall, when he becomes a man, be a skilled workman and capable of earning a journeyman's wages. This theory fixes a certain amount of responsibility upon an employer, which he is not always willing to incur. Business may increase or diminish. At one time many workmen may be wanted; at other times few or none. If lads are employed with the understanding that at the expiration of a certain time they are to be converted into skilled workmen, there may be times during the customary four years of service when there will be nothing for them to do. If retained, they will be a burden on the employer; if discharged, the lad will not unreasonably feel that an agreement has been broken. It is not, however, with the employer that all the difficulty of learning how to work is to be found. The different trades are organised into trades-unions, and one of the accepted theories of the unions is the advantage to be derived from limiting the number of workers. Instead of the fact that work makes work, that one busy class gives employment to other classes, it is assumed that there is a certain amount of work to be done, and the fewer there are to do it the higher wages will be. It is, therefore, sought to make each trade into a monopoly, and although these efforts have been uniformly unsuccessful, they have marred the lives of thousands of young men, and still continue to do so. Such monopolies are not possible, because foreign mechanics, attracted by wages several times greater than they could earn at home, with living but little, if any, dearer, cannot be prevented from crossing the ocean to better their condition in life; neither can mechanics be prevented from coming to the cities from country towns, and as the strength of a union depends upon the enrolment of nearly all the workmen in the trade the union represents, these mechanics are not only invited to join, but pressure is used to force them to do so. Thus, as the exclusive policy of the unions is powerless against the stranger, its force is directed against city-born young men. This term is used because in country towns there are no unions, and consequently no opposition is made to a lad's learning a trade, if he can find some master workman who is willing to employ him. In the country, however, the standard of workmanship is not so high as it is in cities, and country mechanics cannot usually compete on even terms with city workmen. Under union rules the employer is usually allowed from two to four lads, the term of service being from four to five years. This does not allow an employer to graduate under the most favourable circumstances more than one skilled workman each year. As there are not many employers even in the largest cities in any one trade, and, as already stated, some do not want young men, it becomes a matter of no small difficulty to learn how to work. So it often happens that although a lad may be willing to work, and may have strong predilections for certain kinds of work, he is more likely to meet with rebuff than encouragement. His first lesson in life teaches him that he has been born into a world where there is nothing for him to do. This lesson as he grows older he will unlearn. He will discover he was standing in a busy market-place, importuning the crowds to buy when he had nothing to sell. He was willing to do anything; there was nothing he knew how to do.

The old apprentice system is not likely to be revived. The life of the system was the personal supervision of the master, which the lad cannot have again. It may be for the interest of the master mechanic to train good workmen, but it is not his duty. The attempt to teach any large number of lads would be troublesome, even if permission could be obtained from the unions. The workmen of the future must learn how to work before they seek employment. All professional men do this. What scientific schools are to the engineer and architect, what the law school and the medical college are to the lawyer and the physician, or what the business college is to the clerk, the trade school must be to the future mechanic.

Manual instruction in schools especially designed for the purpose is not a new thing. Its rapid development in modern times is due less to the decay of the apprenticeship system than to the discovery that without such instruction the trades themselves were deteriorating. Transmitting a handicraft from man to boy carries with it wrong as well as right ideas. The practice of a trade may be taught; the theory on which that practice is based may be forgotten. The tendency of all shops is to subdivide work. A boy learns how to do one thing, and is kept at it. He has no chance to learn his trade. Trade schools first came to be regarded as important to the welfare of the State on the continent of Europe about the middle of the last century. In England, as in this country, they are of more recent origin. The report of the Royal Commissioners on Technical Instruction, London, 1884, shows not only the extent of technical instruction in European countries, but the value that is placed upon it by the people. This report gives descriptions of schools for the building trades, for weaving in wool and silk, for iron-work, furniture, clock and watch making, pottery, for the making of beer and sugar, indeed for almost every industry in which men and women are engaged. Many of these European schools, both those for general instruction in the mechanic arts and for special trades, are on a magnificent scale. At the Imperial Technical School at Moscow the annual expenses are 140,000 dollars per annum. The Technical School at Verviers, in Belgium, chiefly a school for weaving and dyeing, was built at a cost of 100,000 dollars, the annual expenses being upwards of 13,000 dollars. The Chamber of Commerce of Crefeld, in Prussia, a town of 83,000 inhabitants, having reported that the silk industry was languishing because of the superiority of the French training-schools, an establishment costing 210,000 dollars was begun, to which the State contributed 137,000 dollars, and the municipality 60,000 dollars, the remainder being raised by subscription. This town exports upwards of twenty millions of dollars of silk products, nearly all of which goes to England and the United States. At Chemnitz, in Saxony, now the rival of Nottingham in the hosiery business, and also the centre of an iron industry, is a technical school which costs 400,000 dollars. The report referred to says there is not a manufacturer in Chemnitz whose son, assistant, or foreman has not attended this school. At Hartman's locomotive works in the same town, employing nearly three thousand men, all the boys between fourteen and sixteen years of age are obliged to attend the technical school. To allow sufficient time to do so their hours of labour terminate at four o'clock in the afternoon twice each week.

THE NEED OF TRADE SCHOOLS

At Arco, in the Austrian Tyrol, the founding of a small school with one teacher to give instruction in the manufacture of those articles in olive-wood which find so ready a sale to travellers, developed an important industry, orders being now filled from all parts of Northern Italy and from America. The city of Paris maintains a school on the Boulevard de la Villette for workers in wood and iron. Full wages are obtained, it is claimed, by the graduates from this school. A similar school is maintained in Paris by the Roman Catholic Church, with the idea of combating the irreligious sentiments of Parisian workmen. Besides the technical schools in various parts of France, free evening lectures are given in the large towns on scientific subjects connected with the trades. In Sweden, according to a report made by Professor Ordway to the Massachusetts State Board of Education, there are about three hundred schools where manual instruction in the use of tools for wood and iron work is given. As a curiosity of technical education, it may be mentioned that in Ireland the Royal Agricultural Society maintains a model perambulating dairy, which, mounted on wheels, is drawn from village to village, the inhabitants being invited to witness the most approved methods of making butter and managing a dairy. In England the subject of technical education is now attracting much attention. A very fine school for apprentices has recently been completed by the city and guilds of London, and these guilds also encourage technical education by subsidies to schools in different parts of the kingdom.

Some idea of the need of instruction in the mechanic arts in the United States was probably present in the minds of the Senators and Representatives when the Land Grant Act of 1862 was passed. A clause in this Act reads as follows: 'The leading object shall be, without excluding scientific and classical studies, and including military tactics, to teach such branches of learning as are related to agriculture and the mechanic arts in such manner as the States may respectively prescribe, in order to promote the liberal and practical education of the industrial classes in the several pursuits and professions of life.' The report of the Secretary of the Interior, on Industrial Education, 1882, gives a list of forty-two different schools and colleges in various parts of the union which owe their existence to this land grant. Most of these are agricultural and engineering colleges. The words in the Act in regard to teaching such branches of learning as are related to the mechanic arts being usually interpreted to mean instruction in the use of carpenter's and machinist's tools. Of these land grant schools, the best known are the Massachusetts Institute of Technology in Boston, and the Hampton Institute at Hampton, Virginia. Each of these illustrates an interesting experiment in industrial education. The Massachusetts Institute of Technology might properly be called a school for foremen, as its graduates can be found superintending industrial establishments all over the United States. The pupil in weaving, for instance, is required to design or copy a pattern, and then work it out on the loom. In moulding he makes a drawing, models the wooden pattern from it, and casts the pattern in the metal. The course of instruction is four years —mathematics, chemistry, history, and the modern languages forming a part of the educational scheme. Hampton Institute was founded by General S. C. Armstrong as a normal school for coloured teachers. General Armstrong, while serving as a staff-officer at Fort Monroe, during the war, was brought in contact with the fugitive slaves who took refuge at the fort. When slavery was abolished, and four millions of men, women, and children became the wards of the nation, General Armstrong conceived the idea that they could best be educated and civilised by the aid of their own people. It was as necessary to teach this vast multitude who had never been beyond the sound of a master's voice how to work for themselves, and how to care for themselves, as it was to teach them to read and write. Manual instruction was therefore a necessity at the Hampton Institute. The male graduates were to be leaders on the farm or in the workshop as well as teachers. The female graduates were to be capable of cooking, sewing, or caring for the sick. How thoroughly and successfully this scheme has been carried out need not be stated here. Another type of the industrial school is to be found in the Worcester (Mass.) Free Institute. At this institution three and a half years of general education is combined with instruction in mechanical engineering, in carpentering, and in machinist's work. This school more nearly approaches the trade school, as many of its graduates are returned as 'journeymen mechanics.' The Worcester school was founded by private liberality. Without such aid, it may be added, neither the Massachusetts Institute of Technology nor Hampton Institute could have reached its present usefulness. In the European technical schools provision is made for instructing young men already in the trades by a course specially adapted to their wants. In this country this important branch of industrial education has received but little attention. The Carriage Makers' Association in this city maintain a school in designing and construction for the young men in their trade. The Master Plumbers of Philadelphia, Baltimore, and Chicago have plumbing schools for their 'helpers.' The Cambria Iron Works in Pennsylvania, and several private firms like R. Hoe & Co. of this city, give scientific instruction to their lads; while two railroad companies, the Pennsylvania and the Baltimore and Ohio, have shown not only what it is possible to do, but how much can be done at a trifling cost for the young men in the employ of great corporations. Beyond this short list, little has been done to supplement shop-work with systematic instruction. In the Baltimore and Ohio R. R. Company's shops at Baltimore* five hundred young men are employed. They are placed in charge of a graduate of the Stevens Institute, whose duty it is to see that they are not employed too long at one kind of work. He can change their work as often as it may seem desirable for their future interests. He can also take parties of them from their work at any time to explain to them the machinery they may be engaged upon or may see around them. A neat building has been erected for their use, which contains a library and class-rooms for instruction in mechanics and drawing. The lads are required to wear a uniform, which, besides giving them a jaunty appearance, tends to habits of personal neatness. What is done by the Baltimore and Ohio R. R. Co. could be done in any manufacturing town by the union of a few large employers.

The difference between manual instruction and trade instruction is not always clear in the public mind. By manual instruction is meant teaching a lad how to handle certain tools, usually carpenter's and blacksmith's tools, for the purpose of developing his hands and arms, precisely as other lessons are given to develop his observation or his memory. This is not teaching a trade, although it would render the work of the trade school much easier. A lad who has gone through a course of manual instruction at a school would be more likely to be a better mechanic than one who had reached seventeen or eighteen years of age without ever having held a tool in his hand. Manual training-schools are meant to make a lad handy; trade schools to make him proficient in some one art by which he can earn a living. Manual instruction has already been incorporated in the public school systems of Boston and Philadelphia. The New York Board of Education has maintained for several years a workshop at the Free College. It now proposes to open schools all over the city where boys and girls will be taught to use their hands. A great impression was made last spring by the exhibition, held by the Industrial Education Association of New York, of children's handiwork, and of the different methods of teaching them how to work. Not only was it shown what varied and excellent work little fingers could do, but school-teachers and superintendents came to testify that the brain-work was benefited by the hand-work.

Admitting that trade education is practicable, and that it is advisable both for the purpose of giving young men an opportunity to learn how to work and to keep the trades from deteriorating, it may be well to consider how such education can best be adapted to the wants of the American people.

In most of the foreign trade schools the technical instruction is combined with a general education, the course extending over several years. This system is also followed at the Hampton Institute, at the Indian school at Carlisle Barracks, at the Worcester Free Institute, and at the reformatories and asylums in this country where trades are taught. Except in special cases there seems no need of combining instruction in the trades with a general education. It is duplicating the work of the public schools, and adding greatly to the cost of industrial education. A lad can hardly be taught and boarded, even at a school or college which is liberally endowed, for less than 250 dollars per annum. For a four-years' course this would be 1,000 dollars, and to this sum must be added the cost of clothing, travelling expenses, &c. Such schools would be beyond the reach of those who are likely to lay brick, cut stone, or work at any of the mechanic arts. A simpler, shorter, more economical course of instruction is wanted for the future mechanic. It must be remembered that, although the law requires the parent to support the child, it is an established custom that after a certain age the child shall in some way contribute to the family support. No system of trade instruction will be successful that does not recognise this fact. From eighteen to twenty years would seem to be the best age to enter a trade school. The lad is then old enough to know what sort of work he likes, and for what his strength is adapted. As regards the amount of instruction given, it would be wisest not to attempt to graduate first-class journeymen. That it is possible to do so in many trades there need be no doubt, but it would appear to be better to ground a young man thoroughly in the science and practice of the trade he has chosen, and leave the speed and experience that comes from long practice to be acquired at real work after leaving the school. Such a system would be more economical, as by it the cost of teaching and the waste of material would be greatly lessened. This probation course, as the time spent between leaving the trade school and becoming a skilled workman may be called, need not be long. Six months will suffice in most trades. Young men who begin work in this way are likely to get on better with their fellow-workmen than if taught entirely at a school, and they will understand better how to accommodate themselves to different situations. Trade schools should not be free. They will be best appreciated when an entrance fee is required. Lawyers, physicians, engineers, architects, and clerks are expected to pay for their instruction, and there is no need to treat mechanics as objects of charity; neither do they desire it.

At the Hampton and Worcester schools the work of the pupil yields a revenue. At Hampton, contrary to the usual experience, a student's labour has been found to be of sufficient value to pay for his board and tuition. When the course of instruction at a trade school is short, it is best not to seek for any return from the pupil's work. The same temptation, otherwise, will exist as in the shop, of putting a lad at what he can do best instead of teaching him what he knows least about. The pupil's future is of more consequence than the material that may be wasted. In a well-organised trade school the waste is not a serious item, as the same material can be used many times.

In the belief that the most practical system was a combination of the trade school and the shop, of grounding young men thoroughly in the science and practice of a trade at the school, and leaving them to acquire speed of workmanship and experience at real work after their course of instruction was finished, the New York Trade Schools on First Avenue, between Sixty-seventh and Sixty-eighth Streets, were opened in the autumn of 1881. The schools were designed to aid those who were in the trades by affording them facilities to become skilled workmen not possible in the average workshop, and to enable young men not in the trades to make their labour of sufficient value to secure work, and to become skilled workmen in a short period after leaving the schools. The instruction was given on three evenings each week from November until April. Skilled mechanics were employed as teachers. How much it would be possible to teach during that limited time was unknown, neither were there any means to ascertain what effect the instruction received at the schools would have on the young man's success in life. Instruction was given the first season in two trades, plumbing and fresco-painting. The charge for instruction was made nominal to induce attendance. Twenty young men joined the plumbing class, about two-thirds of whom were in the trade as plumbers' 'helpers,' and thirteen joined the fresco class. Of this number one-third dropped off during the winter. The schools have now completed their fifth season. The attendance has increased from 33 the first season to 304 the fifth season. The charges have been increased to a sum which it is hoped will ultimately meet the expenses of the schools. Instruction is now given in plumbing, fresco-painting, bricklaying, stone-cutting, plastering, carpentry, wood-carving, and gas-fitting. A class in pattern-making was abandoned for lack of support. Those who came to the schools from workshops surprised their employers and comrades by their suddenly acquired skill. Those who came to learn a trade have usually found work.

There is a record at the schools of many of this latter class, who, to use the expression of more than one of them, owe their success in life to having joined the schools. Serious difficulties have to be encountered in obtaining work on account of trades-union rules, but these difficulties have not been found to be insurmountable.

As the time spent at the schools is short, the instruction is given on a prescribed course. Each pupil is required to begin at the beginning, and is advanced as rapidly as his proficiency will allow. Although the classes are kept as much as possible on the same work, no one is allowed to leave his work until he can do it well. Progress is necessarily rapid. A skilled workman is constantly on hand to show how the work should be done, and explain why one method is right and another wrong. Attention is also given to the way a lad stands and how he holds his tools. An awkward habit once contracted is not easily overcome. On two occasions additions were made to the schools by the bricklaying class. The work was done at the termination of the regular course of instruction, the young men being paid in proportion to the number of bricks laid. This practice was found to be of so much value, that the evening instruction for the bricklayers is now supplemented by two weeks' day work. The brick-work of three stores and a large apartment-house has also been almost entirely done by trade school young men. Better or more conscientious work it would be difficult to find. Those young men who are old enough to do a full day's work usually get from one-third to one-half a day's wages on leaving the schools, and full wages in from six to eighteen months afterwards. Thus it seems to be proved that a course of carefully arranged instruction on three evenings each week for a term of not quite six months puts it in the power of any young man to learn how to work. He no longer need beg the employer to teach him. He stands in the labour market with something to sell.

Although the system followed at the New York Trade Schools could perhaps be improved, it has the merit of giving those who are likely to attend such schools what they want. Many well-meant schemes have failed because this point was overlooked. A longer course would be better; indeed, some young men lengthen their term of instruction by labouring two seasons, but to many, and often to the best, even a single season is a heavy tax on their strength. To work all day for a present living, and then to begin again and work during the evening to acquire the skill necessary to obtain a living in the future, requires no small amount of energy and self-denial. Work in the shop ceases at six o'clock. Work at the school can hardly begin later than seven. This leaves one hour only for food, for rest, and for travel. The young men in the New York Trade Schools come from all parts of New York, from Brooklyn, Hoboken, and Jersey City. Some have come from Staten Island, Newark, and Orange. Between two and three hundred young men thus assembled to learn how to work, and who have paid their hard-earned money for the privilege, may almost be said to form an impressive sight. These young men are employed in offices and stores, in mills and workshops, and at the various occupations for which boy labour is needed, but which have no future for the man. During the five winters the schools have been open, no rude or profane word has been heard within their walls. The young men are attentive to their instructors, and although often inconveniently crowded are courteous to each other. Costly tools are scattered about, but they are cared for as if they belonged to those who used them. If they are fair specimens of a class which comprises fully two-thirds of the young men of this city, New York has reason to be proud of her sons.

It is often said that American parents are not desirous of having their children learn trades. The mothers, perhaps, may be responsible for this idea. The present custom of requiring a lad to work for four or five years before becoming a journeyman necessitates his beginning at an early age. Placing boys during ten hours a day with men of whose antecedents nothing is known is undoubtedly objectionable. Although less evil comes from it than is usually supposed, still injury may be done which a careful parent would guard against. A trade school not only avoids any danger of this kind, but it gives the parent an opportunity to ascertain for what sort of work the boy is suited. As it is now, the lad may work for several years at a trade and then find he has no taste for it. New places are not easily found; to change his trade may be impossible. He becomes a poor workman, without interest or heart in his work. Six months at a trade school would be time well spent if it only taught the lad for what work he is fitted.

Could the opposition of the trades-unions to young men learning trades be overcome, a great source of wealth would be opened to those now approaching manhood. This opposition comes almost entirely from foreign-born workmen. The effect of their policy is a matter of indifference to them. Unlike the American, the foreigner cares but little for the future. He looks only to the number of dollars it is possible to extract for a day's work. He willingly surrenders his liberty and his judgment to his union officers. To keep their places, these officers must be able to force the employers to obey the union rules. They not only believe in the advantages to be derived from limiting the number of workers, but they fear that, if many lads are allowed to work, the employer, with the aid of his apprentices, can withstand a strike. This fear is as groundless as the theory of the benefit of trade monopolies is mistaken. Skilled work can only be done economically by skilled workmen. The master mechanics put but a small value on boy labour. Even the Chicago Master Plumbers, in their effort to educate their 'helpers,' do not make it easier to enter the trade. The Journeymen Stone-cutters' Union is the only union in New York which has shown any interest in the welfare of young men. The Journeymen Plumbers' Union lately passed a resolution which, if acquiesced in by the Master Plumbers' Association, will prevent three out of every four of the young men now learning the plumbing trade in this city from becoming mechanics. Until lately, the right of a man to follow any honest calling he may see fit, provided he does not violate the laws, has not been questioned. This right is now being reasserted. It is not the province of any body of men, certainly not of any self-constituted organisation, to decide who or how many shall be allowed to work. No legislature is intrusted with such power. If a trade needs protection, it can be obtained in a legal manner. Lawyers and physicians seek to guard their professions and the public from incompetent men by legal enactments. The law requiring the examination and licensing of journeymen plumbers in the cities of New York and Brooklyn was intended to protect the public from ignorant workmen. Its provisions, with slight alterations, could be made to apply to any trade. The higher the standard of workmanship is made by which admission to a trade could be procured, the better for the trade and the public. Such a system would be better than 'cards of protection' obtained by favour or by purchase. 'An equal chance and no favour' are not idle words to the American mind. Mechanics did not invent their trades, they have no proprietary rights in them. Some trades have been handed down from remote antiquity. Some have deteriorated instead of improving. Roman masonry was better than our own. In metal-work we do not excel the mechanics of the Middle Ages. Furniture of the time of Louis XVI. is preserved in art collections for its elegance and the beauty of its workmanship. The demand for skilled labour all over the United States far exceeds the supply. To such work city-born young men are admirably adapted. They are handy, quick, and generally well educated. They should not only supply the home demand, but the demand which comes from villages that are becoming towns, and towns that in a few years will be cities. A thorough knowledge of a trade often yields its possessor, if he works but two hundred days in the year, an income equal to that received from twenty thousand dollars invested in Government bonds. Is this harvest to be reaped by the stranger and the foreigner, or are our own people to have a share?

MANUAL TRAINING IN SCHOOL EDUCATION.[1]

BY SIR PHILIP MAGNUS.

'Manual labour is the study of the external world.'—EMERSON.

THE first object of education being to bring the mind of man into direct relation with its surroundings, and as this communion is only possible through the senses, the importance of the cultivation of the senses is duly insisted upon by all educational authorities. Now, of the several organs through which we obtain a knowledge of the external world, the sense of touch and the

[1] Reprinted, by permission, from the *Contemporary Review* of November 1886.

muscular sense have a certain prominence as giving us perceptions which are mainly intellectual. For this reason we should expect that the training of the muscular and tactile sensibility of the hand, and the training of the muscular sense generally, as exercised in the determination of size, shape, and resistance, would form an essential factor of education. But so little has this been the case that, until comparatively recent times, the training of the faculties by which we obtain, at first hand, our knowledge of the things about us has been sadly neglected, and education has consisted mainly in storing the memory with words, with the statements and opinions of others, and with inferences therefrom. Apart altogether from the value of the constructive power which manual skill affords, the knowledge of the properties of matter which is obtained in the acquisition of that skill is considerable, and cannot be equally well acquired in any other way. It is this which gives to manual training its value as an educational discipline, and it is mainly for this reason that it is coming to be regarded as an important part of the educational system of nearly every country. 'The introduction of manual work into our schools is important,' says Sir John Lubbock, 'not merely from the advantage which would result to health, not merely from the training of the hand as an instrument, but also from its effect on the mind itself.'[1] And it is to this effect on the mind that I desire to call especial attention in this article.

By manual training one commonly means exercises in the use of the tools employed in working wood and iron.

It cannot be too often repeated that the object of workshop practice, as a part of general education, is not to teach a boy a trade, but to develop his faculties and to give him manual skill; that although the carpenter's bench and the turner's lathe are employed as instruments of such training, the object of the instruction is not to create carpenters or joiners, but to familiarise the pupil with the properties of such common substances as wood and iron, to teach the hand and eye to work in unison, to accustom the pupil to exact measurements, and to enable him by the use of tools to produce actual things from drawings that represent them. The discipline of workshop instruction may be regarded as supplementary to that of drawing, with which,.

[1] *Fortnightly Review*, October, p. 467.

however, it should always be associated, as teaching a knowledge of *substance* in addition to that of *form*. Moreover, under competent instructors, it may be made an instrument of education similar, in many respects, to practical science. In the workshop, the operations to be performed are less delicate, the measurements are not required to be so exact, the instruments are more easily understood, the substances employed are more ordinary, but the training is very similar, and in so far as the faculties exercised are those of observation rather than of inference, the training, educationally considered, is a fitting introduction to laboratory practice. At the same time, the skill acquired in the workshop is particularly serviceable to the laboratory student in enabling him to make and fit apparatus, and in giving him that adroitness on which progress in scientific work so much depends. But whilst a certain amount of manual training is valuable in the education of all classes of persons—a fact which is already recognised by the head-masters of several of our best secondary schools—the usefulness of this kind of training is much greater in the case of children of the working classes, whose education is too limited and often too hurried to admit of any practical science teaching, such as older children obtain, and to whom the skill acquired is of real advantage in inducing in them an aptitude and taste for handicrafts, in facilitating the acquisition of a trade, and possibly in shortening the period of apprenticeship, or of that preliminary training which in so many occupations takes the place of it.

An objection is sometimes raised to the introduction of manual training into elementary schools on the ground that, as the children of the working classes necessarily leave school at an early age, and spend their lives for the most part in manual work, such time as they can give to study should be occupied in other pursuits—in cultivating a taste for reading, and in the acquisition of book knowledge. This objection is due to a misconception of the true objects and aims of education, and to an imperfect knowledge of what is meant by workshop instruction. To assume that the best education can be given through the medium of books only, and cannot be equally well obtained from the study of things, is a survival of the Mediævalism against which nearly all modern educational authorities protest. But there is another and more deeply rooted error in this argument. People often talk and write as if school-time should be utilised for teaching those things which a child is not likely to care to learn in after life; whereas the real aim of school education should be to create a desire to continue in after life the pursuit of the knowledge and the skill acquired in school. In other words, the school should be made, as far as possible, a preparation for the whole work of life, and should naturally lead up to it. The endeavour of all educators should be to establish such a relation between school instruction and the occupations of life as to prevent any break of continuity in passing from one to the other. The methods by which we gain information and experience in the busy world should be identical with those adopted in schools.

It is because the opposite theory has so long prevailed, that our school training has proved so inadequate a preparation for the real work of life. This was not the case in former times; and the demand for technical instruction, both in our elementary and in our secondary schools, is a protest against the contrast which has so long existed between the subjects and methods of school teaching and the practical work of everyday life.

We are always justly complaining that in this country children leave school at too young an age, before they can have had time to properly assimilate the knowledge they have acquired, with the result that they soon forget a great part of the little they have learnt. At the age of fifteen or sixteen, when they begin to feel the want of technical instruction, they are wholly unprepared to avail themselves of the opportunities for obtaining it now brought within their reach. It is to remedy this state of things that Continuation Schools and Recreative Classes are much needed. But there can be little doubt, if elementary education were made more practical, that parents would be more willing, even at some sacrifice, to let their children benefit by it. They are often led to take their children away from school, because they do not see much use in the 'schooling.' Of course, the desire to secure the child's early earnings operates in very many cases; but I am convinced that it would be easier to persuade parents to forego these earnings if the school teaching had more direct reference to the work in which the children are likely to be subsequently occupied.

Now, in order that manual training may serve the purpose of an intellectual discipline, the methods of instruction must be carefully considered. That the training of the hand and eye, and the development of the mental faculties, are the true objects of the instruction should never be lost sight of. In many respects, the instruction should partake of the character of an ordinary object-lesson. Before the pupil commences to apply his tools to the material in hand he should learn something of its nature and properties. The teacher, in a few words introductory to each lesson, should explain to his pupils the distinguishing characteristics of different kinds of wood, as met with in the shop and as found in Nature, and also the differences in the structure and properties of wood according to its sections, treatment, &c. And he should illustrate his lessons by reference to specimens and examples, a collection of which should be found in every school workshop. Something should be said of the countries from which timber is imported, and the conditions under which it is bought and sold, and in this way the material to be manipulated should be made the centre of a series of scientific object-lessons.

Concurrently with the practice in the use of any tool, the pupil should learn its construction, the reason of its shape, and the history of its development from other similar forms. The saw, the plane, the chisel, and the callipers should each be made the subject of an object-lesson to the pupils. In the same way, the teacher should explain the purposes of the different parts of constructive work, and should have models of tennon, mortice, dovetailing and other joints to illustrate his explanations.[1] Fifteen or twenty minutes thus spent might be made the means of stimulating the intelligence and of exercising the observing and reasoning faculties of the children, and of enabling them to fully understand the work they are doing and the instruments they are using.

Further, the children should be taught, from the very first, to work from correct scale drawings, made by themselves from

---

[1] Collections of these models for school purposes are sold by Messrs. Schröder, of Darmstadt.

their own rough sketches. How simple soever the object may be which the pupil is to construct, it should exactly correspond with his own drawings. In this way the workshop instruction supplements and gives a meaning to the drawing lesson, and the school teaching is made to have a direct bearing upon the subsequent work of the artisan. Dr. Woodward, the instructor of the St. Louis Manual Training School, who has had considerable experience in organising and superintending workshop instruction, tells us that 'the habit of working from drawings and to nice measurements gives to students confidence in themselves altogether new;' and he justly claims 'that it is the birthright of every child to be taught the three methods of expression—1st, by the written, printed, or spoken word; 2nd, by the pencil and brush, using the various kinds of graphic art; 3rd, through the instrumentality of tools and materials, which enable one to express thought in the concrete.'[1] The Committee of Council on Education, in their recent report, speaking of the teaching of cooking to girls, say:—'After the three elementary subjects and sewing, no subject is of such importance for the class of girls who attend public elementary schools; and lessons in it, if properly given, will be found to be not only of practical use, but to have the effect of awakening the interest and intelligence of the children.' Surely, what is true of sewing and cooking in the case of girls, is true to a greater extent of drawing and handicrafts in the case of boys.

In many parts of the Continent, manual training has now for some years been associated with elementary instruction. In France, Belgium, Austria, Holland, and Sweden the workshop is a part of the school-building; and in the United States the number of manual training schools of higher grade, somewhat similar to the well-known apprenticeship schools of France, is steadily increasing. Indeed, judging from the published accounts of these schools, and from the writings of some of the most prominent educationists in the United States, an enthusiasm is spreading among Americans in favour of workshop instruction, which is likely to have an important influence on the industrial progress of this eminently practical and inventive people.

[1] *Proceedings of International Conference on Education*, London, 1884, vol. ii. p. 58.

In the Report of the Commissioners on Technical Instruction, notices will be found of some of the principal Continental schools which are now fitted with workshops. Sir John Lubbock, in the article above quoted, has supplemented this information by reference to the ' Slöjd ' system of manual instruction which is adopted in Sweden. An interesting account of this system has been written by M. Sluys, who is well known to educationists from his connection with the Ecole Modèle of Brussels. Since the Report of the Commissioners was published, the movement in favour of workshop teaching in schools has advanced rapidly in France. Nearly every large town has now its higher elementary school (a type of school as yet scarcely to be found in this country), fitted with workshops for wood and iron; and out of 174 primary schools supported by the city of Paris, 95 are now provided with workshops, 90 for instruction in carpentry and wood-turning, and 5 for metal-work. In these schools the manual teaching has hitherto been given either before or after the ordinary school hours; but the Municipal Council of Paris attach such importance to this training that it is proposed to make the workshop instruction a part of the regular school curriculum. This change will necessitate a re-arrangement of the school hours and the provision of workshops in the remaining 79 schools in which they have not yet been fitted. But it is confidently expected that the Municipality of Paris, which has done so much for the technical education of its artisans, will not hesitate to incur this additional expense. The action of the city of Paris gives additional weight to the recommendation of the English Commissioners on this subject.

Experiments of introducing workshops into elementary schools have been tried in this country, with results sufficiently encouraging to justify the extension of the system. In Sheffield, Birmingham, and Glasgow the results have been eminently satisfactory. In London, the experiment has recently been tried on a small scale, and under not the most favourable circumstances, in the Beethoven Street Schools; but the report of Mr. Tate, the energetic head-master, is so encouraging that the School Board of London is very desirous of extending the system of instruction to a large number of the schools under its control. In his report to the Board, Mr. Tate says:—

'This class was started on September 28, 1885, in a shed or workshop built by the Board in a recess in the playground, and the instruction is given by the school-keeper, a carpenter by trade, under the direct supervision of the head-master.

'The boys are chosen mainly from the Seventh Standard, and attendance at the workshop is considered a privilege, and a reward of merit in ordinary school subjects. It is therefore a stimulus and incentive to industry and thoroughness of work. This plan has been so effective that a boy once chosen values the teaching and practice so much that he continues to be chosen each week, and the instruction is therefore continuous, for the class has been virtually the same since it started.

'Boys who have been trained in a good school, and have acquired soundly the rudiments of education, too often when they leave school think that their proper career is a City counting-house, and that to wear black clothes and appear as a gentleman is a fair summit of their ambition. I certainly think that this workshop for upper standard boys will help to dissipate this idea, as it will show boys that, after we have given them the best education which the school offers, we then lead them into the workshop, and so practically show them that the end and aim of our training is to enable them to learn some useful trade and so become good workmen.

'The workshop, I believe, is a valuable training to enable the eye and hand to work in harmony. It is intended to make the school drawing, especially the scale drawing and geometry, apply as much as possible to the work done in the workshop. It is certainly a pleasant relief to ordinary school work. Should a boy not follow a trade when he leaves school, he will at least be able to make his home work comfortable by using the skill and facility which he has acquired in this workshop.'

At the expense of the Rev. S. Barnett and a few of his friends, a workshop has recently been fitted in the school attached to St. Jude's Church, Whitechapel. Arrangements have been made for giving instruction in carpentry and turnery to boys, and in modelling and wood-carving to girls of the upper standards, and the results of the lessons have fully justified the most sanguine expectations of the advocates of this kind of instruction. Those who have visited these schools have been struck with the cheerful interest shown by the children in their work, and by the effect of the teaching in quickening their perceptive faculties and in stimulating their intelligence. The contrast between the listless and often inattentive attitude of children, occupied with some ordinary class lesson, and the eager eyes and nimble fingers of the same children at the carpenter's or modelling bench is most instructive; and no one who has seen it can have any doubt of the educational value of this kind of training. These results, it must be remembered, have been attained by teachers most of whom have themselves been trying experiments, and have been working by the light of Nature without any well-considered methods. Under properly trained instructors, the results would doubtless have been far more satisfactory.

There is good reason to believe that the stimulating effect of workshop instruction on the intelligence of children will be such that, notwithstanding the loss of the time spent in the shop, their progress in their ordinary studies will be in no way retarded.

Mr. Swire Smith, a member of the late Commission on Technical Instruction, states that 'the half-time children of the town of Keighley, numbering from 1,500 to 2,000, although they receive less than fourteen hours of instruction per week, and are required to attend the factory for twenty-eight hours per week in addition, yet obtain at the examinations a higher percentage of passes than the average of children throughout the whole country receiving double the amount of schooling.' This answers the objection so often raised, that the curriculum of elementary schools is already overcrowded. Possibly it may be with literary studies, but not with practical work, and the combination of the two will go far to correct the tendency to over-pressure inherent in our system of payment by results.

As a general rule, children should be required to have passed the Fifth Standard before being admitted into the shop. They should receive two lessons a week, and each lesson should be of about two hours' duration. No fixed rule can at present be given as to the number of children who can be taught by one instructor. For convenience of supervision the shop should be fitted for the accommodation of not more than twenty-five children. On starting a class, each pupil requires more individual attention than later on. A class of beginners, therefore, should not consist of the full complement of children. Where the same shop is used for bench work and lathe work, it will be found that a double lathe will occupy four pupils, that eighteen can be accommodated at three carpenters' benches, each of not less than 14 feet 6 inches in length, whilst two may be engaged in sawing. Besides the benches and lathes, the school should contain a large blackboard, a cupboard, which is better than boxes for holding tools, and a grindstone.

In estimating the expense of adding this subject to our elementary school course, we have to consider the cost—first, of equipping the workshops; second, of the material used; third, of the teaching.

Supposing a shed or some other room to be found, which can be used as a workshop, the cost of equipping the shop with benches and with the necessary tools need not exceed thirty shillings for each pupil's place, and the workshop can be used by different sets of pupils at different times. Moreover, a shop need not be fitted at once with the full complement of benches; for, after a time, the more advanced pupils may be employed in making some of the additional fittings required.

The cost of material is inconsiderable. The children soon learn to construct the various articles for their own homes, which, on payment of the cost of the material consumed, become the property of their parents. Some, too, might be employed in making models and other objects, including certain workshop fittings, which might be purchased for the use of other schools. At the same time, care must be taken that the work is always subordinated to the educational purpose of the instruction.

Of the actual cost of the teaching no very exact estimate can as yet be formed. Much depends on the system adopted. If the instruction were given during school hours, it would take the place of some other lesson, and, by a proper arrangement of time-tables, might be given at very little additional expense. In some of the schools in which the experiment has been already tried, special teachers have been appointed, who have received a certain fee for each lesson. But if several schools in the same district combined, one teacher might be engaged, and either the children might be brought to a common centre, as in the case of the cookery classes, or the teacher might go from school to school, as in the case of the science teaching in Birmingham and Liverpool. The latter plan might be more convenient for the schools; but the former plan would be more economical, as enabling one shop and certain tools to be used by several sets of children.

It would be necessary under any circumstances that the instruction should be encouraged by a system of grants, or by some equivalent external aid. A system might be organised of paying grants on the results of the individual work of each pupil; but all the disadvantages of the method of 'payment by results' would be emphasised in the case of workshop instruction, and the teaching would lose much of its disciplinary value. The amount of the grant should depend mainly on the average number of children in attendance. A grant of four shillings, as in the case of cookery lessons, and the recognition of the subject by the Education Department, would afford sufficient encouragement to induce certain School Boards and School Managers to make manual training a part of the curriculum of the schools under their control. The total amount of these grants would be but a slight addition to our education expenses. According to the last report, the whole number of children presented for examination in the Sixth and Seventh Standards was 112,445. Of these, we may assume that about 60,000 are boys. Supposing half this number to elect to receive workshop instruction, the grant would amount to 6,000*l.* a year. But even this estimate is excessive as an addition to our present expenditure. For many of the children might take handicrafts in lieu of one of the specific subjects on which grants are now paid.[1] It may therefore, I think, be asserted that, the workshops

[1] It may be well here incidentally to call attention to the relatively small amount of grants earned for specific subjects. Out of 352,860 children who last year were examined in elementary subjects in the Fifth, Sixth, and Seventh Standards, only 64,376 presented themselves in specific subjects, the total amount of grant paid being 14,662*l.* 11*s.* 8*d.* Of the children on account of whom these grants were earned, Sir John Lubbock tells us that less than 25,000 were examined in any branch of science.

being once equipped, the additional cost in grants of introducing handicraft teaching into the curriculum of our elementary schools would not exceed 5,000$l.$ a year; and for this comparatively small expenditure about 30,000 boys might be annually sent out into the world from our elementary schools endowed with practical skill at their fingers' ends, imbued with a taste and aptitude for the real work of their life, and so educated as to be able to apply to that work the results of scientific teaching and scientific methods.

In organising a scheme of technical teaching in connection with our elementary schools, the difficulty has to be met of obtaining good teachers and competent inspectors. The artisan, who is a skilful workman and nothing more, may succeed in teaching the elements of carpentry and joinery; but he is not the kind of teacher needed. It is of the utmost importance that the instructor should be a good draughtsman, should have some knowledge of physical science, should be an expert workman, and should have studied the art of teaching. To obtain at first such ideal instructors would be impossible; but there is no reason why, gradually, they should not be trained. Two processes suggest themselves. We might take a well-trained elementary teacher, having an aptitude for mechanical arts, and give him a course of instruction in the use of tools, either in a technical school or in an ordinary workshop; or, we might take an intelligent artisan, who had studied science and drawing in some of the excellent evening classes which are now found in almost every town, and give him a short course of lessons on method in relation to workshop instruction. Good teachers might be obtained by either of these processes. Perhaps the latter is preferable, as it is most important that the teacher who is to inspire confidence should be a good workman to start with and thoroughly familiar with the practice of his trade. For such intelligent and educated artisans there is, 1 hope, a future of profitable employment. It would be well, however, that in all our technical colleges opportunities should be afforded to teachers in elementary schools of acquiring practice in the use of tools; and that special training classes should be formed for artisans in the organisation of workshops and in the best methods of workshop teaching.

Nearly all educationists have pointed out the many advantages of enabling children at an early age to realise the connection between *knowing* and *doing*. Commenius has well said: 'Let those things that have to be done be learnt by doing them.' Rousseau has pithily expressed a similar idea in saying: 'Souvenez-vous qu'en toute chose vos leçons doivent être plus en actions qu'en discours ; car les enfants oublient aisément ce qu'on leur a dit, mais non pas ce qu'ils ont fait et ce qu'on leur a fait.' Locke, speaking of the education of a gentleman—for in his day the education of the poorer classes was scarcely thought of—says : ' I would have him learn a trade, a manual trade ; ' and Emerson, in the choice words, ' Manual labour is the study of the external world,' tersely states the whole aim and purpose of my remarks. Rabelais, Montaigne, Pestalozzi, Fröbel, Combe, Spencer, and others have urged the importance of practical teaching, of studying things before words, of proceeding from the concrete to the abstract. But, as yet, such has been the inertia of school authorities and teachers, and such the force of tradition, that we are only now beginning to employ the methods of instruction that have been advocated for years by the most eminent educational reformers.

In what I have said, I have endeavoured to show that workshop instruction may be made a part of a liberal education ; that, as an educational discipline, it serves to train the faculties of observation, to exercise the hand and eye in the estimation of form and size, and the physical properties of common things; that the skill acquired is useful in every occupation of life, and is especially serviceable to those who are likely to become artisans, by inducing taste and aptitude for manual work, by tending to shorten the period of apprenticeship, by enabling the learner to apply to the practice of his trade the correct methods of inquiry which he has learnt at school, and by affording the necessary basis for higher technical education.

Possibly, the latest authoritative expression of opinion on the importance of manual training was a resolution, unanimously agreed to at the International Congress on Commercial and Technical Education, recently held at Bordeaux, to the effect

MANUAL TRAINING IN SCHOOL EDUCATION 105

that it is desirable that manual work should be rendered obligatory in primary schools of all grades.

It is satisfactory to know from a circular [1] that has recently been sent to school managers, that this important subject is engaging the serious attention of the Royal Commission on Education now sitting, whose labours, it is to be hoped, may result in making our elementary teaching more practical, less mechanical, and better adapted to the future requirements of the working classes.

[1] The circular, as published by Lord Brabazon in a letter to the *Times* of October 11, contains the following questions :—
    1. Is the course of teaching prescribed by the Code suited to the children of your school?
    2. What changes, if any, would you desire in the (Education Acts)? in the Code? in the administration?
    3. Would you recommend the introduction into your school of practical instruction? A. In any of the industries of the district? or in the use of tools for working in wood or iron? B. (for girls) in the domestic duties of home?

TECHNICAL EDUCATION.[2]

(TRANSLATION OF A PAPER READ BEFORE THE INTERNATIONAL CONGRESS AT BORDEAUX, BY H. CUNYNGHAME.)

BEFORE making my contribution to the labours of this Congress, I must explain the circumstances under which I am present here. I am employed by the Charity Commissioners, by whom the charities of England and Wales are regulated and controlled, and I am here by their direction, with a view of acquiring any information that may be of value to them.

But, so far as I am aware, the Commission has no particular educational opinions, nor, if it had, should I be the person to expound them. You will therefore please understand that any remarks I make are simply my own opinions, formed during several years of experience, but which I hope to correct and modify in proportion as I learn more of the subject. I may, however, remark that I am greatly strengthened in them by the fact that they coincide in principle with the report of the

[2] Reprinted, by permission, from *Eastward Ho!* of January, 1887.

important Commission on Technical Education which has lately been presented to the English Parliament.

The present system under which an artisan is prepared for his calling must be considered very defective. As a rule, the sons of workmen in England, from the age of eight to thirteen years, attend the primary or Board schools established under the Education Acts. After this they usually obtain some light form of employment for a year or so; they are then put to their trades, commencing usually at about five shillings a week, and gradually rising during seven years to about eighteen shillings a week, after which they obtain full workmen's wages.

The model of our school education throughout England has undoubtedly been taken from our great public schools, which are justly regarded by us with pride and affection.

These public schools are highly successful in forming principles of generosity and honour; habits of self-reliance, and the art of living amongst others. Added to this is a fair amount of Latin, a little Greek, and mathematics; and boys destined for public examinations are allowed to acquire a smattering of languages, chemistry, and physical science.

This system of instruction has come down by an almost unbroken tradition from the Middle Ages, and has set the example to schools throughout the kingdom. It still preserves some characteristics of its origin. Knowledge is imparted more from books than from things—facts are made to depend rather on the dicta of authority than upon experiment. Sciences are taught without apparatus; geometry without models; trigonometry without scales and protractors. To these schools it is almost as though Lord Bacon had never lived.

For boys who are to become divines or lawyers or statesmen, or to enter the public service of the country, a purely literary education may, perhaps, be the best. But, considering that the majority of the boys will become soldiers, doctors, engineers, manufacturers, merchants, or colonists, it may well be doubted, not only whether the subjects taught at our public schools are sufficient, but whether the method of learning only from books is not pushed too far.

The English are a people with minds of a concrete order; that is to say, they learn better from things than from books, and dislike abstractions. This tendency finds utterance in the contempt for theory which we find commonly expressed, especially by the working classes. It is a mistaken contempt, but one which has arisen, to some extent, from an observation of the defects of the merely book-system of instruction.

Almost all our great men have learned rather from experience than from precept, and, so far as the sciences are concerned, nearly all our great discoverers have been handlers of matter from their childhood.

A careful examination of their biographies shows this. It is customary, for instance, to regard Sir Isaac Newton as a mathematician, locked in his study and immersed in papers, and making no more experiments than to observe the fall of an apple—in fact, studying mathematics according to our present school-method, by means of unrealised abstractions. But if his works and life are consulted, we find that the story of the apple is a myth, and that he made his own apparatus and ground his own optic-glasses, like any optician. If I speak only of our own great men—of Priestley, Wollaston, Sir Humphry Davy, Hooke, Wren, Watts, Faraday, or Wheatstone, all of whom were ardent experimenters—think not that I have forgotten the illustrious mathematician Fresnel, who discovered the true laws of light, which even the great intellect of Newton had failed to grasp, with the aid of some apparatus made by his own hands, out of thread and wire, and with only the occasional help of the village blacksmith. It is, in fact, not too much to say that, from the time of Bacon and Descartes, no mathematician or physicist or philosopher has ever or will ever again be able to dispense with constant experiments, and it will therefore be necessary to effect, in our educational system, a change corresponding to the change which has taken place in our mode of thought and discovery. It is, however, not my intention to dwell further upon the merits and defects of our school teaching than to show that if that system be of questionable utility for many boys of the upper classes, it will almost certainly be imperfect when applied to the children of artisans. Of course, in the first place, the greatest object of all in the national schools, is to imprint on the children sound principles, so as to make them good men and good citizens. In the next place, writing and arithmetic, which are the avenues to knowledge, should be thoroughly taught. But when once it is resolved to go beyond this, how absurd it becomes to try and teach these children, from books, things which even a very clever man could hardly learn, except from observation. This method only widens the gulf between theory and practice, which it should be our aim to unite, and under it the boys soon learn to look on all book-learning as something of a metaphysical nature, not applicable in any practical manner. And no wonder, if physiology, physics, and botany are attempted to be taught without models or apparatus, by men who never made an experiment. Not only, however, is the method of the elementary schools insufficient, but the training of the artisan after leaving school is also very defective.

In ancient time the education of the artisan was provided for by the apprenticeship system. But this has now broken down—a result which may be attributed to the operation of several causes.

In the first place, the spread of printing is tending rapidly to make public all arts, so that the ancient trade mysteries are almost things of the past.

In the next place, the recent advances of science have so revolutionised industries that most of the old methods and secrets are obsolete; so that the mysteries, for which formerly a good premium was payable by an apprentice, are now either well known or else useless.

Again, the factory system, and the modern application of machinery and capital to manufactures on a large scale, has so divided labour that small manufacturers have almost ceased to exist, and, consequently, the personal supervision of the master over his apprentices has disappeared.

Facilities of locomotion have also mixed up the populations of town and country, so that an apprentice can easily run away and find work in a new position, whereas, in old times, he would have had great difficulty in leaving his master and embarking in a new career.

As a result, good workmen are becoming scarce, for few get a proper training. The number of men who are mere factory-hands, possessing no general knowledge or power of adaptation, is increasing, and most of the boys who have served a few years in a workshop, instead of remaining to complete their training, are only anxious to gain an immediate increase of wages.

This picture, therefore, of the education of the workman is unsatisfactory. The boys leave the primary schools with a certain amount of mere book-learning, but without any practice in the art of learning from things; they become apprentices in shops or factories where it is no one's business to teach them their trades; they often leave before their education is completed, and, during their apprenticeship years they find neither encouragement nor opportunity for self-improvement.

These defects are being widely felt in England. Manufacturers complain that good workmen are daily growing more scarce, and the keenness of foreign competition is beginning to make English workmen feel their deficiencies.

Hence has arisen the call for technical education. Much has already been done in England in this direction. The Charity Commission, for many years past, has devised every year schemes for technical education; the City Guilds Institute has founded several schools, and encouraged others; and private beneficence has established some excellent institutes in our large towns. But more still remains to be accomplished. In France and Germany attempts at technical education have been made on a wider scale than in England. The direction which such attempts have usually taken is in the establishment of technical day-schools for teaching various trades. But these day-schools have, in general, laid themselves open to three objections.

In the first place, the expense has been very large, as compared with the results. Schools for teaching handicrafts cost upwards of 20*l*. per head per annum to establish and to subsidise—an amount which it is clearly impossible to provide on a large scale in any country. Moreover, even at this cost, they are not thoroughly effective. For trades are so numerous and varied that a properly-fitted technical school for every trade in each town would be an impossibility. Moreover, such a school could, even if founded, never be able to afford to introduce, from time to time, all the newest machinery; and, therefore, it would soon, as an educational establishment, fall behind the best factories. Added to this, there must be, in all technical schools, a want of reality in the work done. The work is not for sale or use; it is of a more or less experimental character. So that there is a tendency for the boys to develop into amateurs, unaccustomed to the ways of workmen, and unfitted for work on a serious commercial scale.

In a few instances it has been attempted to remedy these evils by establishing a system of payment of the boys for their work. This, however, has only the effect of turning the school into a small and imperfect factory; the amount earned from the sale of work is insignificant, and the evils of the factory system at once become apparent.

But, although apprenticeship schools are open to these disadvantages, it would be wrong to condemn them wholesale: there are some instances in which they may be beneficially established. First, when the plant required is exceedingly simple and cheap, the objection on the score of expense disappears. Thus, bootmaking, tailoring, and wood-carving can be taught without much plant, and at a small expense.

Again, cases may arise in which a valuable trade is in danger of disappearing from a country, owing to some temporary depression. Thus the watch-making trade is suffering greatly in England, owing to the keen competition of Switzerland and America, and will never revive until the system of machine watch-making on a large scale is introduced.

In the meantime, the trade is in a state of such depression and confusion that it is hard for an apprentice to learn it. To meet this difficulty a small but excellent school of watch-making has been established in London, to which boys come from all parts of the country.

Moreover, technical schools have occasionally been the means of introducing new arts and manufactures. The Royal factories at Sèvres and Dresden, in which china-painting was taught, had a considerable effect upon the art of the surrounding districts; and the needlework and wood-carving schools established at South Kensington, and the schools of design throughout the country, have already exercised a considerable influence on English art.

The above are, however, exceptions; in general the fact remains that day technical schools are an impossibility, on the score of their expense, as well as being imperfect as a training for the artisan.

Even, however, if these objections could be surmounted, a third remains, which alone would be fatal. During the stay of a boy at a technical school he must be lodged, boarded, and clothed by his parents, and few working men are willing—and fewer still are able—to forego the weekly wages earned by the boy during his apprenticeship years. And therefore it usually happens that even the few apprenticeship schools, for the establishment of which money can be found, naturally gravitate away from the children of the working classes and become frequented by the sons of men in a better station of life. They become schools not for workmen, but for foremen and captains of industry. I believe that I am correct in saying that in the Ecole Diderôt in Paris, which is largely supported by the State, and in which even *bourses à déjeuner* are given gratuitously to the scholars, one-half the boys are the sons of well-to-do persons, entirely above the artisan class. If this be so, it shows that this school, established originally for artisans, is fast drifting away from the class for which it was provided.

Here, then, we have two defects to remedy in the education of our workmen. We must provide them with some additional instruction in the Board schools more suited to their wants, and we must devise some system which, while it cannot replace workshop education, shall, nevertheless, supplement it and rectify its shortcomings.

This is to be accomplished—firstly, by the introduction of manual work into the Board schools; and, secondly, by the establishment of evening schools for apprentices and artisans; and I believe that it can be shown not only that these remedies are the best to meet the evils which I above exposed, but also that they can be established at a cost so moderate as need in no way alarm the taxpayer.

The manual work to be introduced into elementary schools should, I think, be most strictly limited to two subjects, and two only—namely, elementary carpentry and elementary modelling in clay.

. It must be remembered that the boys here rarely exceed the age of thirteen years, and for such youths a more extended course would be a mere waste of money.

But it is of the very highest importance that these subjects should be properly taught. Simply to allow the boys to trifle with the saw and hammer, or to learn, in amateur fashion, to make elegant trifles with the chisel and plane, is to waste their time and to impair their capacity for labour; or, again, to endeavour to teach them the tricks and little secrets of some particular branch of the carpentry trade would be impossible and futile. What is proposed is not to turn out ready-made carpenters, but to train the mind. Hence, therefore, the acquisition of mere manual dexterity is not what is aimed at. What is desired is to teach the application of geometrical form to matter, and wood is selected as the matter to be dealt with, because it is the cheapest and easiest for the purpose. To carry this into effect it is needful that instruction should be given in elementary geometry—working as far as possible with the rule and compass—not aiming at too extended a course, but endeavouring to be thorough. If the elementary principles of the line and circle could be mastered it would be amply sufficient for boys up to fourteen years of age. The geometry class, having first learned a few properties of the straight line, should next be exercised in drawing simple wooden forms, such as a halved joint, or mitred joint. These drawings, having been inspected and found correct, would next be taken into the carpentry class, where the abstract form, represented on paper, would be realised in substance. The carpentry class would commence with a few easy lessons on the nature of wood and of steel tools, and then the boys would be allowed to use them. The instruction should be progressive—first beginning with the use of the saw, then passing on to the hammer, chisel, and plane. And as these tools were successively introduced their nature and properties should be expounded. Thus, the hammer would familiarise the boys with the idea of potential and kinetic energy; the chisel would introduce them to the wedge and lever; the screw would teach them the properties of the spiral inclined plane, and so on —all these not being called by hard names, but made simple and easy to be understood. But in this work certain rules should be inflexibly observed. Such, for instance, as the following:—

1. No boy should be allowed to make any article whatever, unless he had first drawn it to scale on paper, and understood the geometrical principles involved in it. Most simple articles, such as boxes, trays, and even ladders and tables, only involve a knowledge of the properties of the line and right angle.
2. No boy should ever be allowed to work, except to measurement, exactly as if he were in an engineer's fitting and model-making shop.
3. Every piece of wood should be truly marked out with the pencil before being cut or planed.
4. No work, however good, should be allowed to pass unless it was made correctly to the drawing.

By this means the carpentry class and the geometry class would re-act upon one another. Geometry would give direction and aim to the carpentry studies, carpentry would give reality to the geometrical teaching, and all the while, from their early years, the boys would be learning that in which the workman is so deficient, namely, the application of theory to practice.

A system like this would be amply sufficient for all practical purposes. To extend it to turning or wood-carving, or to follow out carpentry into all its branches, would not only lead the boys away from their true course of study, but would introduce endless difficulty and expense. If a boy of fourteen could use his hammer, saw, chisel, and plane really effectively, he would have learnt more than many adult journeymen now can do. So restricted, the system would not be expensive. In a school of 300 boys a room fitted up to accommodate thirty pupils would be sufficient, and the total prime outlay on tools and benches would not exceed 60*l*. The instructor's salary would not exceed 2*l*. per week, the wear and tear of tools would be exceedingly small, and that part of the wood which the boys took away in the shape of manufactured articles would be paid for by them, the rest serving for fuel. A standard of deal, of good quality, costs about 12*l*., and would probably last for a year.

The teacher selected should be a carpenter, or, better still, a pattern-maker, but should have gone through a course of instruction in geometrical drawing, so as to be able to teach geometry as well as carpentering. Or else, on the other hand, a school teacher might qualify himself in carpentry. But it is of course clear that, to carry out the system properly on a wide scale, some training establishment for the teachers would have to be organised. In all this there is nothing that need alarm the taxpayer.

Instruction so organised need cost no more than Board school instruction costs at present.

In observing a school of boys no one can fail to notice that a portion of them seem to develop literary ability, another portion mechanical ability, and a third portion the artistic powers. In our elementary schools we already provide for the first of these; I have tried to show how, at a moderate cost, we might provide for the second, and I now pass to the third or artistic side. Here, fortunately, expense stands even less in our way than on the mechanical side. All that is needed is some clay, some wooden boards and cloths, and a few simple wooden tools. With these you have sufficient for even a Michael Angelo to realise his conceptions, and for a class of thirty children the whole apparatus would not cost 15*l*.

Just as the carpentry class hangs on the geometry class, so here should the modelling class be associated with the free-hand drawing classes. The children will be made to draw a few simple forms, such as a cone, or a cylinder, or a pyramid, and will then make them to scale in clay. Then they can go on to ornament, drawing some simple form from a cast, or from nature, and then modelling it in clay from the original and the drawing. But similar rules will here be observed to those in the carpentry class, so as to secure that the work shall be both useful and thorough, and elegant trifling with the matter must be sternly repressed.

And I venture to assert that, if the system is properly pursued, the children so trained will be better fitted to become mechanics and artisans than those educated in a purely literary manner. It is interesting to compare the earnest delight of a child in seeing even the most simple little model grow up under its hands with the bored attention of a class during a lesson on grammar or syntax. But, unfortunately, all the mechanical energies of our poor children are at present directed to the making of tip-cats and catapults, and all their artistic powers to the construction of mud-pies and oyster-shell grottoes.

The literary side of their education ought not, of course, to be neglected; but for those who are to become artisans, the mechanical and artistic ought not to be ignored.

I have mentioned the exceedingly unsatisfactory state of the apprenticeship system, and the impossibility of curing it effectually by means of apprenticeship schools, or in fact by any sort of school which shall supersede the workshop. It remains, therefore, to inquire whether evening schools are sufficient to supplement workshop instruction. This has been already proved to be the case. Such schools already exist in England. An excellent one at Finsbury, in London, has been established by Sir Philip Magnus; another has been established by Mr. Quintin Hogg, in Regent Street, and there are several more in various parts of London. In the Midlands of England, and in Scotland, others also exist, and especially in Manchester the evening school system is developing into very large proportions. Such schools, not being designed to teach trades, but rather the principles and modes of applying science to trades, do not need expensive apparatus, and therefore need not be costly. Some excellent classes at Finsbury, on the application of geometry to working in tin, are carried on with the simplest possible plant; and Professor Guthrie has shown that science can be taught with apparatus which can be manufactured for a few pounds. But it is necessary that these schools should be true to their principles, being rigidly restrained within certain limits, and not being allowed to waste their funds in costly attempts to teach trade details that are better learned in the workshop.

And, lastly, it is needful that every effort should be made to induce both masters and parents to permit and stipulate for time for the children to attend these evening schools. It is not enough to devote to study the fag-end of an exhausting day's work. During youth some of the best and freshest hours must be given to it, and it will amply repay both employers and employed.

Hitherto, however, but little has been done to give apprentices leisure to study. Masters have been too anxious to secure a full day's work, and too neglectful to teach their apprentices; while trades-unions, instead of being desirous of helping the apprentices to learn, too often throw every difficulty in their way by restricting the number of apprentices employed in trades, and by raising every barrier to the rise of men from labourers to be mechanics; thus, by a short-sighted policy, impairing the trade of their country and promoting competition from abroad.

I have thus endeavoured to point out the defects in our present educational system, and to show how they may be remedied, not by attempting to give State teaching in trades, or to found technical apprenticeship schools, except to a very limited extent, but by some improvement in institutions already existing; not by endeavouring to teach details, but rather to impart methods and principles, and to prove that this can be done cheaply and effectively, thus offering, at all events, one solution of the difficult problem of technical education.

It is by no means sought here to underrate the many excellent technical schools which already exist, but rather to show that they have not as yet reached the working classes, who require an education which, while not being on the one hand purely literary, shall on the other not attempt to be too technical, and shall aim at imparting to the workmen what Sir Lyon Playfair has happily called the 'Rationale of Empiricism.'

EDUCATIONAL REFORMS.

'THE TIMES,' DECEMBER 28, 1886.

THE New South Wales working man, who, according to Mr. Stephen Thompson, reckons himself in poverty unless he has three 'square meals' a day and plenty of time and money to enjoy himself, is evidently a person who fully accepts the philosophic advice to take short views. He is providing himself with a lazy kind of comfort, but he is not going to work in the right way to make his country great or to raise himself and his children in the scale of being. He is clearly much in want of information and education. Here at home the efforts of the benevolent are hampered by the same want among those whom they seek to help. Miss Davenport-Hill, in a letter which we print this morning, gives striking illustrations on this point, and goes to the root of the matter with the practical suggestion that we should make knowledge of our colonies, their climates, resources, and modes of life, essential subjects of instruction in our schools. We are not aware of any reason why that instruction should not be made at least as efficient an instrument of education as any of the subjects for which grants are now paid. It is true to a far greater extent than most people have any idea of that 'the people perish for lack of knowledge.' We have that fatal want in evidence both here and in our colonies. Would it not be well in organising our Imperial Institute to keep that fact much more constantly before our minds than we have hitherto done? Knowledge of the world they are born into is the crying need of the people on both sides of the ocean, and what need is there to which an Imperial Institute could more fittingly minister? It is not fossil knowledge that is wanted. Mere museums will not supply the need of the day. We require living knowledge, and vivid teaching, using museums merely as its tools.

There is even a good deal to be done in the way of educating those who direct education. In this country our higher education has for generations been exclusively literary, and under an aristocratic constitution it served its purpose fairly well. It does not suit a democratic constitution, and is being slowly and reluctantly modified. But the literary training of the upper classes is a positive hindrance to due appreciation of the fact that what the lower classes imperatively require, if they are to hold their own in the world, is an education in things, not in books. Mr. Stephen Thompson tells us to-day what are the classes that can emigrate with advantage and what classes are useless. We have been told the same thing thousands of times by everybody who knows the colonies, but the lesson has never been practically applied. The colonies do not want 'educated men without capital,' and they want none of that class which has attained such enormous dimensions here—the class vaguely denominated clerks. This country absolutely swarms with men who are not 'educated' in any true sense whatever, and who at the same time are totally destitute of the practical knowledge and aptitudes of the artisan. Their youth has been spent in fumbling with an education which they never attain, and which is only fitted for men possessed either of exceptional abilities or of the means of living without their aid. If we are going to contemplate State emigration, the first thing to do obviously is to fit our people for that end. What we call education is brought to the hard test of the question—Does the world want [this kind of thing? We do not want it here; we are glutted with it. The colonies will have nothing to do with it. They want men who can lay bricks or paint houses or make chairs, men who in some way or other are conversant with things, not with what ancient and modern writers have said about things. We are already inconveniently crowded in this country, and we have three hundred thousand new inhabitants added every year. We are driven to contemplate their exportation upon a large scale by the State, and it is surely high time to begin manufacturing them into an article for which there is a demand. We have to face the fact that there is no community on the globe that is willing to take what is of no use to us merely to oblige Englishmen. If we are to carry out emigration on any large scale, we must make it our business to train our people in such a way as to meet the needs of our colonies. The article they want may seem a very inferior one to persons nourished upon literature and conversant with books. But the colonies will not take any other, and unless we meet their views we shall have to keep our redundant population at home.

COLONIAL TRAINING.

To the Editor of the 'Times.'[1]

SIR,—I have read your wise leading article in the *Times* of to-day with great interest. Having come lately from a two years' experience in Canada and the North-West, I can truly endorse your sentence, 'the people perish from lack of knowledge,' by which I mean that clerks and artisans, finding the labour market overcrowded in the cities, are helpless on farms and ranches because they have never learnt to plough, harness a horse, or milk a cow. On my advice Professor Wilson has added ploughing with oxen and horses to the colonial course of

---
[1] *Times*, December 29, 1886.

his college at the Crystal Palace, and other colonial training farms are doing the same.

The field for agricultural labourers is practically unlimited in our great colonies; it is therefore necessary to extend the simple instruction now being given to young gentlemen to the clerks, artisans, and labouring men wishing to emigrate, so that they could at once find employment on farms if the labour markets of the cities were overstocked.

The question is—How is this simple instruction to be given? I wrote to the secretary of the committee of the Imperial Institute to the effect that, should the Institute undertake such instruction on small plots of land near our large cities, it would be advisable to have colonial instructors. These would turn the minds of would-be emigrants from the United States to our colonies. I further point out that, having carefully inquired on the spot, I found a good Canadian instructor could be obtained for 100*l*. a year and his food, and he would live on the plot in his log hut. I have now two instructors ready to come on these terms. The course should be ploughing with oxen, milking cows, harnessing horses, and, if possible, a little riding. I received an answer from the secretary of the committee that the subject would be considered.

Having succeeded with the schools for young gentlemen I hope yet to succeed for our working men. I maintain it is the duty of the State to place such simple instruction within reach of the people, if the Imperial Institute cannot do so, and thus save the hardships I have witnessed. After going through the course the working man should have a certificate given him, showing his conduct during instruction and his acquirements. Armed with his certificate, the emigrant would have nothing to fear.

Last week Mr. Kennaway, Assistant Agent-General for New Zealand, told me that when selecting emigrants he limited himself to two questions, 'Can you plough?' and 'Can you milk cows?' Having great experience in New Zealand farming, he considered satisfactory answers to those questions sufficient, and found it to be so.

I predict the time is approaching when the ploughman instructor will begin to elbow the schoolmaster. The thin edge of the wedge has been got in with the upper classes, and working men will shortly discover that an education that admits of some of their sons becoming possessors of freehold property in the colonies is better adapted to the future welfare of their families than Euclid and algebra, though they themselves may prefer to remain at home following their occupations.

Your obedient servant,
EDWARD PALLISER.

Army and Navy Club, Pall Mall: December 27.

EDUCATION AS IT IS AND AS IT OUGHT TO BE.[1]

TO THE EDITOR OF THE 'TIMES.'

SIR,—Permit me to add a word in confirmation of your argument to-day on education as it is and as it ought to be.

Some years ago, as treasurer of Barnardo's Homes at Stepney, I was much struck by the fact that the waifs and strays educated there are better prepared for the battle of life than are the children who attend our Board schools. No child, as a rule, leaves the Homes without having learnt some handiwork as well as the three R's.

But, under present arrangements, any training of the hands (except as to the needle) is impossible at a Board school. It has always seemed to me that children who spend part of the day in an active employment, where their hands as well as heads are occupied, lead a far more pleasant life, and, therefore, learn more effectually, than those who always pore over books or writing, however skilfully varied and illustrated. And the result to an emigrant child must be invaluable. Such a child need not compete as a clerk, but can earn his living at some trade, and can learn another trade far more easily than a child whose hands have never been trained.

It is needless to dwell on this. What I desire to insist on is the necessity of a change in our system, so that our Board schools may do better work, and may teach both boys and girls more of what is really useful.

I know well that any change involves a vast expense, but it is better to amend our system, even at a heavy cost, than to persist in what we admit to be defective in a most important

[1] From the *Times* of December 29, 1886.

sense. It is no doubt aggravating to confess a failure in what has cost so much time and money and thought, but nothing is gained by closing our eyes to facts.

I remain, yours faithfully,

Grosvenor Square: December 27.   WILLIAM FOWLER.

SPEECH ON TECHNICAL AND TRADE INSTRUCTION.[1]

BY THE MARQUIS OF HARTINGTON, AT THE POLYTECHNIC,
LONDON, MARCH 16, 1887.

THE Marquis of Hartington, presiding at the distribution of medals, prizes, and certificates to the successful students of the Polytechnic Science, Art, Technical, and Commercial Classes for the Session 1885-86, and to the successful exhibitors at the Annual Exhibition of 1886, said: The division of labour amongst us at the present time was so marked, that it was very difficult for anyone to travel only for his own business, and his trade was almost entirely that of a politician. He did not profess to be one of those with knowledge so various, and grasp of mind so far-reaching, as to be able to devote himself to politics and also to the other questions which were being discussed, such as the progress of Science and Art, and the bearing of that progress upon the industry, trade, and commerce of our country. His first duty was to congratulate the members of this Institute and their numerous friends present upon the work in which they were engaged. The work of the Institution he understood to be classes for science, art, and technical education. Through their classes there had now passed 21,000 individual students, and the numbers were continually increasing. Alluding to their having gained nineteen medals given by the City and Guilds of London in competition with the whole of the United Kingdom, he said the fact of having gained these prizes in such subjects as electric lighting, photography, plumbing, painting, watch and clock making, metal-plate working, carriage building, and boot and shoe making, showed the success which had been achieved amongst students drawn principally from the mechanic classes, many of them being apprentices. The average age of the students was from eighteen to twenty-three, and the average fees from 2*s.* to 10*s.* 6*d.* per session, so

[1] From the *Standard* of March 17, 1887.

that the advantages of the classes were fully accessible to those for whose benefit they were founded—viz. the working artisan classes of London. The Science and Art Classes could not show numbers equal, but their numbers were not unsatisfactory, there being 850 students in Science and 350 in Art, of whom 73 per cent. had obtained passes. There was great necessity for such work as this, and for the further extension of technical education in this country. Professor Huxley, speaking at the Mansion House the other day in support of the Imperial Institute, made a very remarkable statement on this subject. Comparing the organisation of the industrial forces of the countries of Europe with the organisation of their great armies, he declared that the conditions of industrial competition at the present time amounted to a state of war. If that was true, and there was little doubt on that point, what were the consequences resulting from it? The operation of economic laws was so certain and so swift, that it was matter of absolute certainty that a nation which ceased to produce, or produced less of what the world wanted, or produced it of inferior quality, was being defeated in the industrial competition, and would soon feel the consequences of that defeat. What would be the consequences of such defeat to us nationally and individually? To the nation the consequence would be a diminution of the wealth and influence which we had acquired from our pre-eminence in industrial position. We might still have our material resources, our coal, our iron, and the muscular energy of what would then be the vastly superabundant population; but, instead of being what we are now, we should be hewers of wood and drawers of water, the slaves and the servants of the rest of the world, instead of being the leaders and masters of the world. If any there were indifferent to the prospect of this national industrial defeat, this national decadence, he would ask them to consider what would be the consequences individually. It would mean the loss of wealth of those who were now rich, the poverty of those who were now prosperous, and to the masses of the country it would be famine, indigence, and starvation. It became, therefore, a very urgent question how industrial defeat was to be warded off. Just as we could not in preparations for actual warfare afford to disregard the teachings and experience of the rest of the world, and allow ourselves to be behindhand in the possession of the necessary scientific knowledge and appliances which modern warfare required, still less could we afford to be behindhand in the preparations for the industrial warfare of which he had spoken. Success in that industrial warfare was not now a mere matter of the possession of great material resources, great industry, and perseverance and energy on the part of our people ; it could only be gained by the most diligent application of the most scientific instruction to the masses of our people. How were we at present equipped for this industrial competition? We knew what other countries were doing. Germany and France were making enormous efforts to provide for the technical instruction of their people, and the smaller nations were following their example. Mr. Mundella had told them that a year ago he saw in Berlin a Technical Institute which had cost the public upwards of 400,000*l.*, while in every industrial centre in Germany vast palaces were devoted to the practical work of science teaching. In France all the class subjects of her Institute were taught at the public expense in nearly every *arrondissement* of Paris. It was a striking fact that Paris, heavily taxed beyond the conception of Englishmen, should adopt such a course. It showed how powerful the motive must be which produced such a result; and he cited the fact that Switzerland, though without natural resources, had by a system of graded schools and the Technical College at Zürich become a prosperous manufacturing country. Here the subject had been a good deal inquired into of late, and the results were some of them encouraging and others less encouraging. The report of the Commission on Technical Education stated that though we were behindhand, as compared with other nations, in the adoption of a national system of technical education, it was not yet too late for us to maintain the position which up to the present time we had held unquestioned in the industrial world, if we only made adequate exertions. But there was an opinion of a somewhat different and less encouraging kind from the Royal Commission on the Depression of Trade, who said that the foreign competition with this country was a matter deserving more serious attention than it had yet received, and pointing out that not only our technical but our ordinary commercial education was not sufficient to enable us successfully to continue industrial competition with foreigners.

It was clearly, therefore, the opinion of all who had studied the subject that greater and more improved technical education must be provided for our people ; and the only question remaining was, how was it to be provided? No doubt it would be satisfactory if it could be provided by voluntary effort. But he was afraid we had not everywhere, we had not even in London, a sufficient supply of men like those to whom their Institute owed so much. They could hardly rely upon an unlimited supply of men who were content to devote a large portion of their income, and almost the whole of their time, to the promotion of the welfare of their fellow-citizens in the way Mr. Quintin Hogg had done. No terms could be too high in which to speak of the valuable services to his country which were conferred by such a man, and, if he might be allowed to say so, the only unsatisfactory feature in their prosperous and useful Institution appeared to be the extent to which it relied upon the efforts and self-sacrifice of one man. It seemed to him that the employers of labour and the trades-unions were hardly yet alive to the urgency of the question how this additional technical instruction ought to be provided, though much had been done by the former, especially in the provincial towns, in the way of providing technical colleges and schools for educating the future masters, managers, and foremen of our great industries; but what was still deficient was adequate technical and trade instruction for the workers, such as their Institute was intended to supply. If they could not look to voluntary effort to supply all that was needed, assuredly they could not look to the State to supply everything. The State already helped to a considerable extent in Science and Art instruction ; but it might do more in technical instruction. The State, however, could not do all that was needed ; what it could best do would be to assist local effort and promote the direction and organisation which was required. If they could not look to voluntary effort to do the rest, then it seemed to him they must look to the municipal institutions we possessed to initiate the local efforts which were necessary to promote this object. He hoped the time was not far distant when, through our Town Councils, our Local Government Boards, and our School Boards, we should have established in every considerable industrial centre technical schools suitable to the wants of the district, supported out of local funds, but aided to a considerable extent by national funds. Their Institution, and others like it, had done, and were doing, very good and useful work in playing the same part in relation to technical and trade education that had been played by voluntary schools in regard to elementary education. Congratulating the managers of the Institute on having established an intermediate school, with divisions for professional, commercial, and technical education, to prepare for well-paid trades many who up to the present had gone to swell the overstocked class of clerks, and also on the sound physical training in gymnastics, swimming, and athletics which the Institute provided, the noble lord concluded by congratulating the students, both the successful and the unsuccessful, on the benefits they had derived from an Institution which he hoped would meet with continued and increased success.

THE ORGANISATION OF INDUSTRIAL EDUCATION.[1]
To the Editor of the 'Times.'

Sir,—When a statesman of Lord Hartington's authority concurs with and enforces the opinions I ventured to express some little time ago, I have every reason for private and personal satisfaction. But the circumstance has a public importance as evidence that our political chiefs and leaders are giving their serious attention to those social questions which lie far above the region of party strife, and are of infinitely greater moment than the topics which ordinarily absorb the attention of politicians.

The organisation of industrial and commercial education is not the least of these great problems. That it has to be solved, under penalty of national ruin, proves to be no mere alarmist fancy, but the belief of an experienced man of affairs, whose imperturbable coolness and strong common-sense are proverbial.

It is an interesting question for us all, therefore. How do we stand prepared for the task thus imperatively set us? My conviction is that we are in some respects better off than most people imagine, in others worse. I conceive that two things are needful—on the one hand, a machinery for providing in-

[1] Reprinted from the *Times*, March 21, 1887.

struction and gathering information; on the other hand, a machinery for catching capable men wherever they are to be found, and turning them to account. Now, I apprehend that both these kinds of machinery are to be found, though in a fragmentary and disconnected condition, in several organisations which, though independent, supplement one another.

The first of these is that of the School Boards, which provide elementary education, and sometimes, though too rarely, have at their disposal scholarships by which capable scholars can attain a higher training. The second is the organisation of the Department of Science and Art. The classes, now established all over the country in connection with the Department, not only provide elementary instruction, accessible to all, but offer the means whereby the pick of the capable students may obtain in the schools at South Kensington as good a higher education in science and art as is to be had in the country. It is from this source that the supply of science and art teachers, who in turn raise the standard of elementary instruction, is derived. The third organisation is that of the technical classes connected with the City and Guilds Institute, or with the Society of Arts, or with provincial universities and colleges, which provide special technical instruction for those who have, or ought to have, already acquired the elements of scientific and artistic knowledge in the science and art classes.

A fourth organisation for the advancement of the interests of industry and commerce, of the nature of that which I imagined it was the intention of the founders of the Imperial Institute to create, and such as is, I believe, now actually in course of creation in the City of London, will complete the drill-grounds of the army of industry, and, so far as I can judge, omit nothing of primary importance. But, leaving the last aside as still in the embryonic condition, these excellent organisations are all mere torsos, fine—but fragmentary.

The ladder from the School Boards to the Universities, about which I dreamed dreams many years ago, has not yet acquired much more substantiality than the ladder of Jacob's vision.

The Science and Art Department has done, and is doing, admirable work, which I regret to see more often made the subject of small and carping criticism than of the praise which is its due. I trust it may not be diverted from efficiently continuing that work by having duties for which it is unfit forced upon it. That which the Department needs, in my judgment, is nothing but the means of doing that which Commission after Commission, Royal and Departmental, have declared to be its proper business.

As Dean of the Normal School I may be permitted to declare that it is impossible for us to perform the functions allotted to us unless the recommendations made by impartial and independent authority are carried into effect.

The school exists; and common-sense surely suggests, either make it efficient or abolish it. The alternative of abolition is not likely to be adopted, as that step would be equivalent to striking the keystone out of the edifice of scientific instruction for the masses of the people which it has taken a quarter of a century to raise, and which is the essential foundation for any sound system of technical education. The alternative of efficiency means spending a few thousand pounds on additional buildings; but the guardians of the national purse do not seem to feel the force of the adage about 'spoiling a ship for a half-pennyworth of tar.'

The state of affairs in regard to that which ought to be the centre of our system of technical education is nearly the same. The central Institute is undoubtedly a splendid monument of the munificence of the City. But munificence without method may arrive at results indistinguishably similar to those of stinginess. I have been blamed for saying that the central Institution is 'starved.' Yet a man who has only half as much food as he needs is indubitably starved, even though his short rations consist of ortolans and are served up on gold plate. And I have excellent authority for saying that little more than one-half of the plan of operations of the Institute, drawn up by the committee of which I was a member, has been carried out, or can be carried out, if the funds allotted for the maintenance of the Institute are not largely increased. At the same time, the Institute is doing all that could be rationally expected of it. Some of the guilds and many provincial towns are making admirable provision for elementary technical education. Such work, in my judgment, ought to be left to local administrators, whatever aid it may be thought desirable to give them. But the local schools should be brought into relation with the central Institute, and this should be put upon such a footing as to subserve its proper purpose of training teachers and giving higher technical instruction.

Economy does not lie in sparing money, but in spending it wisely. And it is, to my mind, highly necessary that some man or body of men, whom their countrymen trust, should consider these various organisations as a whole and determine the manner in which they should be correlated and in which it is desirable that the resources, public and private, which are available should be distributed among them.

Lord Hartington has many claims on the gratitude and respect of his countrymen. I venture to express the wish that he would add to them by taking up this great work of organising industrial education and bringing it to a happy issue.

I am, Sir, your obedient servant,

T. H. HUXLEY.

March 18.

TECHNICAL AND COMMERCIAL EDUCATION.[1]

ON March 21 a large and influential deputation waited upon Lord Cranbrook and Sir William Hart Dyke at the Education Department to urge the necessity of Government action with regard to technical and commercial education. The proposition of the deputation was that School Boards and local authorities should be empowered to found or give aid to schools fitted to promote technical and commercial education, both in day and in night schools. Among the members of the deputation were the Right Hon. A. J. Mundella, M.P., Sir Lyon Playfair, M.P., Sir Richard Temple, M.P., Sir B. Samuelson, M.P., Sir Henry Roscoe, M.P., Sir U. Kay-Shuttleworth, M.P., Professor Stuart, M.P., Mr. Samuel Smith, M.P., Mr. Houldsworth, M.P., Mr. G. T. C. Bartley, M.P., Mr. Wayman, M.P., Mr. F. A. Channing, M.P., Mr. George Dixon, M.P., Sir John Lubbock, M.P., Mr. Isaac Hoyle, M.P., Sir J. P. Corry, M.P., Mr. Sydney Buxton, M.P., Mr. Broadhurst, M.P., Mr. J. Dodds, M.P., Mr. Maclean,

[1] Reprinted from the *Times*, March 22, 1887.

M.P., Sir Charles Palmer, M.P., Mr. George Howell, M.P., Mr. Stevenson, M.P., Mr. P. Stanhope, M.P., Mr. Howard Vincent, M.P., and others.

Mr. Mundella, in introducing the deputation, said their object was to ask the Government to take a very modest step in the direction of the organisation of industrial and commercial education. If he could put in the admirable letter of Professor Huxley, in the *Times* of Monday, he would probably make the best possible statement of their case. The education of the 4,600,000 on the books of the elementary schools was confined to education of a purely elementary character, and anything in the shape of manual or industrial education was treated in a way very disheartening to those interested in the question. At present our industrial classes were like badly drilled soldiers fighting a battle with antiquated weapons—it was like sending our soldiers into the field, armed with Brown Bess, to meet the best armed soldiers of Europe. Dr. Konrad, in a report on the Prussian system in its bearing on the national economy, said the superiority of the Western to the Eastern workman and of the German to the Englishman was well established; and he added that no doubt the Englishman, by his enormous perseverance and his wonted diligence, got through considerably more work in the sphere to which he had been long accustomed, but he was far behind the German in capacity for adapting himself to new circumstances. This was the result of the better and more general training which the Germans got in their schools. There had been repeated attempts to do something in England to improve the condition of things, but where public bodies had interfered they had acted beyond their powers and been punished accordingly. It was from the restrictions under which these authorities laboured that they now asked to be freed. They asked for increased powers to promote industrial, scientific, and technical training, and that for this purpose they should be put in connection with the Science and Art Department. The cost of executing what they proposed would be trifling.

Sir Lyon Playfair, Sir B. Samuelson, Sir R. Temple, Mr. George Howell, Mr. George Dixon, Sir Henry Roscoe, Professor Stuart, Mr. Samuel Smith, Mr. Howard Vincent, Sir U. Kay-Shuttleworth, and others, also spoke.

Lord Cranbrook, in reply, said :—I am quite with you upon this—that one of the great wants in this country is an adequate technical instruction to be got somehow or other. There are two classes of education—the one which may be called elementary, and the other secondary, to which it is impossible not to see that the greater number of speakers have adverted. It is quite clear that in an administrative capacity I cannot reach the objects you wish to obtain. Whatever is to be done must be done by legislation; and whatever is done must cost somebody a good deal. Mr. Mundella called it a trifle; but when you add up these unconsidered trifles and give them to the Chancellor of the Exchequer, he looks at them in the aggregate, and not as separate trifles. You will not expect me to make a declaration of policy on this occasion. I can see no objection to localities rating themselves for the purpose of bringing about a better system of technical education, which naturally would be more suited to the locality than a general scheme. Nor do I see any general objection connecting the science and art training to a certain extent with the Science and Art Department which exists at present in connection with this office. As to the connection between the School Boards and the local authorities, I should not like to pronounce on that subject without consulting my colleagues who have a voice in the matter. When I speak of local authorities I mean that some authority of the locality should be able to find the means for a good industrial training, beginning at a low point and going to that real secondary education which can never be reached by the elementary department over which I have control. It is not in the large towns only that we have to deal with the population: we have to deal with them in villages and small country towns and other places. I have always thought that, with regard to country schools, recreation might take a form of preparation for the work of their life. But all this requires money, and all this requires Parliamentary sanction. Parliament has not really pronounced an opinion upon it. The only real debate which I can find is the one which took place before the Commission was issued, and at that time Mr. Mundella struck a note rather of fear and timidity. He said at that time that the idea of giving technical education to the whole of the working classes was an entire mistake, and he asked how could any one place technical training in the reach of those who had not the talent to use and apply it. Since that argument on the proposal for an inquiry there has been no debate on the subject, and I confess that I should be glad to know what the House of Commons thinks. As to night schools, I agree that they might be more used. We have ventured to open up cookery classes for girls, and I trust that the night schools may be made advantageous for some kinds of industrial training for boys. It has been pointed out that there are many instances in this country in which not only are the poorest classes somewhat better off in the way of training than those a little above them, but in some cases the criminal classes get the advantage of an industrial training. My object is to meet you as far as I can, by advising with others and endeavouring to obtain the means of doing so. I agree that the local authorities, whatever they may be, should have the power of dealing with the question to a great extent. But the whole matter is a subject for legislation and not for my decision. What you have said will receive the utmost consideration at my hands.

The deputation thanked his lordship and withdrew.

SLÖJD.[1]

By Evelyn Chapman.

I HAVE been asked to give some account of the Slöjd system, as practised in Sweden, having lately visited that country in order to study the system both practically and theoretically. This visit convinced me of its excellence, of its claim to be regarded as an important factor in education, and the need there is for something of the kind in our own schools.

The word Slöjd is essentially Scandinavian, and an equivalent for it is not to be found in any other European language. Its original meaning is 'cunning,' 'clever,' 'handy' (compare 'sleight of hand'), but, as at present used, it means rather the different kinds of hand-work used in schools for educational

[1] A paper read before the Teachers' Guild, Brighton, Nov. 25, 1886. Reprinted, by permission, from the *Journal of Education* of Feb. 1, 1887.

purposes. Slöjd is such a convenient word and embraces so much, that I think we shall have to naturalise it in England, and call it *Sloyd*. It has already been adopted in France and Germany, and I believe in Belgium, Austria, and Russia.

There are many different kinds of Slöjd, or hand-work, practised in the schools in Sweden, Norway, Denmark, Finland, Germany, and other countries : simple metal-work, smith-work, basket-making, painting (trade), fret-work, bookbinding, papier-mâché, needle-work, and finally wood-slöjd, which consists mainly of carpentry, but in which carving and turning may play a subordinate part.

Herr Otto Salomon, the Director of the Seminary at Nääs, has drawn up a table in which the above occupations are compared, under the following heads :—

(1) The children's interest gained; (2) work which can be used; (3) order and precision; (4) cleanliness and neatness; (5) development of sense of form; (6) accordance with children's capacity; (7) strengthening and developing of the physical powers; (8) counterpoise to sitting; (9) capability of methodical exposition; (10) general dexterity.

It appears, from a careful comparison of the results obtained by means of these various occupations, that, while several of them answer to the above tests in certain particulars, yet only the *wood slöjd* can answer all.

I will endeavour to give a brief outline of the chief principles of the method for the teaching of manual work which is followed at Nääs, and which has thence been largely disseminated all over Scandinavia and Finland, and is taught even within the Arctic Circle. In Sweden alone, wood-slöjd is practised in 800 national schools, has been introduced into the secondary schools for boys, and is now being adapted even in the upper schools for girls.

It has also been introduced into France, Belgium, Germany, Austria, Russia, and the United States. It will probably be taken up in Abyssinia, through the instrumentality of the Swedish missionaries; and even far-distant Japan is showing an interest in the subject. Are we English to be left hopelessly behind in the adoption of hand-work as an important factor in education ? We have already accepted it—in a very limited way, it is true —in the adoption of the Kindergarten system, the very soul of which is its response to the child's need of activity and production; and Slöjd is the same principle at work, only in a form suited to the growing powers of our boys and girls.

Herr Salomon himself has treated of the results aimed at by Slöjd, the choice and classification of models, and the question who is to be the Slöjd teacher, in a work which has already been translated into French and German, and will soon, I hope, appear in English.

Slöjd aims at the following *Results* :—

(1) To implant respect and love for work in general; (2) to implant respect and love even for the coarser forms of honest manual work; (3) to develop activity; (4) to foster order, accuracy, cleanliness, and neatness; (5) to encourage attention, industry, and perseverance; (6) to develop the physical powers; (7) to train the eye and the sense of form.

The joining of the Slöjd course should be *voluntary* on the part of the pupil; consequently, the work should fulfil the following conditions :—

(1) It should be useful; (2) the preparatory exercises should not be too fatiguing; (3) they should offer variety; (4) they should be executed without help; (5) they should be *real* work, not play; (6) they should not be knicknacks, or so-called fancy work; (7) they should belong to the worker; (8) they should be in harmony with his power and physical strength; (9) they should be of such a nature that they can be finished with exactness; (10) they should allow of cleanliness and neatness; (11) they should demand thoughtfulness, and thus be more than a purely mechanical work; (12) they should strengthen and develop the physique; (13) they should help to exercise the sense of form; (14) lastly, as many tools and manipulations as possible should be employed.

Such are the results aimed at; but here a very important question arises,—Who is to be the Slöjd *teacher?* Teachers are already so overburdened with work, that it seems too much to expect them to undertake another subject. But for them, too, a subject so novel, and necessarily so differently taught from the ordinary school subjects, would doubtless have its attractions, and would illustrate the saying, 'Change of work 's as good as play.'

Whether this be so or not, the Slöjd instruction must be undertaken, NOT by an artisan, who would naturally regard it merely from its mechanical side, whereas the main object of Slöjd is not the teaching of any trade, but the development of the faculties and the acquiring of general dexterity. It must, therefore, be given by a *trained teacher*, who understands the nature of the material on which he has to work, viz. *child-nature*, and, if possible, by the same teacher who takes the other school subjects.

I may mention that by means of Slöjd, which necessitates individual supervision and instruction, the teacher has an opportunity of obtaining an insight into the character, and of establishing a personal relation between himself and his pupils, which it is almost impossible to obtain by means of class instruction. Numbers of teachers can bear witness to the truth of this statement. The teacher should lead, direct, and control the work, but should be careful not to put his hand directly to it. In order to be able to follow with advantage the course of instruction, the pupil ought to have reached a point of development usually attained about the age of eleven.

One word as to the main differences between wood-slöjd and ordinary carpentering, with which it is very apt to be confused. These lie—(1) In the character of the objects made, which are usually smaller than those made in the trade; (2) in the tools used—the knife, for instance, the most important of all in Slöjd, is little used in ordinary carpentry; (3) in the manner of working—the division of labour employed in the trade is not allowed in Slöjd, where each article is begun, carried on, and finished by the same pupil; (4) but the fundamental difference is in the *object* of Slöjd, which is, not to turn out full-blown, or half-blown, or even quarter-blown young carpenters, but to develop the faculties, and especially to give *general* dexterity, which will be useful whatever line of life the pupil may afterwards follow.

As individual instruction is generally required, and as this manual work cannot be taught in class, the same teacher can only superintend a limited number of pupils at the same time. Generally speaking, there should not be more than twelve.

As to the *Choice of Models*.—(1) All articles of luxury are to be excluded; (2) the objects made are to be of use at home; (3) the children should be able to finish them entirely without help; (4) the articles should be made of wood only; (5) no polish should be used; (6) as little material as possible should be employed; (7) the children should learn to work both in the harder and softer woods; (8) turning and carving should only be sparingly employed; (9) the models should develop the children's sense of form and beauty, and for these ends the series should include a certain number of *modelled* objects—for instance, spoons, ladles, and other curved articles—which are to be executed with a free hand, and chiefly by eye; (10) by means of going through the whole series, the pupils should learn the use of all the more important tools. In the choice of models, care should be taken that each one prepare for the next.

Classification of Models.—(1) The series ought to progress without a break from the easy to the difficult, from the simple to the complex; (2) there must be a sufficient variety; (3) each model must be so placed in the series that the pupil shall be able to carry it out entirely without the *direct* help of the teacher, by means of what he has already made; (4) the models should constitute such a series that at each step the pupil may be able to make, not a *passable*, but a *correct* work; (5) in making the first models only a few tools are to be employed, but as the series is carried out new tools and new manipulations are to be employed; (6) the knife, as the fundamental tool, is to be the most used in the beginning of the course; (7) for the first models rather hard wood should be employed.

At the beginning of the series the models should be capable of speedy execution, and objects which require a considerable time should be gradually reached.

Let us now see whether Slöjd, if the foregoing conditions be carried out, may be regarded as a factor in education, whether considered physically, mentally, or morally.

It is essentially a form of work which calls forth every variety of movement, which brings all the muscles into play, and which exercises both sides of the body. It is so arranged that the children can work with the left hand as well as with the right, in sawing, planing, &c. Thus all the muscles are strengthened, a more harmonious development attained, and there is less fear of their growing crooked. There is no reason to dread their becoming left-handed; in more delicate manipulations the right hand will always remain the better man of the two.

Does Slöjd help forward the *mental* development?

Surely work which draws out and exercises energy, perseverance, order, accuracy, and the habit of attention, cannot be said to fail in influencing the mental faculties; and that it should do so by cultivating the *practical* side of the intelligence, leading the pupils to rely on themselves, to exercise foresight, to be constantly putting two and two together, is specially needed in these days of excessive examinations, when so many of us are suffering from the adoption of ready-made opinions, and the swallowing whole, in greater or smaller boluses, the results of other men's labours.

We want *whole* men and women, the sum-total of whose faculties is developed, who have learnt to *apply* their knowledge, not only in the emergencies, but in the daily occurrences of life; and this readiness—this steadiness of nerve, the ordered control of that wonderful machine the body, the cultivation of the practical side of us—can only come by exercise, and this is given by means of Slöjd. Let us also remember that all skilled work, however humble it may appear, is *brain* work too; the hand is the servant of the brain. If anyone doubt this, let him try to make, from first to last, some complete object, however insignificant—be it the modelling of a leaf, cube, or even a ball, or the making of a wooden spoon—and, I answer for it, he will gain a new respect for hand-work, not only from its usefulness, but the skill it requires.

What does Slöjd do for the *moral* training of the child? It implants respect and love for work in general, including the coarser kinds of bodily work. In the fierce competition which exists in all civilised countries—and nowhere fiercer than in our own—which springs in so many cases from the desire to push on to some fancied higher level of life, what a clearing of the moral atmosphere would be effected if the rising generation could be imbued with the feeling, deepening as they grow up into conviction, that it is the *man* who dignifies or degrades the work—that all labour which proceeds from a worthy motive is of equal worth, and that the right work for each one of us, and consequently the noblest, is the work we can do best!

But this is not all which Slöjd effects in the way of moral influence. It tightens and strengthens the bond between school and home. Everything which the child makes is for *home* use, is prized there as his own honest work, and as the product of the skill which he is gaining at school. Among the *working* classes, the *actual* use of the things made by the children (besides the wholesome pleasure and pride they call forth) is found to do much, in the countries where Slöjd is practised, to reconcile the parents to their children remaining at school even when they are beginning to be of use at home, and to be able to earn something. They have tangible proof, in the objects brought home, that their children are learning something which makes them useful and handy, and which will make them readier in future in learning a trade.

I will only mention one other point in which Slöjd bears good moral fruit. I mean, it implants in the child a sense of satisfaction in honest work, begun, carried on, and completed by fair means and by his own exertions. In these days of scamped work, of dishonest tricks to be found in all trades and manufactures, what can we say too much in praise of a system which will give our boys and girls a sense of the dignity of work—a scorn and contempt for what is slovenly or tricky? The Slöjd system is completely opposed to the modern principle of division of labour, which is no doubt a necessity in the present conditions of life, but which would be disastrous in education, where the aim must be the development of each individual, NOT the getting through a given quantity of work in the shortest and cheapest way. I feel sure that a boy or girl who, at a period when impressions are most lasting, has had the solid satisfaction of carrying out a piece of work from beginning to end, will not be satisfied, in adult life, with becoming a mere machine for drilling holes, putting on pins' heads, or turning out chair-legs by the hundred, but will in his leisure hours vindicate his dignity and skill by doing some work, whether practical or intellectual, worthy of a human being. We must remember, too, that a large part of the distress in bad times is due to the fact that, if the particular *fragment* of work which a person is capable of is taken from him, he can do nothing else whereby to earn his bread.

I can only speak in the briefest way of the crying need there is for some such practical training as is given by Slöjd. I am not an enthusiast for the particular form of it which I have studied myself at Nääs, and which I have seen at work in the Swedish schools, where I wish I could transport you, so that you might see for yourselves the earnestness and energy of the young workers, the dexterity with which they handle their tools, their extreme carefulness (for no damaged or careless work is passed), and the independent manner in which they work. But I do say, that we want something of the kind, suited to our national needs and character, and bearing the same fruit of trained intelligence and skill which it is producing in the countries where it is practised. A great deal is being done in England for technical education, and a great deal is said as to its need, for there is a very real danger of English workmen being driven out of the field on account of the superior skill of foreigners and the great advantages they enjoy in the way of technical education. We can but rejoice that we are beginning to recognise this danger, and that so much attention is being directed to the need of technical education; but, even supposing the country were covered with technical schools, if our young people come to them with eyes and hands untrained, with little or no sense of form and beauty, with lack of perception and habits of observation, with untrained and undeveloped muscles, how can they possibly hold their own against the youth of other countries, coming fresh from schools where eye and hand have been trained to *general dexterity* which will stand them in good stead whatever special branch of technical work they may take up, with trained observation and perception, and with a love for work and an interest in it which has been quickened and stimulated by many a victory gained by perseverance, attention, and energy?

Should this Slöjd instruction be given to girls as well as boys? This question has already been answered practically in the affirmative in Sweden, and with excellent results. It is just as important for a woman to have the complete use of her hands as for a man. It may be said that girls have needlework, which is more suited to their sex, and more useful to them in after life. It would be a very sorry thing for our future wives and mothers not to learn the use of their needle, but why should they not learn needlework and Slöjd too ? The use of the tools would develop their muscles, and they would gain an added dexterity which needlework alone cannot give. And, besides this *general* development, which is of paramount importance, the *positive* knowledge gained, and the power of doing little jobs about the house, would be of great service to them when they grow up.

But, it will be objected, even granted that a universal hand-education should be given, including both sexes, and granted that teachers are forthcoming who are capable of giving it, how is it possible to spare time for another subject ? I will only reply, that the schools in Sweden are among the best in Europe, and yet they find time for it. The Slöjd classes—which are entirely voluntary—are held in the evenings, so as not to interfere with the ordinary school work.

For the girls of our higher schools it seems to me even more important than for their sisters of the working classes. The latter have to help their mothers at home in many active ways, and get, at all events, plenty of movement and variety of occupation; but the former, who have not so many active games as their brothers, and who are often unable to be much out of doors in bad or severe weather, are lamentably in want of some interesting *active* work as a counterpoise to the continual sitting and poring over books and exercises. Slöjd of some sort is the very thing they need. I am persuaded that, if only we set our shoulder to the wheel in this matter, we shall find in this hand-education the true remedy for over-pressure of brain, which is not an invention of the doctors.

You will, perhaps, wonder where all the teachers of Slöjd, so universally taught in the Scandinavian schools, are trained. A Slöjd Seminary has been founded by Herr Abrahamson, a wealthy Gothenburg merchant, on his beautiful estate of Nääs, within easy reach of Floda station, on the main line between Stockholm and Gothenburg, and about an hour by rail from the latter.

This Seminary was founded in memory of Herr Abrahamson's wife, in 1872, and he has spared neither time, money, nor effort in making it a worthy memorial. There is also a model school for boys and girls in connection with it, so that those who are in training may see the system actually at work among the children. I may mention, in passing, that this school has a great reputation, and that children are sent from considerable distances to attend it.

The Seminary is directed by Herr Otto Salomon (Herr Abrahamson's nephew), who is quite an enthusiast in the cause of Slöjd, and devotes his life to the spread of the system in other countries as well as his own, and to the improvement of it in practical details.

The Seminary, which is built very picturesquely of timber, in the old Norwegian style, is situated in Herr Abrahamson's park, close to the lovely lake of Sävelängen. It consists of large work-rooms fitted with double rows of carpenters' benches and racks all round for the different tools, a large lecture-room, a sitting-room for the gentlemen, a small one for the ladies, and a room where the models and finished works are kept. Upstairs is sleeping accommodation for 30 men.

In addition to the Seminary, there is a pretty little house close by, called 'Vänhem' (Friends' Home), where the lady students live, who form a very small minority of those who attend the course. There are also other cottages in the neighbourhood, where the overflowing numbers attending the course are accommodated.

There are four Slöjd courses given in the course of the year, two summer and two winter courses. Each course lasts six weeks, and, as the time is so short, the hours are somewhat long and the work rather hard for those who are not accustomed to much bodily exercise. The plan of the day is as follows:—

Prayer, 6.45 A.M.; lecture, 7 to 8; breakfast; Slöjd from 8.30 to 1, with a break of a quarter of an hour; dinner and rest, 1 to 3; Slöjd, 3 to 5. Coffee, followed by discussions, either on the Slöjd models—which are apt to be very lively—or on ordinary school subjects, for Herr Salomon is anxious to take advantage of the presence of so many teachers by giving them frequent opportunities of hearing each other's views, and thus rubbing each other up by means of a little wholesome friction.

The whole number of models, consisting of 100 articles, is

divided into two series—fifty in the first course, and fifty in the second. Many of the teachers return in order to go through the second course, and are sure of a hearty welcome. At the end of the course each member receives a certificate, in the presence of the whole body, stating that he or she has attended the course and has made so many models. No special number is required; everyone is anxious to get on, but strength and ability vary considerably, and those who come with a knowledge of carpentering soon leave those who have had no such previous practice hopelessly behind. But all gain much during the course—quite enough to begin a Slöjd class on their return to their respective schools in different parts of the world.

The difficulty of teaching together representatives of so many different nations is not so great as it seems. As far as the *practical* work is concerned, the chief thing is to be shown *how* to work, handle the tools, &c., and the primitive language of signs goes a long way. The lectures are more difficult to manage, and I can only say how they were given at the course I attended. A daily lecture was given in Swedish *and* in German. The former was attended, not only by the Swedes, but by the Danes, Norwegians, and Finlanders, who understand Swedish well. The latter was attended by the Austrians, Bohemians, and English. If we had known no German at all, I believe we should have received some *private* instruction.

A few words, in conclusion, as to the life at Nääs. I think the thing which above all struck us was its complete novelty. We felt as if we had dropped into another planet. The mixture of nationalities and languages, the simplicity of the mode of life, the early hours, the general kindliness, the absence of all class distinctions, the childlike enjoyment of little pleasures, the good-tempered rivalry in work—made up a sort of hyperborean Arcadia. On the other hand, it is only fair to say that the general arrangements are so primitive, that no one should go there who cannot put up with a certain amount of roughing it and very simple fare.

I may mention here, in case any one should feel inclined to spend the summer holidays in going through a course of Slöjd at Nääs, that £10 would well cover the whole cost of the undertaking. A first-class return ticket from London to Gothenburg is

£5 5s. (this does *not* include food); the journey to and from Nääs is short and inexpensive, and a very small sum, about 1s. a day, is charged for food. Application should be made some months beforehand to Herr Otto Salomon, Nääs, Floda Station, Sweden.

Another pleasure was the excellent singing, generally given in the open air, specially during the long solemn evenings of the North, when the air was alive with song. A choir was formed of the best male voices, under an excellent conductor, a member of the course, who took great pains with them. The quarter of an hour's rest in the morning was often turned to good account in the musical line. We used to sit about outside the Seminary, while the choir would stand on a knoll and give us song after song till the bell rang, summoning us to return to our labours. Will you think it strange that this going to school again was also a pleasure? We quite enjoyed to be the pupil instead of the teacher, and were amused to find how much our point of view had changed since we were *in statu pupillari*. But, let me whisper, we should probably not have enjoyed it had it been for more than a very limited time.

We are proud, and justly proud, of our position as Englishmen; but I think we can well afford to recognise more heartily and generously the quota which each civilised nation brings to the intellectual wealth of all. Even those who are small in population, and not so well endowed as ourselves with natural advantages, do their part *relatively* perhaps better than we—and Swedish education, during this century, has advanced by leaps and bounds. I will only remind you of these three facts · it was a Swede, Captain Nordenskjöld, who, in the little *Vega*, first made the North-East Passage; it was a Swede, Herr Henrik Ling, who has given to the world the most scientific and comprehensive system of Gymnastics; and it is Sweden which again comes forward and offers us the hand-education which, if rightly used, is to give our children a completeness in their training which is at present lacking.

NOTE.—Since the above article was written, a project has been formed by Miss Chapman and her friend Miss Nyström (late Directress of the Slöjd Seminary for Teachers at Nääs, Gothenburg), to hold a holiday course for teachers at some attractive place in England during the next summer vacation. Further particulars may be obtained from these ladies, 40 Lansdowne Street, Brighton.

INDUSTRIAL TRAINING IN ELEMENTARY SCHOOLS.[1]

To the Editor of the 'Times.'

SIR,—A paper containing the following questions has been sent by the Royal Commission on Education to the managers of schools.

1. Is the course of teaching prescribed by the Code suited to the children of your school?

2. What changes, if any, would you desire in the (Education) Acts? in the Code? in the administration?

3. Would you recommend the introduction into your school of practical instruction—A. In any of the industries of the district? or in the use of tools for working in wood or iron?

4. B. (for girls) in the domestic duties of home?

I hope the answers to these questions will be that the course of teaching prescribed by the Code is not calculated to effect the object of education, namely, to enable boys and girls to earn their own living when they grow up, and to perform efficiently the duties to which they will be called when they reach the estate of manhood and womanhood.

I trust that the managers will point out that all boys (no matter what is their station in life) should be taught to use their hands, and that girls should be educated so as to become good housewives.

I feel confident that the majority of managers desire the introduction of reforms into the Education Code, but I fear lest some, knowing the difficulties which attend all reform, and fearing that additional expense might fall on their own schools by the adoption of extra subjects, may give a qualified or unfavourable answer to these questions.

I would earnestly ask all managers to give these queries their most serious consideration, and remind them that if industrial, technical, and, I hope, physical training be introduced into the Education Code, such reform would of necessity have to be effected in a manner that would not increase the work of the teachers or the expense of the institution, by substituting these essential subjects for some which are now compulsory, but less necessary.

[1] From the *Times*, October 11, 1886.

I hope the universal answer will be 'Yes, if the practical difficulties connected with their introduction can be overcome.' Such an answer would throw the onus of overcoming these difficulties on the proper department, namely, the Education Office, and there can be no doubt that the difficulties could be easily overcome by any head of the department desirous of effecting this most necessary reform. The depression of trade, the misery to be found in our large towns, the drunken habits of some of our people, are in a measure owing to the want of proper training in youth in industrial handicrafts and technical arts on the part of the boys, and in household work on the part of the girls, so that able-bodied men are unable to find work, and women when they marry have no idea how to make a home neat or happy, or to make the most of limited resources.

The above was given in evidence by a well-known representative of the working classes before the London Mansion House Committee on the distress in London.

The children of our Board Schools are being taught many subjects, such as French and even Italian, which they cannot possibly retain, looking at the early age at which they leave school and the necessity which drives most of them to earn their living immediately on leaving school. A clever child who had learnt some trade well enough to earn good wages, instead of a miserable pittance, or none at all, could always learn these extra subjects, with a much better chance of retaining them, a little later in life at one of the numerous institutions where evening classes are held. In our very laudable desire to obtain for the nation a high standard of general culture and in omitting to teach them the use of the tools by which the mass of them will hereafter have to earn their living, we are unintentionally leading them to believe that the bread which has been gained by the sweat of the brow is less honourably earned than that which is the result of mechanical quill-driving. Now I am sure this was not the intention of the late Mr. Forster or of the promoters of the Bill of 1870. They did not wish to cast a slur upon labour or to make a difference in the honour attaching to different kinds of work. 'All work is honourable,' says Carlyle.

The practical result of this one-sided training is that every boy or girl on leaving school is desirous of engaging in work which is neither manual nor what is mis-termed menial. As the demand for clerks is limited, the only result of this overstocking of the supply of writers or copyists is that those who obtain employment are obliged to be content with wages which the artisan would reject with scorn, and the remainder, who are not fortunate enough to obtain the miserable pittance—well, they go to swell the ranks of the unemployed. They are useless at home, useless as emigrants, and, with bitterness and despair in their hearts, they are ready to blame everyone—Providence, society, capitalists—for the miserable condition of their existence, the real culprit all the time being, in my opinion, in a great measure the national system of education. What I have said of the boys is, with a slight alteration, true of the girls. These mainly desire to become governesses—a class notoriously overstocked and underpaid. Of the four subjects a knowledge of which is most essential to women of all classes—hygiene (including an acquaintance with the rudiments of the art of healing), cookery, household work, and needlework—only the latter is compulsorily taught at school, and that imperfectly, according to Lady Leigh, who wrote a letter on the subject to the *Times*. For the last fifteen years household work has been taught to girls in America with very great success by means of Miss Huntingdon's attractive 'kitchen garden system,' with music and song. It is now being introduced into England by Miss Headdon, Villa Bullo, Newnham-on-Severn.[1]

America has of late years discovered the necessity of introducing industrial and technical training into her schools. I have lately returned from that country, where I visited several Eastern cities, and was pleased to find that the municipal authorities were aware that their otherwise excellent system of education was deficient on the side of technical and industrial training. In Philadelphia a central institution has been established in connection with the common schools of the city, to which three boys from each school are annually sent. These lads are selected by competitive examination. The three successful lads from each school are educated free of charge for five years in the central institution, and one of the principal branches

[1] See page 157.

of the education they receive during these years is a practical workshop training in the use of tools in iron and wood. In order to avoid the opposition of trades-unions, the boys are not taught any particular trade; but when a lad has passed through the course, he has received such a thorough practical training that he is fit to turn his hand to any trade he likes.

The advantage of this system of selection is that it is impossible for any one to assert that these lads are working with their hands because they are unable to work with their heads, for they have proved themselves by competition to be the intellectual *élite* of their respective schools.

It appears to me self-evident that, unless we are prepared to be left behind in the competition of nations, we must follow the example of America, Germany, France, Belgium, Austria, Holland, Sweden, and Switzerland, and make technical and industrial training a prominent and compulsory portion of our educational system.

It may be said that the trades-unions would oppose technical education. They do not oppose it in America, as care is taken in the schools not to turn out any manufactured article, but only to teach generally the use of tools in wood and iron. I do not believe that they would oppose it in this country.

The leaders of the working classes are men of intelligence, and it is not likely that they would seriously countenance opposition to any scheme of education which would enable the workmen of England to compete on more equal terms with their fellow-craftsmen of the Continent.

Our population is increasing at the rate of 340,000 a year, and we cannot feed that which is with us at present, and yet we continue to educate our children as if the necessity for labour had disappeared from among us.

The country wants handicraftsmen, and we produce scriveners. The colonists are crying out for men who can handle a plough, shoe a horse, and mend a cart, and we send them out clerks or would-be gentlemen. Our farmers and working men want wives who can cook, bake, and wash, who understand a dairy and the management of poultry, and we supply them with young women who are incapable of doing any of these things.

In view of the present distress and depression in trade and

agriculture, when all classes must exercise the greatest economy and thrift, it is imperative that our boys should be taught to labour, and our girls to become good housewives.

I am your obedient servant,

BRABAZON.

FOR LACK OF KNOWLEDGE.[1]
TO THE EDITOR OF 'THE DAILY NEWS.'

SIR,—Will you allow me to trouble you with a few lines, as I am eager to endorse all Lord Brabazon's premises in his letter to you of Friday last? Our people are perishing, drinking, fighting, murdering, 'for lack of knowledge.' In thousands of homes where there is lacking to the head of the family neither work nor wages, the most abject discomfort prevails. I have no wish to exaggerate. I am happy to think that there are thousands of homes where peace and order and a wholesome plenty make the home all that it should be; but will any one assert that this is universally the case, or that it is indeed the general rule? And yet, is there any necessary connection between small means and dirt and disorder? If a woman has but a small house, has she not the less to look after; and if she is the wife of a working man, has she not at least nine working hours in the day during which she can clean her house and make every domestic arrangement? Why, then, with so many daily available hours, is the work of cleaning and of providing good wholesome food never finished? Simply because it is never begun. Oh, what a welcome is that which many an honest man receives after hours of hard work, and when he puts his hardly-earned wages into his wife's hand—a poor fire, a dull light, a dirty room, cold, tasteless, unsatisfying food! Where, oh! where is the pretty girl with whom, on a bright May morning, he went to church not so long ago, with the clean fair face, the spotless gown, the snowy riband? What stands in her place? A careworn, frowsy woman, with careless hair, gown coarsely patched, all the beauty and attraction of woman lost, her voice rising to a fretful scream as she threatens the children who should be the rosebuds of a family, but who, like

[1] From the *Daily News*, November 1, 1886.

pigs in every sense, and to every sense, quarrel on the dirty floor. 'Strange, indeed!' her old teachers would say; 'she was a good grammarian, and could repeat long pieces of poetry, and could scramble very fairly through the needlework that had been cut out for her—without a thought, it is true, of the purposes to which the work was to be adapted; and she was in Fractions in her sums.' And she was for a short—all too short —a time in service, and then she was married; and then very soon she was called upon to become purveyor and cook and laundress and dressmaker and needlewoman and nurse and family doctor all in one; and she had not had the smallest training in any one of these important offices! Then she failed in health for want of the most ordinary knowledge of the rules of hygiene; and then her looks went, and her temper suffered, and love flew out of a very dirty window, and she became the unlovable object I have represented. Talk of Wellington and Napoleon! Why, they were very cowards to any men who can endure such a state of things day after day—through the long winter and chilly spring evenings—without flying to a bright, clean, cheerful public-house away from the fretful face and miserable entertainment which awaits them at home, where their minds are neither cheered, nor their bodies refreshed, nor any of their senses gratified, nor their hardly-earned wages put to profit. Grammatical expressions and intellectual conversation are excellent concomitants of a good dinner, but in no rank of life will they take the place of one. When the wit or scholar asks his friends to breakfast, does he give them credit for being satisfied with the feast of reason? No, he knows much better; he will provide the best of everything, and the hot coffee and the abundant variety will unloosen the tongue. Is good varied food less essential to the poor man who has to support his family and be one of the mainstays of the nation than it is to the rich? Leathery, half-cooked food presented day after day to the best-tempered man in the world must try him sorely, and must fail to supply that vigour which is so essential to himself and to his family. Government has insisted upon having every child given over to it for education. It is taken away altogether in many instances from the training which a judicious mother might have imparted. How infinitely responsible does Government now become for the judicious and reasonable training of the young creatures entirely committed to its care, and unable to procure any other teaching than what is provided at school, and where they naturally conclude that the instruction given is that of all others which the wit and wisdom of their betters has, after weighty consideration, pronounced to be that which it is most imperative for them to acquire! I believe that every afternoon in girls' schools should be yielded to the managers with permission to occupy it on domestic economy, and that unelastic and tyrannous thing, the time-table, should be altogether banished; then there would be time to teach cutting out, and thorough needlework, and cooking, and everything that bears upon the happiness and very existence of the home. Many a child who now makes but an indifferent scholar might prove a good, happy, sensible wife and mother if early taught the beauty of cleanliness, methodical habits, and how to sew and cook thoroughly. The heart of the nation responds when 'Home, sweet home,' is sung. Let it be ours to see that the association of the words never brings to any man the recollection of foul smells and heart-sickening disorder.

I remain, Sir, your obedient servant,
CAROLINE A. LEIGH.

Stoneleigh Abbey : October 30.

A PLEA FOR INDUSTRIAL TRAINING FOR GIRLS.[1]

BY R. L.

THERE is an Italian proverb to the effect that, if one looks at every side of a question, one will never decide upon anything. It might be inferred from this that it is safer not to go too deeply into any subject, nor to make too many inquiries, but, taking up one side, to go loyally and enthusiastically forward on one ground, leaving all the other aspects of the question entirely out of account. The truth contained in the proverb suggests itself to the writer rather in this way, that, as there is nothing perfect in this world, we must not look for nor expect perfection. In every law, from a nursery rule to an Act of

[1] Reprinted, by permission, from *Eastward Ho!* December, 1886.

Parliament, we must look for the defect, the weakness, the blemish. The wisest measure reads hard for somebody. True wisdom, however, should look at every side, hear every argument, and, neither carried away by beauties nor discouraged by weak points, should aim at the greatest good of the greatest number, and, looking a question fairly in the face, accept or reject it on its true merits as affecting the majority, bringing in the remedial or healing measure for the benefit of the minority.

There is a great question now before the country, perhaps the greatest and most important that can exercise the minds of statesmen. The question is education—in other words, How to elevate the masses?

If, therefore, we keep in view, as our aim, the benefit of the greatest number, we must admit, to start with, that the majority of the nation are, and must continue to be, working people. One head can direct many hands, and there is no state of society conceivable in which manual labour could be dispensed with; therefore education, suitable for working people, is what should be provided by the State, and, in collecting evidence, none should be overlooked that might throw light upon the wants of the working members of the community.

An uncomfortable feeling prevails, with regard to education, that there is something wrong—a screw loose somewhere, or a little wheel a-wanting—which is hampering the action of the complicated machinery at work for the production of men and women such as God meant them to be.

Many years ago, people woke up to realise the fact that thousands of children roamed the streets, for whom no man cared, who had never been brought under the sweet influence of education; who could not write their own names; who could not read the heavenly message, and whose voices had never been trained to rise in praise to the Giver of All. Such things ought not to be, was the unanimous voice; we must educate the children; we will build schools—nothing shall be spared—our land shall no longer be disgraced by a boy who cannot read or a girl who cannot sew. The Act of 1870 was passed, the rates were cheerfully paid, money flowed in, and throughout the length and breadth of the land buildings arose, equipped with all the necessary paraphernalia, and the children were driven in.

The close of 1886 is approaching; let us look round the back lanes and courts, and ask ourselves if things are any better than they were in 1870? Are working people more thrifty and intelligent? Are our artisans more capable, or our domestic servants more honest or efficient?

The shivering girl, still in her teens, one encounters in tramway-cars, drawing her poor rags closer round the infant, whose light weight her feeble arms can scarcely support, has passed through our schools. The wedding-ring that glitters on her wasted finger tells us of the vows that bind her for life to the lad of eighteen sitting by her, his head sunk on his breast in drunken sleep. He, too, has passed through those schools. Speak to the girl, she will tell you, 'Jamie has been out of work—can get none.' Little wonder; he is not very workman-like! And she! What has she been taught? She can read— far better that she could not than waste her spare pennies on the worse than trashy papers she buys. She is ignorant of every art that might make her home comfortable when 'Jamie' is earning good wages, or that might augment them when low. Alas, poor girl! one shivers with pity and despair at the thought of her future.

Times have been bad, it is true, and work very scarce, but how much of this is due to the fact that work is being sent out of the country because it can be better done elsewhere for less money? We are educating a race of male and female clerks (whose work is as mechanical as any artisan's), when every day there is less work requiring clerking being done in the country. Let us fit our youths and maidens for the work of colonising our tracts of untilled acres 'across the ferry,' and fire their ambition with the prospect of a life of comfort and prosperity in a new country which they might never hope to enjoy at home, and they will flock there in thousands, sending home for supplies which will set our now silent machinery in motion and make our deserted shipbuilding-yards once more alive with the sound of busy hammers.

I have before me now no less than three Blue-Books— Reports of the Committee of Council on Education, who have been granted full power to call before them such persons 'as you shall judge likely to afford you any information upon the subject of this our Commission, and also to call for, have access to, and examine all such books, documents, registers, and records as may afford you the fullest information on the subject, and to inquire of and concerning the premises by all other ways and means whatsoever.' That the Royal Commissioners are bent on doing their duty is apparent. They have already examined at great length many witnesses, whose evidence occupies in print some 500 folio pages; but there is evidence they will never hear, there are registers they will never see.

There is evidence of an absolute want of suitable teaching for the poor, in their ill-savoured, wretched dwellings, in the dishonest, faithless work of every kind which has such a paralysing effect on trade, in the numbers of girls who cannot work, who cannot starve; who must live somehow, and who drift into early marriage, in the hope of being provided for without exertion on their own part—too soon finding out their mistake. There will be no evidence forthcoming on this question from the thousands of mothers in the poorer middle class, who are aging prematurely, or gliding into untimely graves; broken-down in the battle which has been too hard, the struggle which has been too keen, not to keep their place in society—they see none—but in the daily, hourly struggle to feed and clothe their children; to permit them to enjoy the comforts of a clean house, wholesome food, and daily outdoor exercise, with no adequate domestic help to be found.

Little wonder that there is a leaning amongst all classes to Communism in the home, and that many people are looking forward with complacency to the probability of all classes, at no very distant date, living in huge hotels or boarding-houses, and to the sweet word 'home,' in all its significance, being obliterated from our vocabulary.

There are still, however, many people who have enough of feeling and poetry left, despite the worries of housekeeping, to look forward with alarm to such a complete social reorganisation, and who would see with sorrow the land swept clear of snug cottages and comfortable suburban villas, where the pride of possession gives the owner as much pleasure, unaccompanied by care, as the great lord's fine demesne. It is not the man who toils for his daily bread in field or workshop, nor his wife, wearied with a round of domestic duties, sitting down at night to enjoy their well-earned leisure, who ask the pitiful question, 'Is life worth living?'

That problem has to be solved by the cultured man of leisure, who has not the force of character to bind himself down to some prescribed work or study, but dips into everything, till, sated with art, science, religion (or theology rather), ethics, and philosophy, he becomes confused and bewildered, and overlooks the only Divine command that could settle his restless mind. 'Work while it is called to-day; the night cometh.' True philosophy is a reflection on completed work. They who have not their work to seek, if they only knew it, are the truly blessed. How few, not compelled by circumstances to confine their energies within limits, can escape *dilettantism*? Now is the time for those who believe this blessed gospel of work to come forward and declare it, and demand for the sons and daughters of toil a suitable training for the callings they are to follow in life. Were the same amount of money which is now lavished by School Boards in training the children of the well-to-do classes for so-called 'honourable callings' spent on technical and industrial training for boys and girls, the dawn of a new century might see such a reformation in the social condition of our dwellings, from the tenement-house in the crowded city to the poor cottar's hut in the lonely Western isle, as would eclipse, as far as the mass of the people are concerned, any reformation ever effected. Let manual labour no longer be considered degrading; let us recognise the dignity of true work of whatever kind, and, by providing in our Board Schools practical and efficient instruction in all useful arts, remove the stigma attached by so many to domestic work, and give it its true place in a girl's education.

It would be well that no evidence which might throw light on this education question should be wanting, and the evidence of one who knows well many both well-to-do and very poor working people, and who understands them sufficiently to know what kind of education would benefit them as individuals—evidence drawn entirely from personal knowledge and observation—may be not without value.

Passing along the streets of a respectable locality a few

weeks ago, curiosity tempted me to inspect the stately buildings recently erected for a Board School. One wishes to be a child and at school again, so numerous and delightful are the appliances of the various class-rooms. The bell has just sounded the dinner-hour, the children come pouring out—merry, bright, happy—not a bare-footed child, not a pinched, starved face amongst them—all comfortably clothed and well shod, and I think, with a sigh of content, This is what the Board Schools have done! But wait a moment. Who is this pressing his little wistful face through the iron railings beneath the stone portico with 'Infants' carved on it in large letters?

'This child must come to school, too; he must be more than six years old?' I ask of the attentive janitor, who is directing me on my way.

'He'll be at the school in B—— Street; there's none of that class here. There's a school in B—— Street, over there, for the likes of him.'

'Do you go to school?' I ask the little boy, speaking as pleasantly as I could.

The child was sucking an empty lobster-tin; he was very dirty, and his feet were bare. Looking up into my face, he shook his head; he did not look exactly like a waif or stray child; his clothes were more grimy than ragged.

'Do you not go to school?' I repeated. 'How old are you?'

'Six months,' he replied, and ran off as fast as his little legs would carry him.

'Six years, he means,' said the janitor. 'For all the officers and the Act, there's dozens o' children running wild about the streets that never go near a school.'

Here was matter for reflection. After all, this fine building, with its busts, photographs, museum and modelling-room, was not intended for the poor, but for the children of well-to-do people. The classes for painting, dancing, *high-class* cookery, &c., are attended by fashionably-dressed girls, many of whom would think themselves lowered in the social scale if obliged to earn their own living; while from the B—— Street school, where there is not even a cookery-class, little girls are turned out a finished article at thirteen years old, and begin to maintain themselves running errands or at any other employment which requires no skill.

Thus do we educate the working classes.

There is, indeed, something a-wanting in the machinery of education. The screw that needs tightening—the little wheel a-wanting—is Practical Industrial Training for girls. The greed of the middle class has seized upon the rights of the poor. The well-to-do ratepayers have coveted the schools for their own children.

'Why pay the rates,' they say, 'and not get the benefit?' and two classes of schools are built within a stone's throw of one another; the high fees—although not high enough to be just payment for what is given—excluding poor children from the better class of school.

Could Lord Brabazon's admirable suggestions in his book, 'Social Arrows,' just published, be carried out, and a dinner provided every day in Board schools cooked and eaten by the children themselves, the Board would not require to spend one shilling on the recovery of a penny fee, and girls would gain some insight into work which would really benefit them, and for which there is an unfailing demand. Here are some social knots for the political economist to untie; some facts to prove that, if in some departments of labour there is no work to be had, in other fields the harvest is white and plentiful, but no labourers to be found. A thousand men in this city (Glasgow) are glad to carry sandwich-boards for one shilling a day. In answer to an advertisement for a cook—20*l*. and all found—one woman applies and will not take the place, for she prefers 'a newly-married couple'!

One hundred and forty answers have been received this very day to a *single* insertion of an advertisement for a governess for two little girls. Their Board School education and certificates have not enabled most of the applicants to express themselves in a way that one would wish one's children to be taught.

To an advertisement for a woman to clean out a place of business, eight hours daily, fifty applications are received; some offering to do the work for five shillings a week; this without food.

To an advertisement, in the same paper, for a woman to do washing and dressing (as clear-starching is called in Scotland), four days weekly, at 2s. 6d. per day and all found, three applications are received, in answer to four insertions. Fine ironing is a thing that almost any one, with a little practice and instruction, can do. Yet it is almost impossible, in country places, to find any one who can undertake such work; and when one does meet with a woman who excels in this most useful branch, one finds that she can employ several assistants, for washing, mangling, &c., doing up the fine articles herself.

I know several women—widows, with large families—who live in great comfort, are bringing up their families well, and saving money, who earn their bread by taking in washing and dressing. One woman, who lives at a fashionable coast-place, makes as much in summer as allows her to enjoy quiet and rest the whole winter. Out of her savings she has purchased her cottage and the piece of ground attached.

I always reflect, with some sadness, in passing through our poorer streets, and listening to the audible remarks made by the idle women constantly standing about upon the personal appearance of any one better dressed than themselves, that, had those women—many of them young enough to have passed through the Board schools—been taught while there to iron collars and cotton dresses, they might be well dressed too, and earning money as well, instead of sitting idle on doorsteps, making remarks on passers-by.

The Royal Commissioners on Education have asked the question of the managers of Board and other National schools, 'Would you recommend the introduction into your school of Practical Instruction (for girls) in the domestic duties of home?'

What is the answer to be?

INDUSTRIAL TRAINING FOR GIRLS.

By Miss Headdon.

AMONGST the many questions perplexing our nation at present, surely few are more important than the one which touches upon the training of the children; truly it was a wise man who said he would begin the training of a child 'twenty-five years before he was born'—that is, he would begin with the mother, and teach

her to train the child. Whatever the nation is begins in the family, and what hope can there be for a nation when there is thriftless ignorance on the part of the mothers and thorough inefficiency on the part of the greater number of domestic servants, with the result of extravagance and discomfort in the homes?

This, we are assured, is partly owing to the fact that *the natural womanly taste for domestic work and household management is neglected and its cultivation left out of the girls' education.*

One cannot but notice how happy *little* girls are if allowed to dust mother's chairs or to iron the stockings and handkerchiefs; how deftly they manage the sweeping-broom with a handle about twice as tall as themselves; how delighted to have a small piece of dough and make grimy little editions of mother's tarts. And one cannot but be struck, too, by the fact that as these same little girls grow older they lose this taste and come to look upon domestic work as drudgery, preferring when they leave school any occupation but housework.

Remedy this neglect, give the girl a continuous course of instruction in this branch—the most essential of a woman's education—lead them to look upon dirt as a disgrace and waste as a sin, inoculate into them a love of cleanliness and order (a habit if once acquired is seldom lost); and we may hope in the future that, with *knowledge* and *method* to guide them, we shall have a race of thrifty, energetic women—good wives and mothers, who know how to make home real homes where the husbands and sons will prefer to be instead of seeking what they cannot find there at the public-houses or clubs; helpful daughters who will consider the making of a pie and the cleanliness of their rooms, persons, and wardrobes of equal importance with their drawing, music, or fancy work; conscientious servants who will scorn to leave the corners and sweep round a mat.

To meet this crying need of our times we have—

THE HOUSEWIFERY ASSOCIATION,

OR

NATIONAL SOCIETY FOR GIVING INSTRUCTION IN THE PRINCIPLES AND PRACTICE OF HOUSEWIFERY.

FOUNDRESS—MISS HEADDON.

THIS association is the result of a strong desire to raise the tone of household work by promoting a wide and correct knowledge of, *first*, the domestic kindergarten, teaching in the first step methodical daily work, taking the girls through the day's work; in the second teaching weekly duties, or washing, ironing, and house-cleaning; and in the third supplementary duties, such as marketing, cooking, clothing, &c.; all taught by means of small models of requisites, and accompanied by suitable drill and songs. *Secondly*, a junior course, or advanced practical lessons upon the same system for older girls.

INDUSTRIAL TRAINING FOR GIRLS

Thirdly, a senior course, for imparting a scientific knowledge of housewifery, hygiene, and sanitary subjects to young women.

President.—THE LADY LOUISA EGERTON.

Council.

THE COUNTESS OF MEATH	*L. M. H. (Editor of 'Work and Leisure')
LADY KNIGHTLEY	
MRS. FRANCES LUPTON	THE EARL FORTESCUE
*MISS HEADDON	JOHN RUSKIN, ESQ., LL.D.
*MRS. EDMUND HELPS	EDWIN CHADWICK, ESQ., C.B.
MISS MORLEY	*DR. ROTH

* These form the Executive Committee.

Office and Class-room.—41 Wigmore Street, London, W. Hours, 11 till 4.

Hon. Auditor.—J. O. CHADWICK, ESQ., F.C.A.

Bankers.—LONDON AND WESTMINSTER BANK, St. James's Square, London, S.W.

TRAINING COLLEGE.

Gloucestershire: RIVERDALE, Newnham-on-Severn.

Visitor.—THE REV. T. J. WEIGHT (Vicar).

Hon. Medical Adviser.—DR. SHAW CARLETON.

Bankers.—THE CAPITAL AND COUNTIES BANK, Newnham-on-Severn.

Hon. Sec., Treasurer, and Demonstrator.—MISS HEADDON, Riverdale, Newnham-on-Severn, to whom all communications must be addressed.

Cheques and postal orders to be made payable to M. E. Headdon.

Arrangements can be made for teachers to attend classes, and for a lady (trainer of teachers) to visit any town throughout England, Scotland, and Ireland to give a course of lessons to teachers in the neighbourhood. Certificates of attendance may be gained by such teachers, but the higher grade certificates of merit can only be obtained by a course of training at the training college.

ORGANISING ASSOCIATES.

For Ireland.—THE REV. ANTHONY L. ELLIOTT, 39 Great George Street, Dublin.

For Scotland.—MR. LAURIE, Paternoster Row, London (*pro tem.*).

For the G.F.S.—MRS. MERCIER, Kemerton Rectory, Tewkesbury.

For the Y.W.C.A.—THE HON. EMILY KINNAIRD, 2 Pall Mall East (*pro tem.*).

For Bedfordshire.—{ MISS YOUNG, Ivy Cottage, } Bedford.
{ A. RANSOM, ESQ., 1 St. Loyes, }

For Wiltshire.—MRS. HENSLOW, Zeals Rectory, Bath.

For Yorkshire.—MRS. PEAKE, 13 Cromer Terrace, Leeds.

For Hallamshire.—MRS. JARVIS BARBER, Abbeydale, Sheffield.

For Shropshire.—MISS SMITH, Aston House, Newport, Salop.

BOOKS AND APPARATUS REQUIRED FOR THE INTRODUCTION OF THE DOMESTIC KINDERGARTEN CLASSES INTO SCHOOL ROUTINE.

To be obtained at the London office, and at the Training House, Newnham-on-Severn.

HOUSEHOLD OBJECT LESSONS: First Manual, with music and directions for drill, &c., 1s. The songs: On cards, 4s. the 100; as leaflets, 2s. Further lessons will come out in the monthly paper, *Little Women*.

TOY MODELS FOR THE FIRST STEP, 13s. 6d. the single set. They consist of a table-setting box, 5s. 6d.; table-board, 6d.; bedstead (folds flat), 4s.; bedding, 3s.; two chairs for bed-making, 6d. Particulars of models for the second and third steps to be obtained of Miss Headdon.

Three sets will suffice for small schools, and in poor districts it has been suggested that the managers might combine to purchase three complete sets, and arrange for their monthly circulation and exchange.

For large schools and infant galleries six, eight, or twelve sets are desirable, that number of children being allowed to handle them in rotation, while the rest watch and join in the songs and actions.

It has been proved that one set manipulated before a class of fifty whose ages varied from nine to fourteen is very successful. In this case much depends upon the cleverness of the teacher.

Little Women, the organ of the Association, says:

'Miss Headdon gave evidence on June 8 before the Royal Commission on Education; and a short time before she described her system to the Special Committee to inquire into the subjects and modes of instruction appointed by the London School Board. She pleaded that her system of domestic kindergarten might be recognised as a " varied occupation " for the infant school, and as such take a part of the Government grant; that it might be introduced into the first, second, and third standards in its first, second, and third steps, once a week, as object lessons; but with regard to the advanced practical lessons upon the same plan, she was obliged to admit that she could say nothing until legislation made it practicable, by multiplying kitchens and giving the girls more time to spend in them, which she thought might well be taken partly from the advanced arithmetic. Given more kitchens and more time, the girls might be taught cooking on Mondays, and one other day; washing on Tuesdays; ironing one day, and on Friday house-cleaning; ending up with a thorough cleaning of the schoolroom ready for the next week's work. The whole thing is in a nutshell, if put in this way: " If the *bulk* of our girls leave school when they have passed the *fourth standard*, then it is to the elementary schools that we must look; and I cannot but think more than ever that this plan, which provides in a *methodical* way rudimentary household teaching for the *first three standards*, and *twelve months' practical training* while they are in the *fourth*, must be the system which is *most calculated* to meet the need of some training for the *majority* of our girls, in order that in the future we shall have better wives, better mothers, and better servants."'

Not only does this question touch upon us in England, but it must be considered by those who advocate emigration for women. A knowledge of house-work and household management is specially needed by them. Beyond this comes the wish that Government could in some way supervise young girls in situations, as some protection to the girls, and also some guarantee that they rendered their mistresses assistance and remained with them long enough to compensate them for the trouble of supplementing the teaching they had received at school.

Much has been done; several of the schools of the London Board are at work on the domestic kindergarten. So are schools at Leeds, Dublin, &c., and many private classes are being started. Advanced classes for practical cookery and house-work are begun at the People's Palace, &c., and, what is more to the purpose, great satisfaction is expressed by the girls and young women themselves.

We have only to beg that Government will recognise the movement and give us its support.

COOKERY IN ELEMENTARY SCHOOLS.

By Miss Fanny L. Calder,
Hon. Sec. of the Liverpool Training School of Cookery, and Hon. Sec. Northern Union of Schools of Cookery.

Now that instruction in practical cookery in elementary schools takes so settled a place in the Education Code, any paper on the subject that is to be of general utility needs to be one of explanations and experiences rather than that of recommendation. Still, a few words on behalf of this twin-sister of needlework will not be out of place before we proceed to discuss plans and methods, and report success already attained.

One could almost wonder that 'house-thrift,' which is really the equivalent of the term 'practical cookery,' should not have been considered necessary for the girls of the working class, even before sewing. For, while ready-made clothing can be bought one way or another, and, in fact, *is* bought to a very large extent by the poorest of our people, no amount of money can purchase the well-ordered home, the comfortable, wholesome meal by the clean fireside, outrivalling even the most attractive public-house, which only a thrifty housewife can produce, and which closes the vista drawn out in the mental vision of the promoters of Schools of Cookery.

The lamentable ignorance displayed by such numbers of women of any true domestic management results in miserable homes, waste of hard-earned wages, loss to the country of many useful articles of food, and the too often degraded condition of the poorer districts. It is calculated that sixty per cent. of a workman's wages goes in food; therefore anything that promotes reformation in that line of expenditure will aid most in bettering his general condition. Knowledge and capacity in this department mean health, thrift, comfort, and saving; so that efficient instruction in this branch of education seems likely to have a more direct effect upon the welfare of the people than any other subject in the time-table of our girls' schools.

As a handmaid to temperance, cookery takes also a foremost place. When this movement was first started, one of the oldest magistrates in Liverpool, who is also a leading educationist, stated in support of this cause that most of the cases that were brought before him arose from quarrels about food—either that it was not provided at all, or so badly cooked as to be uneatable. Of course the natural resource was the public-house, for it needs no deeply scientific knowledge of the laws of life or physiology to understand that, if nourishment is not provided in a wholesome way, it can be temporarily obtained from stimulant, though probably at the cost of the health of both brain and body. An excellent, perhaps the best, antidote to the public-house is a wholesome, appetising meal at home. Moreover, if the wife finds her interest and occupation in thrifty housekeeping, there will be neither time nor inclination for the very objectionable afternoon occupation of gossiping on the doorstep or forming drinking parties indoors. It is frequently remarked of the people in poor neighbourhoods that they have 'nothing to cook;' but any acquaintance with life in those parts reveals the truth that those who cook least, spend the most, in proportion, in drink, and that ignorance more than poverty brings degradation.

In the hope of trying to reform some of these social evils, the first efforts of most of the Cookery Committees were directed to teaching the mothers. Many of these really valued and made good use of the instruction given in lectures, but by far the greater number were too prejudiced or too idle to benefit by them. The prejudice of the people against any article of food that is new or cheap is as strong as the national prejudice against eating frogs or dogs, and the slower processes of cookery, always recommended as the most economical and wholesome, will never be acceptable to women long confirmed in feckless, idle habits.

It was soon decided that, to effect any permanent result, instruction in cookery must be given to the girls while at school. From that time the attention of the Committee of the Liverpool School of Cookery, of whose work and plans I specially speak, was chiefly directed to the one object of getting *practical* cooking introduced into the elementary schools as a regular subject with a Government grant. Appeals to this end were made in different ways, but it appeared that no grant was likely to be given unless definite plans were brought forward, showing the exact cost, and the means by which such instruction could be placed within the reach of all elementary schools both in town and country. Prepared with such plans, which had been developed by experience in various elementary schools, a deputation of ladies and gentlemen from Liverpool waited upon the Lords of the Privy Council on Education in December 1881, praying that practical cookery might be made a recognised subject with a grant of 4s. a head. Supported by petitions from other societies, this request was granted, and the Code of 1882 made a grant of 4s. for every girl of twelve years of age and upwards who had received forty hours' practical cookery instruction. In 1883 this came into force. But it was found that the fixed age of twelve years prevented many of those girls who might most need such lessons from obtaining them—as the poorer children frequently leave school as soon as they have passed Standard IV., generally at eleven, sometimes even at ten years of age. This difficulty was at once laid before the Education Department, and received prompt consideration. In the Code of 1884 the fixed age was changed to any age in the Fourth Standard and upwards, thus leaving it to the discretion of managers and teachers to place in the cookery classes such young girls as were likely to leave school before reaching a higher standard. During that year of 1884 the subject was adopted in many more schools in various parts of the country, but in some with this drawback, that for the sake of obtaining large grants classes were formed far too large for any of the children to receive a fair amount of such practical experience as would justify the term *practical* cookery, for which the grant was given. The Liverpool Committee, therefore, sent a petition to Mr. Mundella on behalf of small classes for practice work, the response to which petition appeared in the Code laid on the table of the House of Commons in March 1885. There the grant is made conditional on each separate class not exceeding twenty-four in number, and every girl having spent not less than twenty hours in cooking with her own hands.

Another condition added to the Code of 1885 requires that the teacher of cookery shall have been trained for the work in one of the Training Schools of Cookery.

These are the steps of rapid and encouraging progress with which the Education Department has marked its approval of a subject of which Mr. Mundella says that, 'after the three elementary subjects and sewing, no subject is of such importance as cookery for the class of girls who attend public elementary schools.'

And now the subject of practical cookery stands thus.[1] It is a recognised subject, with a grant of 4s. a head for any girl in the Fourth Standard and upwards who has had forty hours' instruction, twenty of which at least have been spent in cooking with her own hands in a class of not more than twenty-four scholars; on condition that the Inspector reports that special and appropriate provision is made for the practical teaching of

[1] In the Code of March, 1887, a grant is made for cookery in the evening schools also.

cookery by a teacher who has been trained in some Training School of Cookery.[1]

From many schools whose managers are anxious to make their girls useful women as well as clever scholars, and who therefore adopted cookery as soon as possible, reports of a most satisfactory nature are constantly reaching the Committee. One says: 'As to our cookery classes, I can only record continual success and appreciation. The whole country speaks well of them, and I believe I shall make them support themselves. Miss L—— is an excellent teacher; I cannot speak too well of her.' Another: 'The parents have given frequent testimony of their appreciation of this cookery teaching for their girls. The people of the neighbourhood say that nothing so successful has been attempted in the way of education, and at several meetings lately, gentlemen have praised the effort and given expression to the general approval of the cookery classes.' And yet another: 'The cookery classes have been an enormous success.' The head-mistresses have also written in cordial support of these lessons, and their opinion is extremely valuable, because on them devolves the only real trouble connected with the matter, the arrangement of the classes. They say the girls stay longer at school to obtain this instruction, often even waiting for a second course; they are more regular in attendance, and are perceptibly more intelligent and capable in their other work. After having taken cookery lessons they take great pleasure in the work, and (a point much to be noted) bring for their school dinners meat pasties, rice puddings, and such

---

[1] The Code of March, 1887, offers a grant of 4s. a head for cookery in evening schools, and now cookery can be taken as the first subject after the three R's. Unfortunately the grant is made on the same condition of *time* as in the day schools, viz., forty hours. In the evening schools of large towns this condition is an impossible one, as the pupils are girls in various employments who can never be so perfectly regular in attendance during the twenty-two weeks that these schools are usually open so as never to miss a cooking lesson. And even if regular the hour and a half lessons would not make up forty hours. It is therefore much to be desired that all who are interested in the recreative evening classes, or other night schools, should combine in appealing to the Education Department before February, 1888, to alter this condition of time to, perhaps, twenty hours, with a smaller grant even. Cooking is now much in request in some of the recreative evening schools, and such a concession would greatly aid the managers in responding to such a sensible demand.

dishes, instead of their usual scanty provision; and one writer adds: 'Instead of teaching girls the higher branches of arithmetic, let them devote more attention to those subjects which form the basis of domestic comfort and happiness.' Here we are evidently working in the right direction, and domestic skill, glorified as an educational subject with a Government grant, seems on the eve of regaining its proper place in the eyes of schoolgirls, who had begun to think home-work quite beneath their attention, and to be left to those who had not enjoyed the same intellectual opportunities as themselves. Hence the number of unemployed and too often incapable young women that abound now.

The importance to girls of such preparatory training is realised when we consider how much emigration schemes are being pressed upon the public as a necessity for the country, schemes in which, of course, the women largely share; and all reports from the Colonies urge the value of manual skill even above the much-desired intellectual attainments. Any woman who can cook or wash is sure to make a competency, if not a fortune; while those who offer only brainwork are often compelled to return to England.

The plan of lessons adopted, and recommended by the Liverpool School of Cookery, and which has been in successful operation for some years now, has been drawn up in conformity with the required forty hours of the Code. These are divided into twenty lessons of two hours each, these two hours giving time for the dishes to cook, and for the girls to clean and put away everything before they finish. No assistant-maid is needed, as the children are required to do all themselves. The twenty lessons comprise the elementary knowledge of the nature, use, and preparation of the various classes of food, as meat, vegetables, fish, soups, puddings, bread, and invalid cookery, with practice in the best and most economical methods of cooking them. There are a great variety of ways of cooking both fish and vegetables, and to these much attention is now being directed. The lessons are alternately demonstration and practice, that the faculty of imitation—generally large in children—may be called into exercise. At one lesson the children are shown how, nicely and neatly, to prepare and cook certain dishes; at the same time explanation is given of the nature and use of the food then being dealt with, and they are questioned as to cost, time, and quantities. At the next lesson the girls cook these same dishes themselves under the direction of the teacher. They work together in sets, and take it in turns to do the cleaning, which is as important as the cooking itself, cleanliness being essential to comfort.

On two points the Liverpool School lays great stress. First, the size of the practice class, which should not exceed fifteen girls, but twelve is the best number. And next, the use of plainly-printed recipes, with which each girl is supplied at the beginning of the lesson, so that she can give her full attention to the teacher's manner of working instead of wasting time and attention in writing and spelling words which are often new and strange to her. The classes are usually held once a week. During the lessons the children receive marks for work and conduct, and at the end of the course go through a verbal and practical examination, for which certificates are awarded by the Liverpool School of Cookery. A lady examiner is now officially engaged for this work, and the certificates are greatly appreciated by both parents and children. The last public speech of H.R.H. the late Duke of Albany was on the occasion when, by the kind consent of the Liverpool Council of Education, he presented these certificates to girls of the elementary schools, in January 1884. He then strongly advocated the subject of cookery, and expressed a hope it would extend even to the poorest schools, a hope now accomplished, and lessons are being given to the elder girls, and even to some boys, of the night ragged schools. If through illness or other cause any girl should miss one or more lessons of the course, and so have failed to complete her forty hours, extra lessons can be given at special times on the omitted subjects. When the girls remain long enough at school to receive a second course of cookery lessons, a quite different set of dishes is arranged for this second course, so that their experience may vary as much as possible. At the request of some managers a simple manual, price $2\frac{1}{2}d.$, has been compiled for the girls to use at home, as many of them like to do.

There was but one point wanting to make the Liverpool

cookery system complete, and that has recently been supplied by the liberality of Mr. Samuel Smith, M.P., who has given the Committee of the Liverpool School of Cookery some scholarships to be awarded in the elementary schools to such girls as combine proficiency in work with praiseworthy behaviour. A Cookery Scholarship consists of a complete course of household cookery lessons at the Central School of Cookery, such as are given to ladies and cooks, and valuable to any girl either for home life, or service, or emigration.

The cost of the food for the whole course of twenty lessons is about 1*l*. 17*s*. This is easily repaid by the sale of the dishes cooked, either to the teachers, to the children, to the parents, or for the sick poor of the neighbourhood. There is rarely any difficulty in disposing of the food at cost price, and some schools make a profit by it. In one instance 10*s*. was made during one course of lessons. The dishes to be cooked can always be arranged suitably to the season of the year and the possibilities of each locality.

The necessary requirements for carrying out this scheme are far less formidable than the uninitiated seem to think. The list of utensils needed for a practice class of fifteen girls, including crockery, linen, and materials for cleaning, can be obtained for 5*l*., and are easily stowed away in an ordinary cupboard. This is an expense that will not recur for some years. The tables can be improvised of boards laid across the backs of desks or trestles, and are easily put away, forming no hindrance in a class-room. A moderate-sized class-room is quite sufficient, and if this is not attainable the kitchen of a neighbouring house or cottage can be employed instead. The scullery work *can* be accomplished with ordinary washing-bowls, but it is, of course, neater and more comfortable to have some scullery arrangement, which can now be made at a small expense. A sanitary sink costs from 10*s*. to 15*s*. The stove depends greatly upon existing local circumstances. If there is a small kitchen range, an extra gas table-stove holding two or three pans will quite suffice. If there is only a simple fire-place, a stove with an oven is essential, and can be supplied either by a small gas oven, or by a small fuel stove with an oven, in addition to the fireplace. If there is no fireplace at all, a small range with a boiler, for about 3*l*. 10*s*., is very suitable for the purpose. Should a movable stove be preferred, a gas stove can be had for 5*l*. 5*s*., or a fuel stove for 4*l*. 10*s*. The old fear of teaching with gas has proved groundless; no girl has ever found any difficulty in working with the utensils she has at home because she learnt on a gas stove. Laying aside any objection, there is difficulty in some villages in obtaining gas. In that case an oil stove is a good substitute, though, of course, not so cleanly to work with as gas. Still, it has been found extremely convenient, and does not need to be lighted long beforehand, like a fuel stove. Either of these stoves can be boarded over when the cooking is not going on, and serve as a table instead of being an inconvenience in a class-room.

These preliminary expenses are of course the difficulty in poor schools, but in the present zeal for education and social reform supporters of this movement will be found if school managers are really anxious to take it up. For some years now the Liverpool Council of Education has been making grants to poor schools for the purchase of utensils, but of course in Liverpool only.

Efficient teaching is the vital point, and the one that needs co-operative arrangements in order to secure first-rate instruction at the smallest cost. Managers and head teachers see at once the impossibility (as a rule) of adding this to the duties of school-mistresses, whose time and strength are already fully taxed, and who by no means desire to take up an additional burden. The teaching of cookery is not simply the preparation of certain dishes, which might be shown by any good cook, but includes much instruction in the difficult art of choosing suitable, nourishing, and at the same time economical, articles of food, in order that the smallest incomes may stretch to meet the needs of even the largest families—such instruction as gives the children an intelligent interest in the matter, so that, understanding the true purpose of eating, and what things serve that purpose best, they may eventually become thoughtful, thrifty women, not mechanical or unintelligent drudges.

Teachers trained in the Liverpool School of Cookery are sent forth to all parts of the country. Many of these go from the Liverpool Committee for a term of weeks or months, and under local arrangement have a circuit of schools placed in their charge for the required course of twenty lessons. A teacher can give two lessons a day for five days a week throughout the school year, so that she can take ten classes in ten different schools, or several classes in one school during that time. And the managers of the different schools combine to share the salary according to the number of classes each school has had. By neighbouring places combining in this way the expense is reduced to a minimum for each. The usual plan is one lesson a week, but, of course, this is settled by the managers and headmistress. Several neighbourhoods are being worked in this way. To secure to the public a supply of duly qualified teachers, thoroughly trained for elementary school work by experience in teaching children, the Northern Union of Schools of Cookery, of which the late Duke of Albany was patron,[1] was formed in 1876. When it was ascertained that there was no probability of one good general standard of marks and requirements for diplomas being arranged for the whole country, leading Schools of Cookery agreed to unite in a scheme for adopting a uniform method of training teachers, and to offer diplomas on a basis of such thoroughly efficient instruction and examination that the public might always feel secure of good work when engaging a teacher holding one of them.

The result of this Union has been to create a supply of teachers who, beyond the usual training in cookery, are well informed in methods and plans of conducting elementary school classes, and have already done much good work in this department.[2]

[1] H.R.H. the Duchess of Albany has now kindly consented to become patroness of the Northern Union.
[2] The Training Schools which are connected with the Northern Union are Liverpool, Leeds, and Glasgow. These, with the National Training School of Cookery, South Kensington, may be said to be the chief centres from which trained teachers are supplied for the whole country.

TECHNICAL INSTRUCTION.[1]

SIR,—The Technical Instruction Bill has passed the second reading, but its scope is so limited that unless public attention is called to its defects it will be powerless to influence for good the very classes of our population who need it most.

I have put down an amendment on the committee stage, the object of which is to provide evening schools, as in Germany, for the mass of our children who leave elementary schools at the age of twelve or thirteen, and often younger; and I trust to have your powerful support in advocating this most necessary change.

Speaking broadly, the advocates of technical education may be divided into two classes—first, those who expect to regain our former commercial and manufacturing supremacy by giving a higher scientific education to those who shall direct the future trade of the country; and, secondly, those who desire to see the great mass of the people of this country better equipped for the battle of life, in consequence of better education in youth.

There is no necessary antagonism between these two objects; each is excellent in its own way; but my sympathies and knowledge of the requirements of the poor, derived from many years' practical experience, leads me to attach more importance to the latter.

Now the bill before Parliament mainly contemplates the first object. It provides for the establishment of technical schools by such local bodies as voluntarily adopt the Act, the cost of which is to be thrown on the rates. If successfully carried out, it will lead to the foundation of technical schools in our large towns similar to those created by the City Guilds, which will be attended by a limited number of clever boys, such as now attend the science and art classes. Mr. Goschen anticipates that only some 12,000 children will be attracted to these schools, while some 5,000,000 attend the elementary schools, of whom some 600,000 leave annually, at the age of twelve or thirteen on an average.

There is no distinct provision in the bill for a scheme of

[1] Reprinted by permission from the *Liverpool Daily Post*.

evening schools to meet the wants of this great class, though I am told that it is possible under it to institute such schools; but, what is still more fatal to its usefulness, there is no compulsory power to secure the attendance of children at those schools.

Now I conceive that the time has fully come to graft a system of evening continuation schools on our national system of education; and I should like to see the attempt made under cover of this bill. To show the necessity of this is the object of my letter.

It is perfectly well known now to all educationists that primary education in Germany, Switzerland, and indeed in most of the advanced countries of Europe, is far ahead of ours. The children are infinitely better taught, and, above all, they are kept at school to a much later period of life. The usual age of leaving school in Germany is thirteen and a half to fourteen, with two years' compulsory attendance at evening continuation schools; so that the State enforces continuous education till about the age of sixteen. Need we wonder that in all walks of life the Germans are beating us? Their people are vastly better educated in all ranks of life, and in none is the comparison more against us than in the children of the working classes. Can we be surprised that German clerks, artisans, and merchants are supplanting ours wherever they come into equal competition?

What is the usual history of an English child of the working class? It leaves the elementary school as soon as the exemption standard is passed—that is to say, at an age which is always becoming earlier as the children are more quickly passed through the standards. I notice that last year, in the town of Wolverhampton, 97 per cent. of the children left school at the age of eleven! In many of our towns the average age of leaving is as low as twelve; in a few like London, where the sixth standard is the exemption one, the age varies from twelve to thirteen; in very few cases are children kept after thirteen.

Moreover, night schools have steadily declined since the Act of 1870; and last year, I believe, only 26,000 children attended such schools in all England. The movement in favour of 'recreative evening schools' is somewhat improving the attendance this year; but, speaking broadly, it may be asserted that the education of the English working-man's child comes to an end at about twelve; and so slight a hold has it taken of the intelligence of the child that in very many cases hardly a trace remains at sixteen, except the power of reading the wretched trash which is the chief pabulum of the children of the poor in our large towns.

Nothing, to my thinking, is more deplorable than the deterioration of the children that takes place after leaving our elementary schools; their chief educators are the street, the low nasty serial, and the music-hall. At that crucial time of life, when the character is being formed, the environment of multitudes of children is such as to ensure a poor stunted existence hereafter. When the child in Germany is having its intelligence expanded by elementary science and literature, and when the eye and hand are being trained in drawing, modelling, wood-carving &c., the English child in too many instances is becoming a proficient in the low vice of the streets and slums, or else is cruelly overworked in stuffy workrooms and factories. We allow parents, to our shame be it said, to work their children ten hours a day when they reach thirteen years of age, if they have then passed the exemption standard. Need anyone wonder that the pauper and semi-pauper population of England is vastly greater than in Germany, France, Switzerland, Holland, or the Scandinavian countries; or need we wonder that we have a larger layer of population utterly incompetent to look after themselves than any other civilised country in the world? I speak of what I know from long personal contact with these classes, and lest I should be thought to exaggerate, let me quote from that accurate observer of city life, Mr. Walter Besant:—

From thirteen to seventeen.—Boys and girls at thirteen have no inclination to read newspapers; after their day's work and confinement in the hot rooms they are tired; they want fresh air and exercise. To sum up: There are no existing inducements for the children to read and study; most of them are sluggish of intellect; outside the evening schools there are no facilities for them at all; they have no books; when evening comes they are tired; they do not understand their own interests; after a day's work they like an evening's rest. The street is always open to them. Here they find their companions of the workroom; here they feel the strong swift current of life; here something is always happening; here there are always new pleasures; here they can talk and play unrestrained left entirely to themselves, taking for pattern those who are a little older than themselves. As for their favourite amusements and their pleasures, they grow yearly coarser; as for their conversation, it grows continually viler, until Zola himself would be ashamed to reproduce the talk of these young people. — *The Contemporary Review*, March, 1886.

These are the facts, vividly stated, which make many philanthropists so anxious to graft a system of night schools on our elementary course, and to make attendance on them obligatory, at least to the age of fourteen or fifteen.

I confess that the moral advantage outweighs in my eyes even the intellectual. It is simply a question of life or death for multitudes to be kept under wholesome restraint at that age. The mind then quickly takes the colour of its surroundings. If those surroundings are bright attractive classes, where musical drill and gymnastics play a part, where the hand and eye are trained by the pencil, the compass, and the magic-lantern, where the teaching is a real recreation, as it is quite possible to make it, and where the silent influence of refined teachers creates a true ideal of life, I say we should change the character of the next generation, we should do more to kill intemperance, the social evil, and pauperism than by all the legislation in the world.

No country spends so much effort as ours in attempting to cure evils after they have become incurable, none spends so little in preventing their growth. If you wish to cope with the horrid life of the slums, you must begin with the children; if you want to stop the squalid pauper marriages which take place in London often at seventeen or eighteen years of age, if you want to transform our beery casual labourer into an intelligent self-respecting artisan, if you wish to fit our superabounding population to be good emigrants and colonists, you must begin with the children. Keep them at school till habits of industry and application are formed, till they get a higher ideal of life, and till they are filled with a divine discontent with the animal life in the slums.

Till you do this commissions on the dwellings of the poor will report in vain, the United Kingdom Alliance will preach to unwilling ears, social purity societies will yield scant results, and

England will remain cursed with a degraded proletariat till doomsday.

In conclusion, I would say there must be some further restriction on child labour to make it possible for the mass of our working children to attend evening schools. It is high time that the Factory Acts should be revised in the interests of children. Ten years of age is too young to begin working even half time, and thirteen is too young to begin working full time. No wonder our factory population is physically stunted. How is it possible that the soft tender frame of a child can stand such grinding toil ? We should aim at raising the half time age to twelve and the full time age to fifteen, and then it will be easy to get attendance at evening continuation schools till the latter age.

The effect of this would be to increase the demand for adult labour, and somewhat relieve the excessive over-supply we have at present; and it would prevent a low class of parents from trading on the earnings of their children.

I have only roughly sketched out a plan which needs much filling in ; but I fear I have already encroached unduly on your space. I will conclude with another quotation (from Dr. Paton, of Nottingham), which aptly describes our present wasteful system; and I invoke your kindly aid to bring this waste to a speedy end.

First we build up at immense expense a colossal system of primary education, and then see and allow the results of it to be very largely wasted and lost. Teachers speak dismally of the havoc of the fruit of their labour in the first two years after school is left. The garden which by daily culture has been brought into such an admirable and promising condition is given over to utter neglect; the money, the time, the labour bestowed upon it are lost. We cease to educate at the most important, most plastic, most receptive period of life.

Yours, &c.,

SAMUEL SMITH.

Westminster, S.W., August 13, 1887.

P.S.—The above letter was published in several newspapers, and was sent to every member of Parliament. It is now republished in order to be sent to every School Board in the kingdom, in the hope that it may aid the movement now started in favour of a general system of evening schools.

The Technical Instruction Bill has been withdrawn for this session, but it is promised to be re-introduced at the beginning of next session, and our aim must be to widen its scope, so as to bring it within the reach of the mass of our elementary scholars.

I should wish to add to what I have said above some further remarks on the subject of compulsion. I am aware that many persons feel great repugnance to a further extension of this principle, and I would call attention to the plan proposed by Dr. Paton, which avoids all new methods of procedure, but simply expands the old ones. It is well known that at present a large body of children leave school after passing the fourth standard, and another large body after passing the fifth, and a smaller number after passing the sixth. I am informed, indeed, that in rural districts it is not uncommon to exempt children from school attendance after passing the third standard, at the age of ten!

Dr. Paton's proposal is to raise the exemption standard to the seventh, but allow children to leave the day school after passing the sixth, and work out the last standard in the evening school. Possibly that would be too sudden a change, but I would suggest that the exemption standard in the day schools, when it is now the sixth—as in London—should be raised to the seventh, and in all other schools should be made the sixth; and I would allow children to be excused passing the last standard in a day school, on condition that they attended an evening school for two years in lieu of it.

There can be no doubt that the great bulk of the children would be withdrawn from the day school as soon as possible, and sent to the evening school in preference; and so, without direct compulsion to attend evening schools, we should secure that nearly all the children would pass through them, and so the school age would be extended to fourteen or fifteen on the average. Those evening schools would, of course, be carried on in existing buildings, and the hours would probably be from seven to nine for five evenings in the week, and for eight or nine months in the year. There should be a long summer holiday, and in rural districts it should cover the time when children are engaged in field work. There can be no objection to children early beginning to learn agricultural work, if it does not seriously interfere with their lessons. In Prussia a large number of the schools in rural districts are on the half-time principle.

But my plan is more suitable for urban than for rural districts, and if insuperable difficulty should be experienced in applying it to the latter, it might in the first instance be confined to towns. It should be borne in mind that two-thirds of the population of Great Britain now live in towns, and it is in them that the demoralisation of the children is so lamentable, from the absence of healthy occupation in the evening.

The difficulty of the Factory Act may be got over by providing that no permission to work full time be given till the two years' course of evening education be completed, or the maximum standard of the day school be passed, if that be preferred by the parents.

Most of the children, however, are engaged in small workshops or trades not coming under the Factory Acts, and it might be necessary to limit the hours of child-labour in those miscellaneous trades till the exemption standard was passed. Nothing but good would accrue from moderate restrictions on child-labour up to fourteen or fifteen years of age.

Some discretion must also be left with the school authorities for granting excuses in special cases of necessity, such as elder girls nursing younger children, &c. The scheme at its inception should not be worked with overmuch rigidity, and the attractiveness of schools should be relied upon to draw the children quite as much as the visits of the attendance officer.

I see no reason to doubt that in a few years we might have a million of children in attendance at these night schools; and when the beneficial effect was felt, people would marvel that we were so long in adopting this common-sense method.

In conclusion, I will only add that these night schools should be free of charge to the children. We cannot expect our labouring classes to assume a new burden when the project of gratuitous primary education is coming so fast to the front. I would further suggest that the cost should be put upon the

Consolidated Fund, and not on the rates, which are already over-burthened. By doing this I believe we should make the scheme far more popular.

SAMUEL SMITH.

APPENDIX.

The wretched character of the literature which is so widely circulated and read among young persons of the lower orders is vividly presented in an interesting and instructive article in the *Edinburgh Review* of January last, entitled 'The Literature of the Streets,' which may be advantageously studied by all who are interested in the baneful influence exercised by such writings on young and impressionable minds. The writer concludes :—' The indisputable fact remains, that the worst of modern novels are too often among the most popular. Pure, healthy fiction is indeed to be had, and in fair abundance, but public taste seems to devour unhealthy trash, of every kind, with a higher relish than it can find for the good gifts of the most gifted artists. There is no possible lack of good work, and they who choose trash do so of their own free will and choice. But the case of those for whom this article pleads is wholly different. To them no choice whatever is allowed. They must be content with the garbage of the 'penny dreadfuls,' or nothing. Yet the fancy and the imagination, the innate thirst for novelty and excitement, for a touch of mystery or of tender passion, are as potent and as true in the heart of the street Arab or the shop girl as in the fiercest devourer of romance on Mudie's list. But this desire can be gratified in one way alone. The feast spread for them is ready and abundant, but every dish is a false one, every condiment vile. Every morsel of food is doctored, every draught of wine is drugged ; no true hunger is satisfied, no true thirst quenched ; and the hapless guests depart with a depraved appetite, and a palate more than ever dead to every pure taste, and every perception of what is good and true. Thus entertained and equipped, the wide army of the children of the poor are sent on their way, to take part in the great battle of life, with false views, false impressions, and foul aims. The pictures of men and women to whom they have been introduced are unreal and untrue. The whole drama of life, as they see it, is a lie from beginning to end, and in it they can play none but a vicious and unhappy part.'

A NATIONAL NECESSITY.

By Edward J. Watherston.

We have experienced for many years past, and, I fear, we may yet for several years to come experience, a very great depression in trade and manufactures, and side by side with this great depression (which has caused so much loss and suffering to individuals, and profound anxiety to our statesmen), it is found that there is an increasing competition on the part of foreign countries for the trade which, some years back, Englishmen were inclined to regard as absolutely and peculiarly their own.

Our ribbon and silk industries, our weaving and spinning manufactures, our brass and cutlery, our iron and steel trades, and many others, are meeting with formidable rivals in France, Holland, Belgium, Switzerland, and Germany, and, if we wish to maintain, in wealth and power, the mighty Empire which the valour, intelligence, and enterprise of our forefathers have built up, it is time that we inquired diligently into the causes militating against us.

For good or for ill, we have staked our existence, as a great nation, upon our manufacturing and commercial supremacy. Singularly deficient in raw materials, we cannot even raise food enough to maintain ourselves, and, if our foreign competitors beat us in the field we have deliberately self-chosen, the beginning of our decadence will have set in. The handwriting on the wall has been written so plainly that it requires no Daniel to interpret it.

If, then, it be agreed that, whatever other qualities may be needed for the permanence of our national greatness and prosperity, it is of the first moment that we should call to our aid all that science can dictate or art suggest in our various arts and industries, I shall have made out a *primâ-facie* case for the importance of the subject on which I have the honour to address you this evening—viz., the Technical Education of the children of our working classes. By the term 'Technical Education,' I mean special instruction in some scientific, artistic, or mechanical process or handicraft, as distinguished from purely literary instruction. It has been elsewhere described as 'Special Training for an Industrial pursuit, as distinguished from a general preparation for any calling hereafter to be chosen.'

In dealing with this subject, I propose to show what is the nature of the instruction at present encouraged by the State in our public elementary schools, and how mistaken, in my humble opinion, much of it is, considered as a preparation for the child's future career. I shall also venture to show how it might be improved, in the direction of technical education, to the benefit of the children and the nation.

I may preface my remarks by reminding you that this matter had assumed so much importance that, in Mr. Gladstone's second Administration (August 1881), a Royal Commission, with Sir Bernhard Samuelson, M.P., at its head, was formed 'to inquire into the instruction of the industrial classes of certain foreign countries in technical subjects, for the purpose of comparison with that of the corresponding classes in this country,' and it is to the voluminous and valuable reports of that Commission that I am mainly indebted for the facts I shall lay before you. The conclusions and recommendations in this paper are my own; though I may add that they do not differ very widely from those of the Commission, which are much too lengthy for quotation here.

Now, you are all aware that, in consequence of the Education Act of 1870, which will never be dissociated from the name of the remarkable man but lately departed from us, William Edward Forster, there is school accommodation in England and Wales for every child of school age. Last year—I quote from the report of the Education Department—there was accommodation in State-aided, or public elementary schools, as they are technically called, for five millions of children; and, by the action of the law of compulsory attendance, there were four and a half million names on the registers. The annual income of these schools, from all sources, was six and three-quarter millions sterling, of which sum the State contributed from the Imperial Exchequer two million seven hundred thousand pounds, the remainder being made up of school fees, voluntary contributions, endowments, and rates. I do not desire to underrate the significance of these figures. They are an eloquent proof that the people are desirous for the spread of light and learning. Well, having got the children into school, and spending this immense sum annually upon them, what use do we make of this great opportunity? Are we on the right lines? Are we getting the best thing possible for our labour and outlay? It is here that I regret not to be able to speak with satisfaction. My complaint is that the education of the children in our elementary schools is almost solely literary, and that, instead of raising a body of skilled artisans and mechanics, we are manufacturing only clerks, male and female. For, of what do the subjects of instruction consist? The following:—

Compulsory—Reading, Writing, Arithmetic, and Needlework.

Optional—Singing, English, Drawing, Geography, Elementary Science and History.

These subjects are called class subjects. The more advanced scholars are allowed to be presented for individual examination in the following subjects, viz. :—

Latin, French, Animal Physiology, Botany, Physics, Chemistry, Algebra, Euclid and Mensuration, Mechanics, and the Principles of Agriculture.

'Surely,' you will exclaim, 'you do not desire to add other subjects to this vast programme?' No, indeed, I do not. I wish rather to reduce them; not, be it understood, from any jealous or grudging motive. While I wish to see all clever boys and girls have every chance of fostering and developing their talents, I do think that we should look broadly and practically at the needs of the population as a whole. For one clever and lucky youth who rises from the national school to the university, a thousand, aye more, will, and must, remain at the bench, the anvil, the loom, the engine, the plough.

This being so, I contend that, after the child has learnt to read, write, and cypher well, he should at once be inducted into at least the rudiments of some branch of technical industry that would be of use to him immediately upon his leaving school, thus enabling him to master, far more accurately than now, the handicraft he adopts. For it must be remembered that the great mass of the children leave school before they reach the age of thirteen. Out of the four million five hundred thousand children on the school registers last year, not one-tenth had reached twelve years. This being so, I desire to ask how much Latin, French, or physiology could be taught to, or be retained by, a child of twelve, in a school for children of the working classes? Very little, indeed, beyond the merest elements of the subject; yet for every scholar who passes in such a specific subject the State pays 4s. annually. I venture to think that this money might be far better laid out. I submit that the moment a child has reached a fair standard of proficiency in the three R's (by which I mean good legible writing, distinct reading, of a pleasurable character to himself and his auditors, and arithmetic, which should include proportional and fractional calculations) such child should become a half-time scholar, spending one half of his time in the literary department, where instruction in drawing and mathematics should be the main features, and the other half in a workshop school, to which it might be affiliated. Of course, in country districts, a dozen of the elementary schools could contribute towards the maintenance of one central workshop school.

In the workshop school, which a boy might reasonably be expected to enter at the age of ten, I should give instruction of two kinds: first, theoretical teaching, including geometrical drawing, machine drawing and construction, mechanics, and chemistry; secondly, practical workshop teaching, which should aim at the most careful and accurate workmanship. This latter would include the production of simple geometrical forms in metal or wood, such as the cube or prism. Wood joints, dovetailing, and other simple work might be added.

If the child's school education terminated at this curriculum, we should have achieved very valuable results; but I should propose to offer exhibitions from these schools to higher grade technical schools, for the most promising of the workshop scholars. Into these higher grade schools, which on the Continent are called 'Apprenticeship Schools,' might be gathered the more skilful boys from the lower school.

What should be the curriculum in these apprenticeship schools? Well, these would vary according to the social and economical conditions of the district. In an agricultural district, the pupils should be taught the principles of agriculture and horticulture. The nature and properties of soils and crops and their rotation would, of course, come in. In a manufacturing district the technical teaching should aim at the inculcation of the scientific principles which underlie the particular processes of production. In a district, for example, such as Kidderminster, the scholars would, besides being taught the processes of weaving, have special instruction in design and the artistic grouping of colours. In this way our great centres of agriculture, of manufacture, and commerce could easily establish central technical schools, dealing especially with the productions of their own districts. As another example, Clerkenwell would have an eye to the watch, jewellery, silver plate, and furniture trades.

Now, this programme sounds very well, but two questions arise: First, is it practicable? Secondly, by what means can it be carried out? Well, as to practicability, not merely is every nation in Europe alive to its importance, but in some, notably France, Belgium, Germany, Italy, Switzerland, and even Holland, some splendid and successful schools of this sort have already been established. Take France—instruction in manual work has of late been introduced into a considerable number of primary schools in Paris, and school museums are extending rapidly throughout the country. This instruction consists in teaching the rudiments of a trade or art concurrently with the ordinary school instruction, or in accustoming the children to the use of tools commonly employed in working wood and iron. But the greatest success in this direction has been achieved in the technical schools of the Society of Christian Brothers; and their example is being followed by the great municipalities. This Society of Christian Brothers (whose educational section at the Health Exhibition was, perhaps, the finest in the building), besides having superior elementary schools for a quarter of a million children, has technical schools for some three thousand scholars. They have produced greater educational results than any other institution in Europe. At Beauvais, they have an agricultural school; at Lyons, a silk school; at Paris, a technical school for delicate handicrafts; at

Havre, a great commercial school, in which everything is taught that goes to make a first-rate man of business, such as commercial arithmetic, foreign exchanges, bookkeeping, statistics, &c. In the Lyons silk school the scholars are instructed literally 'ab ovo'; the rearing and nurture of the silkworm, its food, its ailments, are carefully taught, as well as everything relating to the preparation, dyeing, and weaving of silk. Botany and chemistry are most carefully taught. But it is to the Ecole St. Nicholas, in the Rue de Vaurigard, that I desire to draw particular attention. It contains 720 scholars, besides 250 apprentice scholars. The pupils of the ordinary schools are not received until they can read, write, and cypher. Admitted with these acquirements, they are immediately put to a course of algebra and geometry, surveying, linear and ornamental drawing, modelling, and, among other things, the elements of chemistry.

They pass on from this preparatory school to the apprenticeship school. Here a select body of workmen, chosen for their special skill in their craft, joined with capacity to teach it, take the boys under their care, the Brothers themselves exercising supreme control. The Royal Commissioners say that the following trades are taught:—

> Bookbinding, optical and mathematical instrument making, type-setting, printing, working and chasing in bronze, brass instrument making, gilding, joiners' work, saddle making, wood carving, wood engraving, map engraving, and engine fitting.

They add that the apprentices are well taught, and find employment readily after they leave the workshops.

As I observed just now, the great success of this and the other technical schools of the Christian Brothers has stimulated the public spirit of the municipalities, and Paris can boast of a highly successful school for workers in wood and iron in the Boulevard de la Villette. The boys are admitted after they have left the ordinary primary school, on presenting the certificate of primary studies, or on passing an equivalent examination. The instruction is gratuitous, and is divided into general and technical; the general instruction, besides comprising those subjects which are obligatory in primary schools, includes some which are optional in those schools, such as the elements of mathematics, physics, mechanics, and chemistry, in their relation to industry. The trade instruction in the workshops is subdivided into two courses. In the first, the pupils are taught the nature and conversion of materials. In the second, they pass on to actual construction. The first or preparatory course is the same for all pupils, all in rotation passing through the workshops for both wood and iron. One of the reporters on the school says that 'This is done in order to give suppleness and certainty to the hand, and to enable the scholars, when they have become workmen, to take up, in case of need, at any rate for a time, a trade different from their ordinary one, and thus to gain a living in bad times.'

The choice of a trade takes place at the commencement of the second course, which coincides with that of the second year, and it is only then that they begin to execute actual constructive work. No apprentice is allowed to commence any work, whether complete in itself or a part of a machine, without having made a sketch or a drawing of it to scale, so that the pupil must necessarily acquaint himself with its proportions and connections, and fully understand the nature of what he is doing. The entire course occupies three years. The boys enter the school at 7 A.M., and leave at 7 P.M. During the first two years, six hours daily are spent in the workshop and four in the school; in the third year, eight hours in the workshop and two in the school, leaving, in each case, two hours for meals and recreation, the latter including three hours of gymnastic exercises per week.

And let us not forget the numerous 'Ecoles Professionnelles pour Jeunes Filles' to be found upon the Continent. In nearly every country Her Majesty's Commissioners found schools established for the industrial training of girls. In France, Germany, Austria, Holland, and Italy girls share equally with boys the advantages of manual and technical instruction. One at Brussels deserves mention—the Professional School for Girls. The basis of instruction in this school is drawing, which underlies all the special trade work which the pupils are taught. The teaching comprises a general course, which is obligatory on all pupils, and subsequently special courses in preparation for various trades. The general course is intended to carry forward the education received at the primary schools; the trade courses comprise lessons in bookkeeping, the application of arithmetic to commercial occupations, English or German language and correspondence, botany, applied art, dressmaking, embroidery, artificial flower-making, china-painting, and lace-making and designing. It is most important to note the extent to which drawing is made the basis of instruction in such subjects as dressmaking. The success of the school in the department of artificial flower-making mainly depends upon the admirable instruction in botany and drawing. There are six schools on this model in Belgium. It may be remarked, *en passant*, that we import into this country artificial flowers to the amount of half a million sterling per annum. Here I am reminded of the philosophic remark of Mademoiselle Marchef-Gérard, in reply to a pointed question put to her by the Minister of Commerce, as to the necessity of technical education for women. She said, 'C'est de rendre les femmes à la fois plus intelligentes et plus spéciales.' There can be no doubt of the truth of this dictum. At all events, its truth has been recognised abroad.

But the Communal School, in the Rue Tournefort, is one I should like to see largely copied here in England. This primary school is one in which rudimentary trade teaching is combined with ordinary elementary instruction. It was established on its present footing in 1873. Until the beginning of last year trade instruction was commenced at the age of ten years. During the first two years every child was taught drawing, modelling, carving, joiners' work, smith and fitters' work.

In the third year the work was specialised, some of the children being taught modelling and carving, others joiners' work and cabinetmaking, &c. Since the beginning of last year the same plan has been continued, but, in addition, the children in the lowest classes, beginning even at six years of age, have three lessons, of one hour each per week, in handicrafts. Subjoined is the time-table, showing the distribution of the lessons on one day :—

COMMUNAL WORKSHOP SCHOOL, PARIS: RUE TOURNEFORT.

TIME-TABLE—WEDNESDAY.

MORNING

Moral and Civil Instruction.		Modelling and Carving.	French.	
	Rapid Sums.	Joiners' Work, Lathe and Forge.	French.	Memory Exercise.
Joiners' Work, Lathe, Forge, Technology.			French.	Reading.
Technology. Physical Science.			French.	Reading.
Technology. Morals.			French.	Reading.
Technology. Morals.			French.	Reading.

Discourse on Geography or Cosmography.

Reading with emphasis and explanation.

AFTERNOON

Tools and Sketches.	Modelling and Carving.	Geography.	Gymnastics.
Arithmetic.	Writing.	Modelling.	Morals.
Arithmetic.	Drawing.	Geography.	Morals.
Arithmetic.	Writing.	Joiners' Work and Forge.	Exercises of Memory.
Arithmetic. / Writing.	Writing.	History and Geography.	Exercises of Memory.

Permit me here to quote the remarks of the Royal Commissioners on the apprenticeship schools in France. Their remarks are in every way highly suggestive. They say:—

'The authorities of the City of Paris have deemed the experiment of apprenticeship teaching in the school of La Villette sufficiently successful to induce them to decide upon the erection of a number of other similar schools in various parts of the metropolis.[1] The whole subject was referred to a commission, and its president, M. Tolain, in a report to the Préfet of the Seine, says, "that in consequence of the virtual abolition of apprenticeship in most trades, and owing to the specialisation and subdivision of manufactures resulting from the introduction of machinery, the number of skilful and intelligent workmen in all branches of industry and art manufacture has decreased, and that the standard of technical knowledge has been lowered."

'This, he considers, has been especially prejudicial to French manufactures, the distinguishing merit of which he believes to have consisted in originality of design. The vulgarisation of manufactures has, in his opinion, given great facilities for piracy, especially on the part of foreigners. He believes that a remedy for these evils will be found in the establishment of apprenticeship schools, the object of which should be mainly, not the creation of foremen, but the theoretical and practical education of workmen proper. In determining what should be the trades taught in schools founded and carried on at the cost of the municipality, he calls attention to the fact that apprenticeship still exists in those branches of industry which are concerned with the making up of materials into clothing, and he proposes, therefore, that these arts should not be taught in the municipal schools. He would confine them to what he calls "parent industries"; that is to say, those in which the processes to be taught are applicable to a large number of allied trades. He recommends, accordingly, that for the present three apprenticeship schools should be established, one in the Faubourg St. Antoine for the furniture trades, to form workers in wood, who would become chiefly cabinetmakers and upholsterers, but also

---

[1] We are informed that they have within the last few days voted 80,000*l*. for the erection of these schools.

carpenters, joiners, and wood-carvers; and workers in iron intending to become general smiths and workers in metal for the same trades and for decorative purposes. The second school should be for the south of Paris, on the model of that of La Villette, intended, however, to train not only mechanics, but also iron-founders, carpenters, stonecutters and masons, iron and tin-plate workers, slaters and plumbers, so as to be a complete school of apprenticeship for the building trades. A third school in the heart of Paris should comprise the following trades, viz., instruments of precision, telegraphic apparatus, clock-making, surgical instrument-making, and small machinery in general. In addition to these three schools for boys he recommends that a school should be established for girls, which should be not only an apprenticeship school, but also one of domestic economy; the latter division would include general house-work, laundry-work, sewing, and, in addition, the obligatory parts of primary instruction, together with linear drawing, gymnastics, singing, and some special notions of technology having reference to the duties of housekeeping, and to the materials to be used in the workshops. The trades to be taught would be millinery, embroidering, lace-making, dressmaking, artificial flower and feather making, and with these latter there would be compulsory courses of drawing from flowers and nature, and of modelling.[1]

'The estimate for the girls' school, intended to receive 300 outdoor pupils, is for buildings alone, exclusive of the ground, 21,600*l*., and for fittings, 1,600*l*.

'The instruction in all of these schools will be gratuitous, and the pupils, in order to be admitted, will have to present the *certificat d'études* of the primary school.

'A few provincial municipalities have established apprenticeship schools of the same type as that of the Boulevard de la Villette, that is to say, schools to form workmen and not foremen. There is one at Havre, which has undergone various

[1] A girls' school, corresponding in some particulars to the above, and maintained by the Municipality of Rouen, the *école professionnelle des jeunes filles*, was visited by the Commissioners. There are in Paris establishments conducted by nuns, containing a large number of children, who work at artificial flower-making, millinery, and other trades, but these cannot be considered as apprenticeship schools.

transformations, and is now one of the most complete of its kind in regard to building and fittings. The course, like that of the Villette school, occupies three years. The time spent in the workshops is six hours daily throughout the whole course. The book work begins at a much more elementary stage than in the Paris school, and appears not to be carried so far; no *certificat d'études* is required on entrance. Even absolutely illiterate children have been admitted, if they have shown some manual dexterity. The admission or rejection of applicants is, in fact, left to the discretion of the head-master. With the object of inducing the apprentices to remain at school during the third year, the pecuniary rewards are much higher than in the Paris school. A boy here may receive as much as 6*l.* in his third year. Notwithstanding this, the number of boys who completed their third year diminished steadily from 1876-77 to 1878-79; it was 26 in the former, and only 17 in the latter year; 16 of these entered private workshops, and one went to sea as an engineer. The cost of maintaining the school, exclusive of materials used in the workshops, was, in 1880, 1,120*l.* for 160 boys, a small portion of which was recovered by payments for work done by the boys.[1]

'We were told that several of the Paris *syndicats* (guilds) of employers had established apprenticeship schools, but we found on inquiry that nearly all of these were simply drawing schools for evening instruction. The jewellers have founded prizes of considerable value for original goldsmith's work, to be competed for by their apprentices. The only apprenticeship school proper, founded by a guild, that we met with, was that of the clockmakers in the Faubourg du Temple. The trade of clockmaking is carried on in Paris in the house of the workpeople, to whom the parts are given out in the rough, and the masters have therefore no control over the instruction or training of the apprentices. Under these circumstances they established the school in February 1881. It contains twenty-five pupils, the course lasting four years. The present premises are only

[1] Since this report was written, we learn that the municipal authorities of Boulogne-sur-Mer are establishing an apprenticeship school on the model of that of La Villette, which it is expected will be opened before the end of the present year.

provisional, and are about to be extended. The expenses are mainly borne by the *Chambre Syndicale de l'Horlogerie*, which contributes 560*l*. The Government has granted the school a subvention of 80*l*. and the City of Paris 40*l*. The pupils pay 12*l*. per annum, and provide the small tools needed in their work. The larger tools (machinery) are furnished by the school authorities. The pupils receive complete instruction in watch and clock-making; and the teaching is both theoretical and practical. The practical course for the first class [1] is, the use of tools and roughing-out work. For the second class, finishing; for the third class, escapements, and for the fourth, regulating and repairs. The course of theoretical instruction for the first three years includes French, the elements of mathematics, geometry, and machine construction applied to watch and clock making, the theory of the construction of watches, bookkeeping, and linear drawing. In the fourth year they are taught algebra, trigonometry, the elements of physics and chemistry, cosmography, and industrial drawing. Examinations take place at the end of each school year. Students are admitted at fourteen years of age, but not earlier, except in special cases. The working hours, during the winter months (from October to April), are from 8 A.M. to 7 P.M., with an interval of one and a half hours, from 12 to 1.30, for meals and relaxation. During the remainder of the year the hours are from 7 A.M. to 7 P.M., with the same interval as before. Arrangements have been made for boarding the pupils, at a fixed inclusive charge of 32*l*. per annum. Even when machinery shall to a great extent have superseded manual labour in the wholesale manufacture of watches and clocks, a number of skilled operatives will always be required in this trade, so that the school will not cease to be useful.

'The Government has founded, and sustains, certain apprenticeship schools for manufactures; one of them is the watchmaking school at Cluses, under the Ministry of Agriculture and Commerce. It is taking the place of a municipal school for the same trade at Besançon, which has been frequently reported on, but which we were told by a competent authority is now declining. Another is the school of porcelain decoration at the manufactory of Sèvres, founded within the last two years

[1] Each class represents a year's work.

by the director, M. Lauth, of which, as well as of the recently remodelled school of a similar character at Limoges, we shall speak when we come to deal with art schools. There is also an apprenticeship school attached to the *manufacture des Gobelins.*'

These cases suffice to show what is being done in all the great industrial centres of France, where the greatest activity prevails in the foundation and perfection of these schools.

Time does not permit me to tell you, in detail, what is going on in this direction in Belgium, Italy, Holland, and Germany, but anyone who visited the magnificent educational display of the Belgian Government in the Health Exhibition, two years ago, must be convinced that our Flemish rivals are keenly alive to the importance of the subject. During the last few years it has been my good fortune to visit Holland on many occasions, and use was made of the opportunity to inspect the *Ambachts* (artisans) schools, the best of which are at Amsterdam, Rotterdam, The Hague, and Arnheim. The first school of this type, in Holland, was founded at Amsterdam, by the Working Men's Association, in 1860. It has now been subsidised by the town, and has excellent workshops, with every modern appliance for teaching carpentry, joiners' work, smiths' work, painting, plumbing, &c. Rotterdam soon followed, and in 1873-4 The Hague and Arnheim opened similarly subsidised workshop schools. Again, I found that, at Amsterdam and The Hague, girls share equally with boys in the advantages of industrial training.

The school at Rotterdam was established in 1869 by the Rotterdam branch of the Netherlands Architectural Society, in order to train skilled artisans, and thus to remedy the acknowledged defects in the system of apprenticeship. It receives an annual grant from the Town Council, on condition that the programme includes all the branches of theoretical instruction recognised in the three years' course of public middle-class schools. The funds necessary for the foundation of the school were subscribed voluntarily; a building was purchased, and the institution was inaugurated on April 1, 1869. The main building contains the various class rooms; the director's residence and the workshops have been constructed round a small open court in the rear. As the object is to train workmen well versed in the practice of the various trades, the boys are as far as possible engaged on useful work, capable of being sold or employed in the school.

As soon as the boys have learnt the use of the various tools, they begin to make small articles which have a marketable value, and thus realise that they are working with a view to the commercial results of their labour. It has been found, from experience, that his being engaged on a bonâ-fide piece of workmanship serves as a powerful stimulus to the pupil. The workshops are as far as possible kept up to the level of modern requirements, and have frequently been extended to accommodate the increasing number of students. They comprise shops for carpenters, blacksmiths, metal-workers, fitters and turners, cabinetmakers, masons, and stone-carvers.

The articles made in the school are sold to dealers, and orders are also executed for the municipal authorities. Many doors, window-frames, and fittings are made for builders. The metal-workers make locks, hinges, shovels, hooks, smiths' tongs; also stoves and coalscuttles. The lads in the shops work under the direction of practical foremen. The school hours in summer are from 8 A.M. to 7 P.M., or till 6 on Saturdays, and in winter (September 1 to March 31) from 8 A.M. to 5.30 P.M. The mornings are spent in the class-rooms, and the afternoons in the shops. The general instruction is in continuation of the ordinary teaching of the elementary schools; the teachers bear in mind that the boys are to become artisans, and the examples are therefore taken as much as possible from their future profession. Drawing is carefully taught, and is made thoroughly practical. The boys begin with copying rectilinear and curved figures and simple ornament from casts. In the architectural course, as soon as they have acquired sufficient skill, they draw details of construction, and make measured drawings from actual work. In the advanced class they learn mechanical projection and simple perspective, as applied to architectural details and parts of houses. The staff comprises Mr. D. de Vries and twenty masters and assistants. There are over 280 boys, who pay 8s. 4d. per annum for instruction, and the fees are readily remitted to poor parents. The full course lasts three years. Boys from twelve to fifteen years of age, who have completed their education at the primary school, are eligible for admission, and when they have completed their full course of three years they are under the patronage of the school committee, who find them situations for five years longer. It has been found that these lads, on leaving the school, readily earn good wages, and are paid more than apprentices who have been trained in the usual way.

I wish I could pass on to other countries, but time fails me. It is but right to add that we in England have also made a commencement, and that we have already a great central organisation in the Science and Art Department, which, if Parliament would enable them to do so, could rapidly develop a system of technical schools. Meantime, our great School Boards are waking up. The Sheffield Board have maintained a workshop school for two or three years with excellent results. The Manchester Board have a Central Science school under one of the ablest teachers in England, Mr. Scotson, though, I believe, the school at present lacks the essential adjunct of a workshop. The Brighton Board are just following in their wake. There is also a first-rate school at Glasgow, called the Allan Glen's Institute. The object of this institution is to prepare boys to learn trades, the mastery of which requires a considerable amount of scientific knowledge. In London, too, we can boast of the Finsbury Technical School, supported by the City and Guilds of London, which, under my distinguished friend, Professor Silvanus Thompson, D.Sc., promises to many hundreds of students instruction of the best kind in mechanical engineering, electrical engineering, and industries involving the application of chemistry and art applied to industry.

But, my desire is to see what is being done only here and there extended generally throughout the country. No district, or group of smaller districts, with a school population of five hundred, ought to be out of reach of a workshop school. At present, the purely literary instruction in our elementary schools costs, on an average, $2l.$ per scholar, of which the State contributes $17s.$ $6d.$ Now what ought, in my humble judgment, to be done is this. Divide the $2l.$ between the two classes of schools, and let the literary and the workshop school each have a pound per head. The Science and Art Department at

South Kensington should distribute the workshop grant upon results produced, and the admirably equipped institution of the City and Guilds of London might have the training of the teachers. Indeed, it is but very little known what is now being done by the City and Guilds of London Institute for the promotion of technical education. Already a quarter of a million has been spent by the Corporation and thirty-six out of the seventy-nine Livery Companies, the Institution at present having an assured income of at least 33,000*l*. per annum. This is supplementary to what has been done, individually, by the Clothworkers', Turners', Carpenters', and probably other Companies. The two former Companies, indeed, led the way, and to the excellent school of the Clothworkers' Company at Bradford that town owes the revival of trade commented upon by its Mayor, a few months ago. The Textile Industries side of the Yorkshire College, Leeds, erected at a cost of 30,000*l*., supplemented by an annual grant of 1,500*l*. for maintenance, and a technical college at Huddersfield, are also practical examples of the liberality and far-sightedness of this Company.

This reminds me of Mr. Owen Roberts, M.A., Clerk of the Clothworkers' Company, to whom the cause of technical education owes so much. Speaking lately, at the Onslow College of Science and Art, he said :—' For my own part, I am as much convinced as ever of the paramount importance of the Central Institution of the City Guilds at South Kensington for advanced instruction in science and art, specially adapted for the teachers of technical schools and colleges in the centres of localised manufactures, and also for those inheriting or otherwise succeeding to the position of masters and managers of industrial undertakings. It could not have been expected that a scientific institution, such as that, framed on entirely new lines, and intended for a class of advanced students in science and technology, should emerge from the earth like Minerva armed *cap-à-pie* with a full quota of the precise character of students for whom it was designed. Nevertheless there are between sixty and seventy matriculated students there already, who will in two or three years doubtless increase to the full number of 300, for whom the building was planned. But, in addition thereto, some hundreds of students, including teachers in elementary schools and teachers of technological classes, have availed themselves of the special courses of instruction provided for them, and more of these special courses will be developed and organised to meet the wants and opportunities of the times, which our organising director and secretary is so well qualified to gauge. The seed sown must be allowed to grow to the harvest, and we must not, as children in their little gardens of mustard and cress, keep digging up the newly sown ground to find out whether the seed is germinating, or else our harvest will be delayed, if not spoiled altogether.'

The Royal Commissioners themselves refer to the great work of the Institute :—' Nowhere in Europe,' they say, ' does there exist a system of evening instruction similar to that which is carried on jointly by the Science and Art Department and the City and Guilds of London Institute,' . . . and further it is remarked that ' no organisation like it exists in any Continental country whatever, and the absence of such organisation has been lamented by many competent persons with whom we came in contact.'

But recognising to its fullest extent the importance of the work of the Institute, I cannot but endorse Lord Selborne's lamentation (Report to Governors, March 31, 1886, p. 31) :— 'The Council again refer to the importance of encouraging technical education in elementary schools, by the establishment of workshops for instruction in the use of tools, and they hope that the funds to be placed at their disposal may enable them to extend their operations by assisting in the movement.' I am fully convinced that this object should be kept well in view.

But to return to the Science and Art Department. The work already achieved by the Science and Art Department has been of the most valuable character; thousands of our best art workmen, our designers in wood, metal, or textile fabrics, owe their instruction and their success to the Department, notably to the able and painstaking staff at South Kensington. To my mind one of the most interesting portions of the Health Exhibition was the gallery set apart for objects which had been designed or wrought by students of art and science schools.

The fact, then, that this Department has achieved so much

argues that it could do much more if so permitted by Parliament, and a system of workshop schools would very quickly spread throughout the country under their energetic management. The immense building of the City and Guild of London Institute, with its lecture rooms, laboratories, and professors, amply suffices as a great central training school for technical teachers. The teachers should be drawn from amongst the skilled artisans of the country. I am certain that the public-spirited and generous municipalities of this country will not lag behind those of France and Belgium, and if encouraged to do so would quickly raise funds to enable the skilled mechanics of their respective districts to undergo a course of special instruction at this great central institution, in order that, on their return, they should become the teachers of the workshop schools. I do not suggest that the already heavily burdened taxpayers shall contribute a farthing more; the vote for public education, properly administered, and directed to right objects, is quite sufficient, and it might and would be supplemented by public-spirited individuals like Josiah Mason and others. And I am quite certain that this casting of our bread upon the waters would return to us after not many days. We should raise up a body of scientific handicraftsmen who would quickly regain our waning prestige in all the great manufactures in metal and wood and textile fabrics; thus should we be able to defy the keenest competition of our foreign rivals. Our artisans and designers would not be drudging along in the old grooves, using the same methods and achieving no better results than their fathers before them; but they would be alive to the necessity for invention, for skilful adaptation of means to ends, for labour-saving processes and appliances, for more artistic production. With a population such as this, we shall be carried through the bad time which a great commercial nation must occasionally experience, and be ready and able to take instant advantage of any rebound, when enterprise is active and opportunity holds out her hand.

TECHNICAL EDUCATION IN ELEMENTARY SCHOOLS: THE FORM IT SHOULD TAKE.

By Edward J. Watherston.

On July 19 of this year, Sir William Hart-Dyke, Vice-President of the Committee of Council on Education, introduced in the House of Commons a 'Bill to facilitate the provision of Technical Instruction,' and all those persons who, for several years past, have been working and waiting for some national provision of this kind congratulated each other on the step forward which the Bill seemed to promise. It is true that many of us thought it not quite adequate to the necessities of the country; nevertheless it was a genuine advance, and hardly a dissentient or opposing voice was raised against it in the press or on the platform. Yet the Bill was too much for our overworked Legislature, and, amongst the general slaughter, this, the most spotless of the innocents, received its *coup de grâce*. But there is some balm in Gilead. The Bill will rise again next session in a larger and better form, and its discussion during the recess will tend towards that consummation.

While most of us desire that the children in our elementary schools shall have some really scientific instruction such as shall tend to make them more skilful artisans, mechanics, or engineers, and fit them to cope with the ever-increasing competition of their foreign rivals, there is no shirking the fact that the problem is of considerable difficulty. This paper is an humble attempt to suggest the lines on which a system of national elementary technical instruction might be laid down.

My propositions are:—

(1.) That, side by side with the ordinary elementary instruction given at present, all children should be instructed in drawing, and, after seven years of age, in elementary science.

(2.) That children between ten and thirteen years of age should receive definite practical instruction in handicraft work, if necessary, by the exclusion of some of the more purely literary instruction at present given in our schools.

(3.) That children after thirteen years of age should, by

means of scholarships or the payment of fees, have the opportunity of perfecting their earlier instruction in higher elementary schools, or, as they are called abroad, 'Apprenticeship Schools.' Allow me to quote the words of Sir Philip Magnus on this point. They put the case for technical education with singular clearness and force. He says:—

I have suggested that drawing should be taught generally in our public elementary schools; that more attention should be devoted to the teaching of science than at present is given to it; that handicraft instruction should be introduced after a certain standard; further, that higher elementary schools should be established, into which the children who had passed the fifth standard may have an opportunity of being drafted; and that, where scholarships are available, they should be placed at the service of School Boards and the managers of public elementary schools, in order to encourage a better class of pupils—the more gifted pupils, I would say—to avail themselves of the opportunities of further instruction in the higher elementary schools. Lastly, I think that further encouragement should be given to instruction in evening schools, in order that the children may not forget the knowledge and the skill which they have acquired in the elementary schools, and which they will need to apply when they come to take advantage of the excellent science, art, and technical classes which are now organised in different parts of the country.

It is true that considerable difference of opinion exists as to the age at which children should receive technical instruction. In the Bill of Sir William Hart-Dyke, clause 3 ran thus:—
'(3.) Provided that no payment shall be made under this Act out of the local rate in respect of a scholar unless or until he has obtained a certificate from the Education Department that he has passed the examination in reading, writing, and arithmetic prescribed by the standard set forth in the schedule to this Act (being the sixth standard fixed by the minutes of the Education Department in force at the passing of this Act), or an examination equivalent thereto.' But this standard is, I firmly believe, too high. In the first instance it seems to argue that only those children who have attained a high standard in the purely literary subjects are likely to benefit by the handicraft teaching, and it also appears to ignore the fact that only a small percentage of our scholars reach the sixth standard at all.

Let me give you the figures on this subject. Of scholars presented last year in the various standards there were in the

First standard	. . . . .	482,673
Second „	. . . . .	565,485
Third „	. . . . .	549,363
Fourth „	. . . . .	454,752
Total in first four standards	. . .	2,052,273
Fifth standard	. . . . .	265,138
Sixth „	. . . . .	103,124
Seventh „	. . . . .	25,027
Total in the three higher standards	.	393,289

So that, if the Government proposal had been accepted, only 128,151 children, scattered throughout 19,173 schools, would have been eligible for technical instruction, and as from this number would have to be deducted about fifty thousand girls, only about eighty thousand boys (in round numbers) would be eligible for the proposed technical instruction. Surely, if any standard of literary attainments is to be prescribed—a prescription which I think quite unnecessary—the fourth would be more appropriate.

It will be a terrible *reductio ad absurdum* if the School Boards and local authorities are on the one hand to be encouraged to spend money on the schools and appliances necessary for technical instruction, and on the other for the children to find themselves barred by a too high standard from making use of them. Another serious blot on the Government Bill may here be remarked. As drafted by Sir W. Hart-Dyke, the only bodies authorised to provide technical instruction by means of the rates were School Boards, and where School Boards did not exist, Town Councils. But there is a population in England and Wales of no less than 8,007,587, not included either in School Boards or Town Councils. Why should this large population be excluded from the benefits offered to the urban population?

I have said that some technical handicraft instruction should be given, if necessary, to the exclusion of some of the merely literary teaching. This is said in no jealous or grudging spirit;

but while it is eminently desirable that all clever boys and girls should have every chance of fostering and developing their talents, I do think that we should look broadly and practically at the needs of the population as a whole. For one clever and lucky youth who rises from the national school to the university, a thousand—aye, more—will, and must, remain at the bench, the anvil, the loom, the engine, the plough.

This being so, after the child has learnt to read, write, and cypher well, he should at once be inducted into at least the rudiments of some branch of technical industry that would enable him to master, far more accurately than now, the handicraft he adopts at a later period. For it must be remembered that the great mass of the children leave school before they reach the age of thirteen. Out of the four million five hundred thousand children on the school registers last year, not one-tenth had reached twelve years. This being so, I desire to ask how much Latin, French, or physiology could be taught to, or be retained by, a child of twelve, in a school for children of the working classes? Very little, indeed, beyond the merest elements of the subject; yet for every scholar who passes in such a specific subject the State pays 4s. annually. I venture to think that this money might be far better laid out. I submit that the moment a child has reached a fair standard of proficiency in the three R's (by which I mean good legible writing, distinct reading, of a pleasurable character to himself and his auditors, and arithmetic, which should include proportional and fractional calculations), such child should become a half-time scholar, spending one half of his time in the literary department, where instruction in drawing and mathematics should be the main features, and the other half in a workshop school, to which it might be affiliated.

In the workshop school, which a boy might reasonably be expected to enter at the age of ten, I should give instruction of two kinds. First, theoretical teaching, including geometrical drawing, machine drawing and construction, mechanics and chemistry. Secondly, practical workshop teaching, which should aim at the most careful and accurate workmanship. This latter would include the production of simple geometrical forms in metal or wood, such as the cube or prism. Wood joints, dovetailing, and other simple work might be added.

If the child's school education terminated at this curriculum, we should have achieved very valuable results; but I should propose to offer exhibitions from these schools to higher grade technical schools, for the most promising of the workshop scholars. Into these higher grade schools, which on the Continent are called 'Apprenticeship Schools,' might be gathered the more skilful boys from the lower school.

What should be the curriculum in these apprenticeship schools? Well, these would vary according to the social and economical conditions of the district. In an agricultural district, the pupils should be taught the principles of agriculture and horticulture. The nature and properties of soils and crops and their rotation would, of course, come in. In a manufacturing district the technical teaching should aim at the inculcation of the scientific principles which underlie the particular processes of production. In a district, for example, such as Kidderminster, the scholars would, besides being taught the processes of weaving, have special instruction in design and the artistic grouping of colours. In this way our great centres of agriculture, of manufacture, and commerce could easily establish central technical schools, dealing especially with the productions of their own districts. As another example, Clerkenwell would have an eye to the watch, jewellery, silver plate, and furniture trades.

Before drawing your attention to what is being done in this direction on the Continent, I will first place before you the following figures drawn from the latest Statistical Report of the Education Department (House of Commons Paper, No. 5077, 1887).

On August 31, 1886 (the latest date up to which the figures have been tabulated), there were 19,173 separate elementary schools in England and Wales in receipt of annual grants from the Education Department. There was accommodation for 5,200,685 children; but the *average attendance* was 3,470,509 only. It is impossible not to be struck by the immense discrepancy between the places provided and the scholars in average attendance, and this in spite of the costly machinery for compulsory attendance which now exists. Many of us think that the school places will be much better filled when the parents see that the character of the instruction is more likely to benefit their children when they leave school to earn their livelihood. Again, of the total number of children on the register of inspected schools—viz., 4,553,751—there were—

Under seven	1,411,999
Between seven and ten . . .	1,606,479
„ ten and fifteen . . .	1,535,273

In other words, 66 per cent. of the children in our elementary schools were under ten; nearly 30 per cent. were between ten and thirteen; and 4 per cent. were over thirteen.

Table showing the number of children on the registers aged from three to fifteen:—

Under three	. . . . . .	7,862
„ four	. . . . . .	130,947
„ five	. . . . . .	298,056
„ six	. . . . . .	454,006
„ seven	. . . . . .	521,128
		1,411,999
„ eight	. . . . . .	530,272
„ nine	. . . . . .	533,651
„ ten	. . . . . .	542,556
		1,606,479
„ eleven	. . . . . .	519,131
„ twelve	. . . . . .	470,805
„ thirteen	. . . . .	354,964
„ fourteen	. . . . .	149,858
„ fifteen	. . . . .	40,515
		1,535,273

The reason why I give the figures in these groups is because compulsory attendance is now general up to ten years of age, and because, after ten, provision is made for the partial or total exemption of children on their passing in a certain standard.

On this point of the standards for exemption, I may state that the third standard of the Code is the almost universal one for half-time exemption. In the great towns and populous districts, the fifth generally obtains for total exemption, and in the rural districts the fourth. A few more figures, and I shall have given you all the statistics necessary to my case. The total income of all those elementary schools last year (ending August 1886) was 6,827,188*l*. 15s. 5*d*., which was mainly made up in this way:—

	£	s.	d.
From rates	1,169,149	10	7
,, voluntary contributions	742,597	9	5
,, fees of the scholars	1,763,189	9	2
,, grants from Imperial Exchequer	2,866,699	9	10

These figures are an eloquent tribute to the anxiety of the country to deal generously with the children of our industrial population. But we must not merely be generous with our money; we must endeavour to spend it wisely, and I rejoice to think that the purely literary education of our children is to be curtailed.

Now, very nearly one-third of the children in our elementary schools are under seven years of age (1,411,999). There is universal testimony to the great improvment which has taken place in the methods of infant instruction. This improvement is due in great measure to the development of the Kindergarten system, and children, when they move up, at seven years of age, from the infant schools, are now found to be infinitely better prepared than formerly for the higher instruction of the senior school. Not much change is needed in the infant schools, except that more time should be given to elementary drawing and to object lessons. Drawing cannot be taught at too early an age; the moment a child enters a school he should be taught how to use his pencil. As to object lessons, in the hands of a skilful teacher they may be the means of founding habits of clear apprehension and clear expression, which prove of the utmost value later on.

I pass to the children of between seven and ten years of age. Here a certain amount of elementary disciplinary handicraft teaching might well be introduced. Of the kind of handicraft teaching for scholars up to this age, permit me to quote Sir Philip Magnus. He says, in his evidence before the Royal Commission:—'If handicraft instruction is to be introduced on any large scale into our elementary schools, the instruction ought to be distinctly of a disciplinary, and not of a professional, character; that its object ought to be to train the senses, to train the hand and eye to work together; that it should have a moral and intellectual purpose. Such training would be extremely advantageous if it became an integral part of the elementary instruction, just in the same way as reading, arithmetic, and writing, its object being distinctly disciplinary and formative, as distinguished from professional.'

The evidence collected by the Royal Commission is clear on this point, that our Continental rivals have demonstrated that most valuable rudimentary handicraft teaching can be given in the elementary and primary schools. In all the new elementary schools which are being erected in the large towns in France, instruction in handicraft teaching will find an important place.

The commercial school in the Rue Tournefort, Paris, may be mentioned as a successful example of this kind of school. Here rudimentary handicraft teaching is combined with the ordinary instruction. Up to the beginning of 1880, I think, the handicraft teaching commenced at the age of ten. During the first two years, every child was taught drawing, modelling, carving, joiners' work, smiths' and fitters' work. Now, however, the plan has been extended in order that children in the lowest classes, beginning even at six years of age, may have three lessons, of one hour each per week, in handicraft.

It is greatly to be hoped that, under the improved Act of next session, we shall see such schools as this largely prevailing in the country. Every school of over 100 scholars might provide, at no great expense, for this rudimentary handicraft teaching, and the smaller schools might be grouped in convenient areas, and contribute from their annual income towards the maintenance of a common central handicraft school.

The taxpayers need not be called on for much more than they pay now. The total school income is nearly seven millions, or upwards of 2*l*. per head; the State already contributes 17*s*. per child, and what is called for is a judicious distribution of this immense income between the two kinds of teaching—rather than a further large contribution from the State.

Let us pass on to the higher elementary school, or apprenticeship school. Into these schools the boys might be drafted at the age of ten, eleven, twelve, according as they have reached a certain standard of attainments in the elementary subjects, and in drawing, elementary science, and elementary handicraft work; but I should hope, in a few years, to find most boys of eleven entering such schools.

It would not be well to have these higher elementary schools all on the same pattern. They ought to spring out of the industries of their particular districts, and the courses of instruction should be carefully graduated—the first and second year's courses aiming at teaching the scientific basis of the various arts and industries of the neighbourhood, and the third being more distinctly professional in character.

I quote here the description given by Sir Philip Magnus of the Ecole Professionale of Rheims :—

" In this school, advanced instruction is given in the ordinary subjects of an elementary education, and, in addition, instruction is given in science, including mechanics, physics, and chemistry, in art, and technology. The school is provided with ample and well-filled laboratories. There are also rooms devoted to the teaching of freehand and model drawing, containing a large number of excellent models. The teaching of mechanical drawing forms an essential part of the instruction, and the curriculum includes instruction in the technology of those industries which are carried on in the neighbourhood of Rheims. The course lasts three years, and in the third year the boys are divided into sections, according to the aptitude which they display in their preliminary studies, and they are also classified according to the different industrial and commercial pursuits which are carried on in the neighbourhood, agriculture being one, general commerce being another, mechanical industries being a third, and textile industries a fourth. For the purpose of giving these boys some preliminary instruction in the subject of textile industries, there are weaving and spinning sheds attached to the school, all fitted with a large amount of machinery. This school is by no means an uncommon one; there is an excellent school—which is one of the first of the sort that was established—in Lyons, called the ' Ecole Martinière,' which was established by Major-General Martin; there is another one at Amiens; there is one at Rouen; and, in fact, I may say that there is a higher school of this kind in most of the manufacturing towns of France. One of the most recent schools of this kind, which is now in course of construction (at least it was last year—whether it is completed or not I cannot say), is one at Vierzon. Vierzon is situated in the pottery district, and contains, in one set of buildings, a whole series of graded schools, an infant school, a primary school, and a higher elementary school, in which this superior instruction is given. In both the elementary schools and the higher schools the instruction is to a certain extent technical.' What has been achieved in the technical schools of the Society of Christian Brothers is too well known to make it necessary for me to dwell on it here. A school of this kind exists at Sheffield, and is under the School Board of Sheffield. It is a higher elementary school, receiving children after they have passed the fourth standard, and taking them on to the seventh, and giving them an education of the kind which one would very much wish to see in other towns. Sheffield is not the only town which has a higher elementary school. There is a very good one at Manchester; there is an almost similar school at Nottingham; there is a school of a somewhat higher character, but still answering the same purpose, at Glasgow; and there are a few others. What Sheffield has done I hope our other great centres of industry will shortly do. Towns like London, Birmingham, Leeds, Bristol, Manchester, Hull, Cardiff, Swansea, all of large populations, and all provided with School Boards, might well establish apprenticeship schools.

The total population on April 1 of this year under School Boards was upwards of sixteen millions, eleven millions of which were comprised in the great municipal boroughs under School Boards. It is not too much to hope that there will not be lacking in these places the funds and the public spirit required to establish these much-needed technical schools. On the other hand, a judicious union or grouping of the smaller towns would enable them to found common central schools, or establish a fund to go towards exhibitions from their respective districts. There are in England and Wales 14,916 parishes, of which no less than 8,951 have a population of less than 500. It is clear that some scheme will be necessary for grouping these parishes for the purpose of maintaining a good common technical school. It is most earnestly to be wished that they will not remain out in the cold in the revised Act. By judicious management such schools might be nearly self-supporting. It is true that on the Continent they are open gratuitously; but there is no kind of instruction for which English parents, with their essentially practical instincts, would more willingly pay than that to be found in the apprenticeship schools. With the district rate and the school fee, not much more need be demanded from the State. At present the Education Department pays 4s. for each child passing in a specific subject of instruction.

The number of passes last year was as follows:—

Algebra	16,702
Euclid	769
Mechanics	3,331
Latin	224
French	3,089
Animal Physiology	12,959
Botany	1,428
Principles of Agriculture	1,022
Chemistry	812
Sound, Light and Heat, Magnetism and Electricity	2,891
	43,227

Assuming that handicraft teaching be treated as a specific subject, and paid for at the same rate, it is scarcely likely to cause a large addition to our educational expenditure for some years. Personally, I should be glad to see several of the subjects I have named above superseded by handicraft teaching.

In this connection let me draw attention to the excellent work which might be performed by our night schools, which at present are lamentably deficient. Last year there were only 26,089 scholars in average attendance, and only 23,866 went up for examination. I cannot but think, that if the young men found that they could get skilful teaching of a scientific character likely to be of use to them in their daily labour, these numbers would increase ten, nay, fifty-fold, in a very short period.

I would strongly impress on all the municipalities and School Boards which provide apprenticeship schools the great necessity for making night-school classes a leading feature in their programme. Indeed, I think so highly of what might be achieved in night schools, and deplore so deeply the little at present done, that I should like to see a national league for the advancement and extension of evening schools.

The question will be asked as to how I propose to obtain the teaching power. I submit that every training college should be at once called on to provide skilled handicraft teaching for its students. Some of these colleges already have well-fitted laboratories, but they are not so general as they might be, while little or no provision for handicraft practice exists. A professor of handicraft teaching at each college, and attendance at special courses of instruction at the great Guilds Institute, would soon provide the teaching power necessary for the elementary schools.

For the higher elementary schools, if the necessary funds are forthcoming, I do not doubt that the Science and Art Department and the City and Guilds Institute will furnish an abundant supply of teachers. The record of the Science and Art Department is one of unqualified success.

The work already achieved by it has been of the most valuable character; thousands of our best art workmen, our designers in wood, metal, or textile fabrics, owe their instruction and their success to the Department, notably to the able and painstaking staff at South Kensington. To my mind, one of the most interesting portions of the Health Exhibition was the gallery set apart for objects which had been designed or wrought by students of art and science schools.

The fact, then, that this Department has achieved so much, argues that it could do much more if so permitted by Parliament; and a system of workshop schools will very quickly spread throughout the country under their energetic management. The immense building of the City and Guild of London Institute, with its lecture rooms, laboratories, and professors, will amply suffice as a great central training school for technical teachers. The teachers should be drawn from amongst the skilled artisans of the country. I am certain that our public-spirited and generous municipalities will not lag behind those of France or Belgium, and will quickly raise funds to enable the skilled mechanics of their respective districts to undergo a course of special instruction at this great central institution, in order that, on their return, they may become the teachers of the workshop schools. I do not suggest that the already heavily burdened taxpayers shall contribute much more; the vote for public education, properly administered, and directed to right objects, is quite sufficient, and it might and will be supplemented by public-spirited individuals like Josiah Mason and others. And I am quite certain that this casting of our bread upon the waters will return to us after not many days. We shall raise up a body of scientific handicraftsmen who will quickly regain our former prestige in all the great manufactures in metal, and wood, and textile fabrics; thus shall we be able to defy the keenest competition of our foreign rivals. Our artisans and designers will not be drudging along in the old grooves, using the same methods and achieving no better results than their fathers before them; but they will be alive to the necessity for invention, for skilful adaptation of means to ends, for labour-saving processes and appliances, for more artistic production. With a population such as this, we shall be carried through the bad times which a great commercial nation must occasionally experience, and be ready and able to take instant advantage of any rebound, when enterprise is active and opportunity holds out her hand.

TECHNICAL EDUCATION.

(A SUMMARY OF THE REPORT OF THE ROYAL COMMISSION APPOINTED TO INQUIRE INTO THE STATE OF TECHNICAL INSTRUCTION, BY F. C. MONTAGUE, M.A.)[1]

PREFACE.

By SIR BERNHARD SAMUELSON, Bart., M.P., Chairman of the late Royal Commission on Technical Instruction.

My friend Mr. William Rathbone, at whose request the following digest of the Report of the Technical Instruction Commission has been prepared, has asked me to prefix to it, by way of preface, such observations on the subject as may

[1] Reprinted by permission of the Cobden Club.

appear to me to be useful at the present time. Perhaps I cannot do better than to summarise the conclusions and recommendations of the Commission in the fewest words; to state how far they have been complied with by the Government; and to add some information as to what has been done during the progress and since the conclusion of our inquiry towards remedying in various other ways the deficiencies which it disclosed.

Dividing the subject into the three heads of the technical instructions of (1) the proprietors and principal managers of industrial works, (2) the foremen, and (3) the workmen, we found that the education of the first was provided for on the Continent in a way beyond all comparison more complete and effective than in this country, and that this applied as much to their commercial as to what is usually understood by their technical education. The defects of the latter in our case were more conspicuous in the more refined chemical manufactures than in mechanical engineering. In reference to the second class we found that, whilst there are on the Continent, and more especially in France, a limited number of establishments designed for the systematic training of foremen in mechanical engineering, and in some other branches of manufacturing, and in Germany schools for instruction in the principles of textile manufactures and dyeing, on the other hand, the instruction afforded by classes in connection with the Science and Art Department of South Kensington, supplemented by those of the City Guilds, covers a wider area of elementary, and what may be distinguished as lower secondary scientific and technical instruction, in this than in any other country. To this provision, however, instruction in art, in view of its application to industry, forms an exception. This latter we found, partly by reason of its gratuity, far more widely diffused in France and Belgium than amongst ourselves. Lastly, as to the instruction of the artisans, we found that their defective elementary instruction in this country, as compared with that of the corresponding class in Germany and Switzerland, and latterly in the principal cities of France, prevented our people from availing themselves of the opportunities which the science classes already referred to would otherwise afford them. At the same time we ascertained that it was a fallacy to suppose that the workpeople of foreign countries (again excepting as to art) have received a better technical education than our own. The contrary rather is the case, thanks to the training which our people have received for several generations in our workshops.

At the same time we found that the technical skill of foreign artisans was rapidly increasing. We observed that elementary instruction in the use of tools for working in wood and iron was being introduced into the principal elementary schools of France, and that, under the name of higher elementary schools, gratuitous technical schools rendered available by bursaries to artisans for their more advanced technical instruction had been and were being set up in many French cities. We did not approve of the French schools which profess to give instructions to artisans in mechanical engineering and the other more important handicrafts as a substitute for apprenticeship in the workshop, but we recognised the advantage of the schools in some poor and remote parts of the Continent, which afford instruction in such domestic employments as wood-carving and lace-making as a means of procuring some slight addition to the precarious and slender income of families in those districts, and it appeared to us that the circumstances of Ireland might render such instruction very useful in some parts of that country.

As the result of our inquiries we were induced to make the following, amongst other recommendations :—As to elementary schools, that drawing should be taught systematically in all of them; that no school should be considered efficient in which proper appliances—such as casts and models, &c.—for this purpose were not provided; that the limits of age and acquirements authorising the employment of the whole time of children in labour should be raised in England and Ireland to the standard of Scotland; that proficiency in the use of tools for working in wood and iron should be recognised as a 'specific subject;' that in rural schools the principles and facts of agriculture should be taught to the older children.

As to science and art schools, we recommended that local authorities should have power to establish them and to contribute to their maintenance; that the inspection exercised by this department should be more efficient; that greater encouragement should be given to industrial designing; that the building grants should be more liberal; that grants should not be conditional on the payment of fees by all the students in science and art classes, but that artisans might be admitted to them gratuitously.

We desired that science should be more efficiently taught in the training colleges for teachers, and that the students in these colleges should be allowed to avail themselves fully of the instruction in art and science to be obtained in the Government schools of South Kensington and Dublin.

We recommended the liberal application of ancient endowments to secondary schools in which so-called modern subjects should take the place of the classics; that power should be given to local authorities to establish schools of this kind; and that the existing restrictions with reference to the establishment of free public libraries and museums should be removed.

These, and some special recommendations in regard to Ireland, relating to instruction in home industries, to grants in aid of agricultural schools, and to the functions of the Royal College of Science in Dublin, were our chief demands, so far as they depend on the action of the Government and of public authorities.

In addition, we considered ourselves justified in hoping that there would be greater liberality than heretofore on the part of private individuals in the provision of scholarships in technical and other secondary schools for the more promising pupils of elementary schools; that employers and Trades Unions would give greater encouragement to, and, if necessary, insist on, young persons employed in manufactures and handicrafts availing themselves of instruction in science and art classes; that the managers of such classes would encourage more systematic and advanced instruction; and that the great national agricultural societies would promote the establishment of schools in which agriculture is taught.

Successive Ministers of Education have in various ways shown that they concur, on the whole, with our demands; but with the exception of drawing having, under difficulties on the part of the Treasury, been made a class subject in elementary schools, and of more stringent requirements on the part of the Science and Art Department in reference to practical work in the science classes, the Government did not feel itself sufficiently supported by public opinion to give effect to our recommendations until the present session. The Bill for the establishment of technical schools, introduced a few nights ago by the Vice-President of the Council, encourages those who have for so many years laboured perseveringly in the promotion of technical instruction to hope that some real progress will at length be made, not only in a few favoured places, but throughout the length and breadth of the land. The intention of its authors is to give effect to our recommendations so far as they relate to elementary and secondary technical instruction. It is to be hoped that the power to be granted by it to local authorities will not be hampered with unnecessary restrictions. Those conferred on the Science and Art Department are ample, and I believe it has every disposition to exercise them liberally if it can rely on the support of the country and of the House of Commons. A few of the City Guilds, and notably the Clothworkers' Company, have shown great liberality in the judicious provision of funds for the encouragement of technical instruction; and I see no reason why, in the case of those companies who now devote their incomes to less useful purposes, a fair contribution to what is properly their work should not be insisted on, in aid of schools maintained jointly by the localities in which they are situated, and by the State through the agency of the Science and Art Department.

Several such schools are now in good working order. Amongst these are the Technical Schools of the City Guilds in Finsbury, the day and evening classes of which are full to overflowing. The Technical College at Bradford, assisted by the Clothworkers' Company, is in full activity in all its departments. The courses of the dyeing school, conducted by an energetic young professor trained at Zurich, are followed both by middle class and artisan students; and the weaving department is attracting students even from Germany. The Bristol Trade School, erected and maintained by the liberality of the Merchant Adventurers' Guild of that city, intended chiefly for the instruction of chemists, engineers, and miners, is well equipped, both as regards its staff and its laboratories. The school at Keighley is a conspicuous example of a good science school. The Heriot-Watt School of Edinburgh, the Glasgow and West of Scotland College, and the Manchester Technical School are old schools amalgamated or otherwise reorganised. I name these as instances of the higher elementary and secondary technical schools which are already in operation in various parts of the country. As yet they are few; but in Stockport, Blackburn, Wakefield, Preston, Hull, and in several other towns, similar schools are either being established, or the proposal to establish them has been warmly taken up, and is likely to lead to practical results.

Elementary instruction in the use of tools has been introduced tentatively in some of the London Board schools, successfully in Sheffield and elsewhere.

The signs of progress in the highest technical instruction are less hopeful. The Central Institute of the City Guilds, in the Exhibition Road, has an ample provision of professors and of laboratories and class-rooms; but its students are not till now so numerous as might have been wished and expected, even making allowance for the short time that it has been opened; and the various local University Colleges are, with some few exceptions, inadequately provided with funds and not very numerously frequented. It will be seen from the digest of our Report how munificently colleges of similar and of higher rank are supported by the Governments of Continental countries. The highest technical instruction is not—and probably never will be—self-supporting in any country; and if, in consideration of the exceptionally liberal contributions of the State with us to elementary instruction—which in Germany and Switzerland is defrayed almost exclusively from local funds—we can scarcely expect that as much will be done here as in those countries out of imperial funds for this important—perhaps the most important —grade of technical education, some assistance may be fairly asked for from Government, and will not, I believe, be asked for in vain when it shall appear that there is a genuine demand and sufficient preparation for instruction of this advanced type.

A branch of the subject not less important, though, as I have said elsewhere, it has not hitherto been regarded as strictly within the lines of technical instruction, is that of commercial education. Our youths are far behind those of Germany in the cultivation of modern languages, arithmetic, and geography. The Oxford and Cambridge Local Examination Board has recently devised and submitted to the Chambers of Commerce a special scheme of examination in these subjects, which it is to be hoped will act as a stimulus on the secondary schools.

Amongst the encouraging signs of the interest taken in technical instruction, I would mention the recent establishment of an association for its promotion which owes its inception to Sir Henry Roscoe and Mr. Arthur Acland, and of which Lord Hartington is the President. Its chief objects are to stimulate public interest in the subject, to assist local bodies with its advice, and to take Parliamentary action in the direction in which legislation is required.

I will conclude this somewhat hasty review with an expression of the hearty wish that our people throughout the country may at length arrive at a full sense of our educational deficiencies, and at the determination that they shall cease to exist.

B. SAMUELSON.

July 20, 1887.

I. INTRODUCTION.[1]

During the first half of this century we enjoyed an unchallenged industrial supremacy, the result of many contributory causes. Among them were physical causes, such as our mineral wealth, our position, at once safe and accessible, our prolonged sea-board, and our bracing climate; moral and intellectual causes, such as the natural energy and inventiveness of our people; political causes, such as the happy union of individual liberty with public order; economic causes, such as the gradual accumulation of capital in earlier times; and many other causes too numerous to be specified. Full scope for the operation of all

---

[1] The Commissioners and the Report referred to in these pages are invariably the Commissioners appointed to inquire into technical instruction, and the second Report prepared by them. The Report itself may be purchased either directly or through any bookseller from any of the following agents :—Messrs. Hansard and Son, 13 Great Queen Street, W.C., and 32 Abingdon Street, Westminster; Messrs. Eyre and Spottiswoode, East Harding Street, Fleet Street, and Sale Office, House of Lords; Messrs. Adam and Charles Black, Edinburgh; Messrs. Alexander Thom and Co., or Messrs. Hodges, Figgis, and Co., Dublin.

these causes was given by the long Napoleonic war which devastated the Continent, whilst it left us in secure isolation to perfect our manufactures, and to grasp the carrying trade of the world. So conspicuous was the supremacy thus established that some among us came to regard it almost as part of the fixed order of nature. These good people took the same view respecting their country which a Sheffield manufacturer expressed respecting his town :—' Sheffield was really a very fine town, and he questioned whether any part of the world was equal to it.' Although conceivably we might improve ourselves, yet we were so superior to other nations that improvement was hardly a thing of practical concern. Nay, there was some fear of doing harm in the rash attempt to ameliorate that which was already so excellent. In this frame of mind our industrial classes were little disposed to vex their souls with problems of technical education.

Our neighbours, however, saw things more clearly. The industrial supremacy of Great Britain appeared to them the effect of definite causes, not of an indefinite perfection in the British. They were inferior to us in material resources and in natural ingenuity; but their inferiority in these respects forced upon their attention the value of thrift and of education. Thrift multiplied their capital, and education multiplied their industrial efficiency. England served them as a model of organisation and equipment; but their trained intelligence enabled them to improve upon this model. For some time past, whilst we have advanced, they have advanced faster still; they have driven us from several of their domestic markets, and they are sharply competing with us in the markets of other nations. We find that our industrial empire is vigorously attacked all over the world. We find that our most formidable assailants are the best educated peoples. Upon this matter let us listen to the testimony of an Englishman, for thirty years manager in a Bavarian engineering works :—

Germany thirty years ago, as compared with England, was simply nowhere; but placing English and German workshops side by side now, we should find that the progress in the latter had been positively marvellous. During all these years the Germans had been following the English step by step, importing their machinery and tools, engaging, when they could, the best men from the best shops, copying their methods of work and the organisation of their industries; but, besides this, they had devoted special attention to a matter which England had almost ignored—the scientific or technical instruction of their own people. And what has been the result of all this? They have reached a point at which they have little to learn from the English.—*Report*, vol. i. p. 335.

This testimony was confirmed by the observation of the Commissioners themselves. In their description of a visit to the factories of Alsace, they tell us that—

Our rivals have possessed themselves outwardly of all the advantages and excellences which have been the growth of English inventiveness and enterprise during the last generation. To the casual observer, strolling from room to room, and watching the varying processes from the soft white sliver to the 'built-up' cop of yarn, there would not appear to be a very appreciable difference between a German and a Lancashire factory. The raw material, machinery, and appointments are equal in both cases. In general appearance the operatives do not compare unfavourably with those of Lancashire.—*Report*, vol. i. p. 295.

We know to our cost that the equality of English and German manufacturers is sometimes real as well as apparent. Thus, weaving firms in the Saxon town of Chemnitz send their fancy goods to London, Bradford, or Manchester, and sell them in the very centres of competition. Similar instances could be drawn from other industries.

The success of our rivals is not to be explained by reference to the low wages and long hours of work general on the Continent. If labour is cheaper there, coal is dearer, machinery is dearer, and imported raw material often pays a tax. Moreover, the artisans abroad have not the energy of our own men, who eat better and more abundant food, and have more rest. The foreign employers questioned by the Commissioners allowed that for strength and spirit the English operative was unrivalled. Some of them thought that they should ultimately gain by such a rise in wages and curtailment of work as would improve the health and strength of their own hands. The Commissioners expressly state that the foreign competition which presses us most seriously is more frequently that in which the conditions of hours and wages approach nearest to those prevailing here. In so far as the competition between ourselves and foreign nations depends on the workman, it is mainly the sobriety and the intelligence of their workmen which give them the advantage. But in that competition it is not only the intelligence of the workman; it is the intelligence of the foreman, the manager, the master, nay, it is the intelligence of the whole people which is of so much weight.

Let us dwell a little longer on this point, for it is one of supreme consequence to ourselves. We have begun to see the commercial value of elementary and of technical education. But our perception of their commercial value will not help us unless it is joined to a perception of their place and relations in the whole scheme of enlightenment. We must again and again repeat that neither elementary education nor technical education can be perfected apart from education in general, or could by themselves have made Germany so puissant a rival as we now find her. The strength of Germany lies in the culture of every class of Germans, in the real love of learning which animates the people and their rulers, in the patient, inquiring, and scientific spirit which has transformed almost every branch of human activity from metaphysics to the art of war. This culture, this love of learning, this scientific spirit, are not rare among us, but neither are they diffused; they are the property of individuals and of small groups. In Germany the problem how to educate the whole nation as well as possible has for many years been constantly present to the minds of scholars and statesmen. In England, and still more in Ireland, it is less the education of the people than the advantage which parties can draw from controlling education that has fascinated journalists and members of Parliament. Education, however, is too grave a concern to be dealt with by men who lack singleness of aim and purity of purpose. In spite of the growth of a genuine interest in the object, we are still far behind Germany in primary, in secondary, in university education, and therefore in technical education, which grows out of and always remains entwined with all three. The education of a people is a whole, and has a unity. Technical education, the education which makes a man expert in his calling, has its allotted place in that wider education which makes him a worthy member of a civilised commonwealth. The education which draws out all the intelligence of the community is a necessary antecedent to the education which draws out the capacity of this or that man for this or that calling.

Technical education falls into two great divisions: the education of those who will be engaged in manufactures, mining, building, and similar occupations; and the education of those who will be engaged in agriculture. Each of these principal divisions may again be subdivided into three grades: the primary, the intermediate, and the advanced. In each of these grades the instruction must be varied according to the nature of the particular branch of industry which is taught. From these considerations we may see how vast and intricate is the subject of technical education. Its full discussion would produce a large library of monographs which only experts could understand. But many persons beside experts are beginning to concern themselves in technical education, and for them a general survey of the field which it covers may be useful. Such a survey, based upon the results of long and laborious investigation, helps to show the ends at which we must aim, the results which we have already achieved, and the principles which should guide us in making good our deficiencies. In the hope of rendering this assistance to the public the following abstract has been written.

II. TECHNICAL INSTRUCTION IN MANUFACTURES, MINING, &c.

A. *Primary Instruction.*

By primary instruction is here understood such technical instruction as is required by the ordinary artisan. The education of the artisan may be divided into the education given in the public elementary schools and the education given in schools purely technical. Accordingly, the Commissioners, in their inquiries and recommendations, constantly kept in view the state of elementary education. So much has recently been done to improve the elementary schools of this country that we are apt to think them even better than they are—to suppose them practically perfect. In truth, we have still many things to learn from countries where the school system has been maturing through a long course of years. If anybody questions this statement, let him take a favourable specimen of our public elementary schools, and compare it with the Swiss school of the same class, described in the following passage of the Report:—

One of the best elementary Swiss schools visited by the Commissioners is that on the Lindescher Platz, in Zurich. The cost of building this school was 43,000*l*. which amounts to 66*l*. per head. Irregularity of attendance is practically unknown ; all the children learn one foreign language ; moreover, they are all taught drawing, and have object lessons in natural history. In the higher classes they are instructed in the rudiments of chemistry and physics, great pains being taken to place before the children well-arranged specimens, which are contained in a school museum. These museums form very noteworthy objects in the Zurich schools. Among the objects we found there were simple chemical and physical apparatus, chemical specimens, geographical relief maps showing the Alps and their glaciers, typical collections of commonly occurring and useful rocks and minerals, excellent botanical models, as well as collections of insects, carefully labelled, a complete herbarium, zoological and anatomical specimens and models : the collection, in fact, serving as a type of what such a school museum should be. Many of the specimens were collected and arranged by the teachers.

All the school subjects were taught intelligently and well. We were specially struck with the clean and tidy appearance of the boys, and there was a difficulty in realising that the school consisted mainly of children of the lower classes of the population.—*Report*, vol. i. p. 20.

The chief faults of our elementary school system are two— the average period of attendance at school is too short and the programme of school teaching is too meagre. It is convenient to examine these defects separately. In England a child can be compelled to attend school when it is five years old ; but as soon as it has passed the fourth standard it may be employed for hire, and as soon as it has passed the fifth standard it is free from any obligation of further attendance.[1]

---

[1] The age at which a child may be employed for hire is fixed by statute; the standard of total exemption from attendance at school is fixed by a by-law of the School Board or School Attendance Committee, which has received the approval of the Education Department. In such by-laws the fifth standard is usually, but not always, selected as that of total exemption.

The fourth standard is ridiculously low, and an intelligent child, fairly well taught, can easily pass it at the age of ten years. Consequently, in those districts which especially concern us here, in the manufacturing districts, where the labour of children is valuable, almost every child has passed the fourth standard at that age, and thenceforward is employed half its time in the factories. It is plain to the meanest capacity that a child's education must be hindered by putting it to work as soon as it has completed its tenth year. The child, even when working half-time, can usually pass the fifth standard in another year, and it is thus released from school when but eleven years old; that is to say, after a school life of six years. In Germany and Switzerland they order these things very differently. They act on the principle, admitted by everybody who knows or cares anything about education, that the way to secure a good training for the mind is not to end the school life as soon as the scholar can pass an examination, but to insist that every scholar shall spend a certain number of years under sound teaching. The period of compulsory attendance at school begins later and lasts longer there than here. In the city of Hamburg it commences at the age of six and continues for seven years; in the kingdom of Saxony it is practically the same. In Baden, Bavaria, Zurich, and elsewhere, young persons leaving the elementary school at the age of twelve, thirteen, or fourteen years are required by law to attend the Fortbildung, or continuation schools, for two or three years more.

These evening schools (say the Commissioners) help to sustain a boy's interest in study at a time when he is likely to forget what he has acquired in the ordinary primary school. For the want of them apprentices or young workmen frequently find themselves too ignorant to avail themselves of the special technical instruction which they have the opportunities of obtaining, and on this account, and also because they serve to give the youth a taste for study at the time when he begins to appreciate the value of instruction, these schools have proved to be most serviceable to German and Swiss artisans in quickening their intelligence, and in affording them useful information bearing upon their trades.—*Report,* vol. i. p. 37.

In Germany and Switzerland there are not only more years in the school life; there are also more hours in the school day.

Having thus secured the necessary time, the law lays down a more liberal programme of elementary instruction than the one adopted here. Examinations, developed here to the great detriment of primary as well as of advanced instruction, are there kept in their proper bounds. There is less 'cramming,' and the instruction is slower, more thorough, and more reasoned, than it can be under our system of hurrying children to the point where they may be rewarded by having their education cut short. To lengthen the school life is, therefore, the first reform needed in our school system. The Commissioners contented themselves with recommending that no child should be allowed to work half-time before it had passed the fifth standard—practically, before it was eleven years old. This is a step in the right direction, perhaps as long a step as can be taken now; but we must not fancy that even this change puts us on an equality with Switzerland or Germany. With us the period of compulsory attendance at school would still average only six years, and would still begin at an unusually early age. It is desirable that children under twelve years should not be employed in factories, and should be compelled to attend school without reference to the standard which they may have attained. Continuation schools, open in the evening, should be established throughout the country, and all persons under the age of fourteen years who are not attending other schools should be required to attend them. We have already seen the opinion of the Commissioners as to the service done by the Fortbildung schools in Germany and Switzerland. In this country they would be still more useful, inasmuch as children leave school in a less advanced stage of instruction. With us, the child who has attended an elementary school too often leaves it at that very period of life when the power of fixing the attention and the taste for knowledge begin for the first time to show themselves; he goes back to a home without intellectual interests, where life is sacrificed to getting a livelihood; he spends his days in a narrow routine of mechanical labour and his evenings in utter listlessness, and, on reaching manhood, finds that he has lost, in great part, the rudiments which he so painfully acquired: that he is, if not exactly illiterate, yet unfit to make progress in any branch of knowledge which may relate to his calling. The true remedy is not to try to crowd much more into the short period of compulsory attendance at school, but to lengthen that period, whilst interfering with industry as little as possible. This can be done only by establishing evening schools to carry further the instruction given in the day schools.

In the second place—and this is a fault which naturally grows out of the fault first mentioned—our public elementary schools do not teach as much as the model artisan should know. There are, at least, three weak points in their system of instruction, as tried by this humble and practical test. Drawing is taught ill, the rudiments of natural science are taught slightly, and the use of tools is taught rarely. Each of these points demands separate consideration.

I. *Drawing.*—All experts are agreed that practice in drawing is valuable as a means both of general and of technical education. It imparts steadiness and delicacy to the fingers, it develops clear and exact perception, and it cultivates the sense of elegance and beauty, which, however feeble in most people, is wholly absent only from the lowest minds. A knowledge of drawing is useful in every handicraft, and indispensable in many. Yet it appeared, from the evidence given before the Commissioners, that drawing is not taught in more than a fourth of the elementary schools in England. Even in these schools it is not taught to every pupil. The teaching is generally bad, because the schoolmasters and schoolmistresses themselves have not been properly taught to draw. When the Commissioners drew up their report, the grant for drawing might be earned by a school which did not allot to the subject more than one hour a week; but this miserable allowance has since been increased to one hour and a half. Formerly the examination in drawing was of the most futile character. A prodigious quantity of work was sent up from every part of the kingdom to South Kensington, and was there judged by the unhappy officials. It should be noted that the drawing in public elementary schools is in the charge, not of the Education Department, but of the Science and Art Department. By the same Minute, which requires more time to be given to drawing, it is provided that the examination in drawing shall henceforward be held in the school itself by a local inspector or by his assistant. These changes are good, but they do not raise the instruction in drawing to the standard attained in France or Germany, nor do they fulfil the recommendations of the Commissioners. The Commissioners recommended—(i.) That rudimentary drawing should be incorporated with writing as a single elementary subject, and that instruction in drawing should be continued through all the standards; (ii.) that a proper supply of casts and models for drawing should be included in that 'apparatus of elementary instruction' which a school must possess before it can receive public money; (iii.) that modelling should be constituted a subject on which grants could be earned; (iv.) that art should be properly taught in the training colleges to those who will subsequently have to teach art to others; (v.) that the inspectors of the Education Department should be made responsible for the instruction in drawing given in elementary schools. To these recommendations may be added another, which they involve; namely, that the time given to drawing in the school programmes should be increased. Mr. Armstrong, the Director of Art for the Science and Art Department, thought that four hours a week should be allotted to drawing alone, before taking any time for such a subject as modelling. This once done, he thought that one hour a week for modelling would be time well spent. Drawing is not a sort of work which harasses or exhausts the mind, and, for its sake, the present school hours might, with advantage, be lengthened.

II. *Natural Science.*—In our infant schools the pupils have object lessons in natural science, and in our elementary schools certain sciences are class subjects, which may be taken up by scholars who have passed the lowest standards. Geography may, however, be regarded as a science, and geography may be taken as a class subject in the lower division of elementary schools. The Commissioners recommended that elementary lessons in natural science, including geography, should take the place now occupied by geography alone. The effect of this change would be to continue the object lessons in elementary science now given in the infant school up to the point at which they would be succeeded by definite teaching of special sciences, so that the impressions made upon very young children should not be allowed to vanish before they are old enough to profit by higher methods of instruction. But when we try to develop the study of natural science in elementary schools, we are met with the same difficulties as in the case of drawing—the want of time, the want of money, and the want of well-trained teachers. Little science can be taught to backward children, whose school hours are so few. The cost of apparatus wherewith to illustrate lessons in natural science is more than most schools can afford. The teachers from the training colleges have often been 'crammed' with science rather than disciplined in science. These difficulties, perhaps insuperable in country places, have been partially overcome in a few large towns by the employment of itinerant demonstrators, or by the foundation of higher elementary schools.

At Liverpool and Birmingham the itinerant demonstrator has proved useful. He works in unison with the teachers in the various elementary schools, and his demonstrations reinforce their lessons. The apparatus used in the demonstrations is kept at a central laboratory, and is transferred from school to school by means of a light hand-cart. The demonstrator visits each school once a week, giving in the week eighteen or twenty demonstrations. In the intervals between the demonstrations the teachers of the respective classes, who have themselves been present, go over the subject of the last demonstration, and frequently illustrate their lectures with simple experiments. For the help of the teachers there has been prepared a simple text-book, with reading lessons on the subjects of the demonstrations, and exercises to be worked by the scholars. Schools not under the control of the School Board may have the benefit of the system on condition of contributing to the expense. At Liverpool the cost of the apparatus used during five years did not exceed 120*l*. These demonstrations have proved equally beneficial to the teachers and to the scholars. The teachers have been improved in their method of teaching natural science. The scholars, when examined in the subjects of the demonstrations, have shown a remarkable proficiency, and this without any detriment to their other studies.

The foundation of higher elementary schools, sometimes known as 'graded' schools, has had good results in Manchester, Sheffield, and other towns. These schools are recruited with the most forward scholars from the common schools. In Manchester all the children attending the graded schools have passed in the fifth standard. They are taught French, drawing, mathematics, physiology, chemistry, physics, and geography. The school fee is only ninepence a week, and there are many scholarships for children entering from the primary schools or leaving for the Manchester Grammar School. The Commissioners stated that they had not seen on the Continent any school which surpassed these in general efficiency or in the tuition in any special subject, except drawing. In a school of the same type, the Central School of Sheffield, all the pupils take the ordinary subjects together with some of the special subjects named in the code. Both boys and girls throughout the school are taught German. All the girls learn needlework and practise cookery; those in the higher classes take chemistry. Drawing is thoroughly taught, and is made the basis for practical work carried on in the school workshops. This work comprises the production of simple but perfect surfaces and solids in wood and iron, of models and of apparatus for the experimental illustration of mechanical principles. It appeared to the Commissioners that the manual work deserved to be encouraged by grant, and could not well be carried on without such encouragement.

The Commissioners expressed in their report the warmest approval of these 'graded' schools, and a desire for their establishment in all our large towns.[1] To these and to the system of demonstrations above described they trusted for the diffusion of such elementary scientific knowledge as must form the basis of ordinary technical education. At the same

[1] It is only right to say that some persons of great experience disapprove of the institution of graded schools, and would prefer to see the higher instruction of advanced scholars given in the same school and by the same masters in which and by whom their elementary training has been given. Their arguments are briefly as follows:—(1) Parents are more easily induced to prolong the attendance of children at an old familiar school than to send them to a new untried one. (2) A child's education is more likely to be systematic and of a piece throughout if entirely given by the same teachers. (3) The teachers are improved both in zeal and in intelligence by having occasionally to give instruction which is not elementary. Considerable weight attaches to these arguments, and it must be owned that the question is one of much difficulty.

time they insisted on the imperfection of the teaching in science given by the training colleges. They suggested that the training colleges should send up every year to the Normal School of Science at South Kensington, or to similar institutions of established merit, the students who show scientific aptitude. They further recommended that the great school boards should be empowered to found training colleges for day students.

III. *Instruction in the Use of Tools.*—Such instruction has been introduced into many, and is to be introduced into all, the primary schools in France. It has been successfully tried at Manchester and at other places. At Manchester the lessons are given by the school board carpenter before and during school hours, in rooms separate from the rest of the school, and fitted with joiner's benches and lathes. The boys work one and a half hours a day. The Commissioners recommended that manual work, like modelling, should be included among the subjects on which grants may be earned. The instruction in the use of tools which can be given in a primary school is, of course, very limited. Children of less than ten or eleven years are not strong enough to use tools properly, and older children have scanty time to spare. The lessons cannot be profitable unless the teachers are skilful and the appliances good, and the expense of providing these for a variety of handicrafts is beyond the means of any one school. All that can be done is to give the scholars a chance of making themselves acquainted with the common tools for working wood and iron. Such knowledge is useful to them, even if they do not afterwards become artisans. The work is agreeable as a relaxation from reading and writing. It helps to foster a taste for active industry, and to check the foolish prejudice that the life of a copying clerk is finer and happier than the life of a skilled craftsman.

Seeing how short is the school life of most children, it remains to consider the education given to the workman in purely technical schools. We are not here concerned with workmen who possess unusual talent, scientific, artistic, or administrative—workmen who will, in the natural course of things, become inventors, designers, or organisers. They should be encouraged and assisted to seek the fullest technical instruction. But here we have to do with the common man, and the problem is how to train him so that he shall be able to execute in the best possible manner his common work. Formerly this training was given by the system of apprenticeship; and now that apprenticeship has lost most of the peculiarities which made it valuable as a means of education, it is proposed to supplement the lessons of the workshop by those of the school. To combine these so as to get the happiest result is a task of extreme nicety. The apprenticeship schools which abound in France, Germany, and the neighbouring countries vary in efficiency and usefulness; but, as a rule, they have not fully met the wants of the class for which they were designed. A few examples taken from the report will give a general idea of all. We shall then take a survey of the means of primary technical instruction possessed by our artisans, notice the recommendations made by the Commissioners, and add a few observations upon the possibilities of improvement.

The school of the Boulevard de la Villette, Paris, is intended for workers in wood and iron. The instruction is gratuitous. It comprises a general literary and scientific course, continuing the course of the primary school, together with a special technical training. The technical training combines lessons on the nature of tools, materials, and processes, with practical manual exercises in the workshop. The manual work is divided into two courses: in the first year the pupil spends six hours in the shops daily, and is taught the nature and conversion of materials; in the second year he spends six, and in the third year eight hours every day in the shop, and is busy with actual construction appropriate to the trade which he adopts. The school hours are from seven o'clock in the morning to seven o'clock in the evening, with two hours of interval for meals and recreation. The students pay visits to industrial establishments, and write descriptions of that which they have seen. A large proportion become engine-fitters or pattern-makers, and are said to earn good wages immediately on leaving the school. There are 250 pupils, and nearly 50,000*l*. has been expended on the buildings.

Another apprenticeship school visited by the Commissioners was the Royal Trade School of Iserlohn, in Westphalia, the first school of the kind established in Prussia. The manufacturers of the district were moved to found it by the ignorance of the pupils who entered their works. In this school industrial art suitable to metal-work is combined with handicraft teaching. The scholars go through a three years' course, and are trained as designers, modellers, wood-carvers, moulders, founders, turners and pressers, chasers, engravers, gilders, and etchers. The theoretical instruction includes drawing in all its branches, modelling in wax and clay, the elements of chemical and physical science, mathematics, German, technology, and the history of artistic work in metal. The practical instruction consists of lessons in the different branches of industry which the pupils are likely to follow, each pupil stating on entrance in which craft he wishes to be trained. In this, as in other technical schools, the hours are much longer than in schools where there is little or no practical work, the alternation of mental and bodily labour giving rest to the different faculties in turn.

Particularly interesting are the apprenticeship schools which have been established in Southern Germany and in Austria for the encouragement of petty manufactures carried on by the peasants. At the present day such manufactures are limited both in number and in extent by the development of machinery, and the consequent development of factories. But if they require the exercise of taste, and if they are carried on by persons who depend largely upon some other calling, such as agriculture, they may still minister to the well-being of great numbers of people. Industries of this sort are wood-carving, clock-making, straw-plaiting, and, under peculiar circumstances, some sorts of weaving and pottery. For all these crafts elementary technical schools have been provided in Baden, Bavaria, and Austria. At Furtwangen, in Baden, there is a remarkable school for wood-carving, recruited among the peasant lads of the neighbourhood. The scholars first draw and then model the copy before carving it. They pay for the wood, but become owners of everything which they execute. The local authorities provide the building, and the State pays the teachers, besides supplying models, examples, and tools. For literary and technical instruction the pupils all resort to the neighbouring Trade School, and for lessons in cabinet work they frequent a joiner's school. At Arco, in the Southern Tyrol, a school much humbler than the one at Furtwangen proved the germ of a flourishing industry. The people of Arco, who had long regarded olive-wood as fit only to be burned, noticed at last that at Bergamo and other places just over the frontier it was manufactured into many pretty or useful articles. Thereupon the authorities opened a school, with workshops for turning and inlaying; skilful teachers and good examples were procured; the scholars became first expert, and then famous; orders poured in from every quarter, even from America, and now many persons are employed in carving olive-wood, either in the factory or in their own homes.

It is worth while to contrast the skill and ingenuity of the wood-carving done in the districts where these schools have been established with the lack of the same qualities in much of the carving done in Ireland, where the artistic power of the peasantry has not been called forth by instruction. And in this context we may notice an instance of the revival of an old peasant industry by timely artistic training.

In the Erz-Gebirge, far from manufacturing towns, the women, to the number of 20,000, earn a livelihood by making lace. At one time the lace made in this district was much admired, and fetched a good price. But fashion changed, and foreign makers undersold the peasants, who could not understand why their lace was no longer wanted, and went on making what they could not sell, until many were at the point of starvation. The Government then held an investigation, established a lace department in the Industrial Art School of Vienna, caused a number of girls to be annually brought up from the country for a three months' course of lessons in designing and making lace, and thus restored comparative prosperity to the unfortunate lace-makers. Instances like these point to the establishment of small technical schools as one of the best means of reducing the poverty and idleness which prevail in some parts of Ireland. People without capital, without knowledge, and without enterprise, must be taught like children. It is perverse pedantry to apply to them maxims of letting well alone, which have only a partial truth when applied even to rich, enlightened, and energetic people.

Compare with the Irish pictures which we know too well the following picture from Thuringia :—

If the neighbourhood through which we passed is fairly representative of the forest country of Thuringia, it is impossible to overrate the importance, in a material point of view, of these home industries. The cottages were pretty and well kept ; most of the windows contained flowers beautifully grown in pots, and many of the houses had gardens attached to them. The people were well dressed, and had the air of being well fed and contented. They are evident y a most industrious race, and their success may depend as much upon their natural disposition and temperament as on the fact that they have been trained for generations in these various occupations. Still, whatever may be the cause of their success in home industries, we think it is impossible to doubt that the influence for good of such work is of vast importance. We found populous and thriving villages, filled with busy workers, in districts remote from railways, and where carriage and transport must be matters of extreme difficulty, and in parts of the country, moreover, where agricultural work would in many cases be wholly insufficient to provide support for more than a small proportion of the present population. It is in such cases as these that the provision of suitable employment for the masses of the people is so important, and the question of the mode in which such industries are introduced, and the way in which they are fostered, is surely one which deserves the most careful attention of the economist.
—*Report*, vol. i. p. 549.

In Belgium the apprenticeship schools give gratuitous teaching, and are supported chiefly by the State and the municipalities. They are open on every evening in the week, and on Sunday mornings. But there is no uniformity in their programmes, which are adapted to the different industries of different places. The general instruction takes in French or Flemish, arithmetic, geometry, the elements of chemistry and physics, technology, the laws of health, and industrial economy. Drawing is the basis of all the technical teaching, and is regarded as the universal language. The drawing lessons follow a graduated course, from drawing lines in chalk on the black-board to the study of projection and ornament, industrial drawing for special trades, and original designing. The course at these schools lasts from three to five years, according to the circumstances of each place. As a rule the pupils must be at least fourteen years old at the time of admission, and most of those attending at any one time are less than eighteen years of age. Many of the pupils intend to become clerks or draughtsmen, but every class of skilled artisan is represented among them.

Holland has some good apprentice schools, of which the Ambachts School at Rotterdam is a favourable specimen. The general teaching continues that given in the primary school, but extends to all the subjects recognised in the three years' course of the Dutch middle-class schools. Drawing is well taught, always with a view to practice. As regards technical instruction, the boys, as soon as they have learnt the use of tools, begin to make small articles, which can either be sold or else used in the school itself. It is found that they become more industrious by being employed upon work which has a marketable value. The workshops, constantly improved and enlarged, now include shops for carpenters, for blacksmiths, for metal-workers, for fitters and turners, for cabinet-makers, for masons, and for stone-carvers. Boys are admitted when twelve years old, and the full course lasts three years. When a pupil has finished his time the school committee finds him a situation. The fees, which amount to 8s. 4d. for the year, are readily remitted to the sons of poor parents. It is unnecessary to say that the school is maintained chiefly by the assistance of the Government, the province, and the city.

The provision made in this country for the technical instruction of the artisan may be considered under four principal heads: I. Schools maintained by private firms for the benefit of those in their employment; II. Schools open to the general public; III. Classes organised by the City and Guilds of London Institute for the Promotion of Technical Education; IV. Science classes organised by the Department of Science and Art. (The Art Schools under the Department will be noticed in the next chapter.)

I. Under this head are comprised such schools as that established by Messrs. Armstrong at Elswick, or those established by the London and North-Western Railway Company at Crewe, or the school attached to the works of Messrs. Mather and Platt, at Manchester. The last-named school was inspected by the Commissioners, under the guidance of Mr. Mather, who explained its intimate connection with the works. The drawings made in the school are of work actually in progress in the shops. One day the teacher gives the necessary explanations and calculations, and the next day the scholars see, as it were, on the anvil, the very thing which has been the subject of his lecture. The teachers are also employed in the works, know what each pupil is doing there, and readily adapt their lessons to his wants. Thus every arrangement is based on the principle that you must bring the school to the workshop, not the workshop to the school—a thoroughly sound principle as applied to certain industries like engineering. The school has well repaid the firm for their pains in setting it up. Mr. Mather told the Commissioners that the works had derived from the school an incalculable advantage.

We desire to send out yearly one or two thoroughly competent men, who shall not be simply mechanics in the ordinary sense of the word, but who shall be able to turn their attention to anything coming under their notice, whether they have done the thing before or not. We had the greatest difficulty in finding such men until we began to take them from the school; and since the school has been established we have been able to send boys of twenty to twenty-one to long distances from England, and to place in their hands work which they have not had much to do with before; and by their own intelligence they have made competent teachers of others, and given the greatest satisfaction. Thus one was sent out only a few years ago not quite out of his apprenticeship, and is now getting 4*l*. per week.
—*Report*, vol. i. p. 430.

We can the better understand the value of such a school to a great engineering firm by comparing Mr. Mather's testimony with that given by Professor Ayrton, of the Finsbury Technical College.

The present workman, to a great extent, is nothing more than a mere machine; he exercises no more independent thought than the chisel or the lathe, and the result is that he becomes deadened, and he works in a careless way, scamping his work and wasting material, the consequence of which is that the price of articles has very much risen.—*Report*, vol. iii. p. 116.

But such schools as that maintained by Messrs. Mather and

Platt for the benefit of their own establishment can never meet the wants of the country at large.

II. Schools available for apprentices generally are few in this country. The Oldham School of Science and Art is one of the best. The Commissioners described it as an excellent sample of the kind of school which should exist in every industrial town in the kingdom. It had its germ in certain evening classes in science and art commenced in connection with the Oldham Lyceum, and is in alliance with the City and Guilds of London Institute for the advancement of technical education. By the liberality of Messrs. Platt the school is now housed in a large and handsome building, with chemical and physical laboratories. It is an evening school, with nearly a thousand pupils. The science course embraces practical geometry, machine drawing, building construction, mathematics, mechanics, sound, light, heat, magnetism, and electricity, inorganic chemistry, geology, steam, freehand and model drawing, and technical instruction in tools, mechanical engineering, and the cotton manufacture. The leading manufacturers of Oldham support the school generously, and speak highly of its work. A member of an important firm of engineers told the Commissioners that it got all its foremen draughtsmen from the School of Science and Art. Before the school existed the firm employed Swiss, French, or German draughtsmen. Now there is hardly a foreigner in the town. Another employer observed,—

The working mechanics are much more intelligent. Now a man can be sent out to work, and can transmit his views to the firm in writing, give sketches, and reason about matters: formerly the man would have had to return to the works, and get personal instructions in all cases of difficulty. The suggestions they make to remedy defects are more practical than before. *Every man may now be equal in intelligence to what the master was before the school was established.*—*Report*, vol. i. p. 453.

III. The City and Guilds of London Institute has framed a system of technical teaching in its outlines not unlike the system of teaching science established by the Science and Art Department. It enters into correspondence with local committees throughout the kingdom, helps them to organise classes, finds examiners, holds examinations, and makes a capitation grant for successful candidates. The qualification needed for a teacher of any of these classes is partly theoretical and partly practical. He must hold a certificate of honours, granted either by the Science and Art Department or by the Institute, and he must have filled some place, such as that of foreman, in the industry which he professes to expound. The Society of Arts had conceived, and in part realised the idea of local examinations in technical knowledge, but, as it did not pay for results, the results were small. Few candidates offered themselves, even in the few places where examinations were held. Since the Institute took over the examinations, and made them the basis of payment, the centres of examination and the candidates at each centre have multiplied exceedingly. In some places technical schools already existing have affiliated themselves to the Institute, and prepare candidates for its examinations. In other places the classes established with the help of the Institute have grown, or promise to grow into technical schools. Some disadvantages always attach to a control over education exerted by a central examining body; but these disadvantages are not to be weighed against the advantages of a uniform standard and a coherent organisation, which the Institute assures to the technical teaching of so many localities, differing so greatly in their knowledge of what constitutes a good technical training, and in their means of providing it. There is some danger lest, for want of skilled teachers, high standards, and adequate resources, our small technical schools may discredit technical instruction altogether. The Institute does what it can to avert this danger. It is now becoming well known throughout the kingdom; but, oddly enough, when the Commissioners visited Ireland it had not been heard of outside Belfast.

IV. The Science and Art Department does not profess to give technical instruction in its science classes. But these science classes do more than any other agency to spread among our artisans that elementary knowledge of natural science which is the only possible basis of technical knowledge. The Department has been so long at work, and its methods are so well known to all who interest themselves in education, that any lengthened criticism is needless here. We have only to note the suggestions for increasing its usefulness which were made in the Report. These suggestions, in so far as they related to science, were briefly as follows :—(i.) That School Boards, and, in places where there are no School Boards, the local authority, should have power to establish, conduct, and contribute to the maintenance of classes for young persons and adult artisans under the control of the Department. (ii.) That the Department should, wherever possible, give a more practical character to the teaching of science, especially in the 'honours' stage; that in the 'advanced' stages the payment on results should be increased for all subjects, and that the grouping of subjects should be encouraged. (iii.) That the subject of metallurgy should be broken up into groups of kindred subjects, such as (a) the precious metals, (b) metals extracted from metalliferous mines, as copper, lead, tin, &c.; (c) iron and steel; and that the subject of mining should likewise be broken up into (a) coal mining, and (b) metalliferous mining. (iv.) That the Department should make more effective its inspection of science classes, with a view to ascertain the quality of the instruction and the adequacy of the laboratories and apparatus. (v.) That the Department should not insist on the payment of fees by artisans attending the classes. (vi.) That the grants made by the Department for the building of schools of art or of science should no longer be limited to 500*l.* in each case, and that the conditions attached to these grants should be revised.

Upon a general view it must be owned that with regard to technical instruction for artisans we still have much to learn from our neigbours. At the same time we possess in the classes of the City and Guilds Institute, and in those of the Science and Art Department, two unique and valuable organisations, which, if constantly extended and improved, may supply most of our deficiencies. By undertaking this work later than other nations we get the benefit of their experience. They have now and then committed the mistake of trying to teach in the school things which can be better taught in the workshop. They have now and then offered to the artisan an instruction too elaborate for his wants, or given at hours when his work has to be done. Our people are of a practical bent; they can distinguish the knowledge which is useful to them, and if they can most conveniently get it in the workshop they will seek it there. But in our first enthusiasm we may found technical schools for workmen such that workmen will not attend them. The technical school for workmen must teach what workmen want to know. It must adapt its hours and arrangements to their leisure and to their convenience, and must, therefore, be an evening school. A day school which keeps boys of fifteen or sixteen years from their work lays a heavy burthen upon their parents, and the pressure of this burthen provokes an agitation, first of all for the remission of school fees, and secondly for the supply of food and clothing at the public expense. The Parisian technical schools for workmen are, as a rule, open gratis, and in one of them each pupil costs the community 75$l.$ a year. A pupil leaving this school at the age of seventeen years would not necessarily or probably be a better workman than a lad of the same age who had spent two years in a good workshop, and had attended evening classes at the Finsbury College or the Oldham School of Science and Art. Even in Paris the schools thus lavishly assisted are not filled solely by young artisans.

The evening school is liable to this objection, that it offers instruction to persons already fatigued with a long day's labour, who may be incapable of application, or at least may feel that they have earned their rest. Yet there is abundant experience to show that evening schools are crowded with pupils, and teach their pupils a great deal. Employers should certainly assist and encourage apprentices to attend these schools. Professor Huxley says, with his accustomed shrewdness,—

Of all the practical measures that could be taken for the advancement of technical education and scientific teaching the most important would be that employers should show that they valued it, and that they would do something for the young people who in any way distinguished themselves.—*Report*, vol. iii. p. 322.

B. *Intermediate Instruction.*

Technical education, we repeat, must always be considered with reference to education as a whole. The establishment of a complete system of public elementary schools has made it possible to organise primary technical instruction. Intermediate technical instruction cannot be put on a proper footing until we have improved our secondary schools. In England we have asserted the right and duty of the State to secure the efficiency of primary schools by regulation and assistance. But we have hitherto confined the action of the State in respect of secondary schools to the business of ensuring that their ancient endowments, if they have any, shall not be wasted. With this exception we have left our secondary education to the mercy of chance. Any person, however ill-qualified, may set up a school for boys of the middle class, and, having set it up, may conduct it as he pleases. No public body undertakes to provide new schools of this order, or to enforce any standard of excellence in those already existing. The consequences are such as we might naturally expect. Test the instruction given in many of the private adventure schools, whether in classics, in modern languages, in natural science, or in drawing, and you will find it thoroughly superficial and unserviceable. Yet these schools exact fees which in France or Germany would be thought high; their masters are ill-paid; their buildings, although not so bad as everything else about them, are seldom satisfactory; and altogether the proof is ample that they cannot afford to be efficient, and would not pay if they were useful. Such schools are no fit places of preparation for youths who are to carry on the commerce and manufactures of a great people.

There are, no doubt, many schools whose celebrity offers a guarantee of their quality; but these schools do not aim at preparing boys for intermediate technical education. They educate boys for the universities, for the learned professions, for public life, and for the pursuits of literature. There are many schools inferior to these, yet richly endowed, which have been re-modelled by the Charity Commissioners, and give the preparation here suggested. But the Charity Commissioners have not proceeded in the re-organisation of endowed schools quite so fast as we could wish. Besides, endowed schools are distributed very unequally over the country. Whilst they are numerous in a small town like Bedford, they are few in a huge city like Manchester. They are naturally most plentiful in those places which formerly were seats of industry and of wealth, places almost without exception left to quiet and forgetfulness by the industrial revolution. So that if all the endowed schools of England could be re-organised in an instant, and with full consideration for those studies which naturally lead up to a technical training, even this would not meet all the wants of middle-class education.

In order to provide for our intermediate education, both as a whole and in its technical branches, we must call in the help of public bodies. Without this we cannot get a sufficient supply of good secondary schools evenly distributed over the whole kingdom. Such schools, experience has shown, cannot be cheap if they have to defray all their expenses out of the fees paid by their scholars. In order that they may be open, not merely to the children of prosperous men of business and professional men, but to the children of the struggling middle class, they must have help, if not from endowment, then from rates or taxes. The local authorities of counties and boroughs must be empowered to establish such schools, and to contribute to their maintenance. There is nothing unreasonable in this proposal. The rich man whose sons are at Eton or Harrow, at Trinity or Christ Church, cannot well deny the claim of the shopkeeper to give his sons an education better than he could provide out of his unaided means. The poor man, whose children are educated largely at the cost of the middle class, can scarcely grumble if the middle class receive public help towards its own education. Nor will any wise patriot grudge an expenditure so necessary, in order that the class which fills all but the highest post in all our industries may hold its own against the corresponding class in France or Germany, educated to the highest point by means of profuse expenditure of public money.

Secondary schools, built and equipped out of local funds, maintained partly by local subsidies, but partly by the fees of the scholars, and inspected by official experts, would differ considerably from the private adventure schools to which the middle class now entrusts its children. They would not supersede the private adventure schools, but they would kill out all that are hopelessly bad, and drive the rest to become better. These public schools should, of course, vary their curriculum according to the needs of different places. Where there already existed schools enough to satisfy all the demand for a literary education, the new schools should chiefly devote themselves to teaching natural science and modern languages. In other places they might be double—might have two 'sides,' as the phrase goes; the one chiefly literary, the other chiefly scientific. The majority of these public schools would correspond with the 'real' schools of Germany, and, besides discharging other functions, would prepare lads for that intermediate technical instruction which we have now to consider.

The term intermediate, as applied to technical education, is necessarily vague. Technical education, which must always drive at practice, and adapt itself to all the endless requirements of a thousand callings, does not admit of that clear and simple distribution which may be used in explaining a scheme of liberal education. The intermediate technical instruction discussed in this chapter is an instruction for students of many descriptions, for that minority of gifted workmen whose talent claims more than elementary training, for managers of departments in large works, for heads of establishments who lack time, means, or inclination for an elaborate culture, and for merchants and distributors who find their advantage in having some theoretical knowledge of the goods in which they traffic. Schools meant for the use of such a variety of persons must needs be very various in character. They may be roughly classified as follows:—I. Schools giving general technical instruction. II. Schools giving the technical instruction needed in particular industries. Among these schools we may distinguish building schools, mining and engineering schools, and weaving schools. III. Schools of industrial art. A few remarks respecting each of the above classes will show how rough is the classification even as applied to schools on the Continent. As applied to schools in our own country it is still rougher. But the absence of concert in our technical education baffles every attempt to classify our technical schools.

I. Schools giving a general technical education. The lower grade school of this class ranks just above the apprenticeship school—in fact, may be combined with it, as in several English institutions; the higher grade schools of this class rank just below technical schools of the first rank, such as the German Polytechnics or the Central Institution at South Kensington. The pupils of the inferior technical school will

R

come mostly from the public elementary schools; whilst the pupils of the advanced technical school will mostly come from the secondary schools. Thus intermediate technical schools may be classified according to the average age for admission in each instance. There will be one set of technical schools for those who wish to begin learning a trade at the age of thirteen years, and another set of technical schools for those who can defer learning a trade until they are sixteen years old. Intermediate technical schools of the lower grade are few in England. In France they are more plentiful. A French example will serve to show what schools of this class ought to be.

The Ecole Professionnelle Municipale of Rheims was founded in A.D. 1875, in order to help the youth of that city in getting a practical knowledge of manufactures and commerce. The pupils were to be drawn from such scholars at the primary schools as had passed their examination with credit, but others are admitted on passing an entrance examination in grammar, dictation, and arithmetic. Boys enter the school at the age of thirteen, and the course extends over three years. During the first two years all receive the same theoretical and practical instruction; but in the third year they are distributed, according to their aptitudes, between the sections of manufactures, mechanics, commerce, and agriculture. In this year eighteen hours a week are allotted to practical work in the shop. For the practical work a complete plant has been supplied at a cost of 20,000*l*. In the weaving and spinning department the student can apply his theoretical knowledge to the production of the various textiles manufactured at Rheims. He can spin and weave the wool which he has washed, carded, dyed, and prepared, and can perform each operation in the school with plant similar to that used in the factory. Drawing is taught on a method which appears to produce accurate and rapid draughtsmen. The students in the first year spend three months in drawing from sketches on the black-board; they then proceed to make freehand sketches of geometrical solids, tools, and parts of machines. These sketches are afterwards carefully figured for dimensions, and from them accurate drawings to scale are prepared. Finally they produce in the same way freehand sketches and finished drawings of the objects that they actually make in the workshop. In the second year seven, and in the third year six hours a week are devoted to drawing. The chemical laboratories are well equipped, and the scheme of instruction is so carefully arranged that the whole cost of 200 experiments performed by a student in his first and second year does not exceed five francs. A special laboratory is set apart for those students of the third year who intend to enter chemical works, and in this the chemistry of dyeing is taught.

The French schools of this class are highly recommended in the Report.

In the whole system of French instruction your Commissioners have found nothing, except as regards art teaching, which seems to them so worthy of attention as these higher elementary technical schools.—*Report*, vol. i. p. 84.

In the grade just above that of the higher elementary schools, the grade of secondary schools properly so called, come institutions such as the technical department of Firth College, Sheffield, or of University College, Nottingham, the Ecole Centrale of Lyons, and the Higher Trade Institute of Chemnitz. The Ecole Centrale of Lyons is a school for mechanical engineers who wish to complete their education at the age of nineteen or twenty years. The pupils usually become managers and superior foremen. The Commissioners thought that schools of this type might with advantage be established in our large towns. The Higher Trade Institute of Chemnitz in Saxony comprises four schools—a higher technical school for mechanists, chemists, and architects; a foremen's school for foremen employed in various industries; a building school for those who wish to follow any branch of the building trade; and a drawing school for everybody who cares to attend it. The age of the pupils is much the same as at the Ecole Centrale of Lyons. The outlay upon the school may show the value which the Saxons attach to technical instruction. The site and buildings cost nearly 82,000*l*. The annual expenses amount to upwards of 9,000*l*., of which the students' fees hardly cover one-sixth part. The rest is made up by a large subsidy from the State and a smaller subsidy from the town.

The efficiency of this school called forth the admiration of the Commissioners.

II. We now pass to the consideration of schools giving special instruction to persons preparing for some one industry. Among the schools of this class the German building schools form an important group. They are large and admirably appointed, supplied with eminent professors, and so moderate in their fees as to be readily accessible to the thrifty, industrious workman. The Building Trade School of Stuttgart is a fine specimen. It is housed in a magnificent building which cost more than 50,000*l*., and its annual expenses are defrayed chiefly by the State. Pupils are admitted at the age of fourteen years. The instruction is organised in two preparatory mathematical courses and three special scientific courses, designed respectively for those employed in the building trade, for land surveyors and land agents, and for mechanical engineers. The subjects taught include mathematics, physics, general geometry and statics, freehand and ornamental drawing, geometrical drawing, building construction, surveying, mensuration, machine construction, and special drawing for joiners.

Drawing in all its applications was most carefully taught, and the studies of the pupils evinced a thorough acquaintance with the subject.—*Report*, vol. i. p. 104.

No practical work is attempted in the school, as the scholars are presumed to be already working in the builder's trade. The attendance is always best in the winter, when building has to be suspended. It is instructive to compare this superb building school, situated in a petty capital, with the starved Building Trades Institute of the great city of Manchester.

The metallurgical school of Bochum, in Westphalia, is a good specimen of another class of special technical schools. It was established by the iron and steel manufacturers of the district, who were desirous that their foremen and leading hands should have some tincture of theory to help out the experience gained in the workshop. Only workmen are admitted, and candidates must have been employed for at least four years in iron-works or mechanical engineering works. Certificates of good conduct, competence, and elementary knowledge are also exacted. The whole time of the pupils is spent in the school. The course occupies three half-years, the first being devoted to general preparatory study, and the two following either to metallurgy or to the construction of machines, according to the vocation of each student. In the preparatory class the programme includes drawing, mathematics, physics, experimental chemistry, the principles of the metallurgy of iron and steel, the German language, and the keeping of accounts. In the metallurgical division these subjects are continued, and the construction of furnaces, smelting, making steel, the analysis of the raw material, and the testing of the finished product are also studied in detail. The mechanical division includes—besides the general subjects—instruction in theoretical and applied mechanics, in the properties of materials ordinarily used in machinery, in the construction of machines, and in the economy of the workshop.

The German building schools are not likely to have any direct result in making more severe the foreign competition which we now experience. The German schools of mining and metallurgy are quite recent; but the German weaving schools call for special notice, as having helped foreigners to rival us in our greatest industries. These schools teach whatever the master, the foreman, or the designer ought to know in reference to his trade, and they also impart to merchants, agents, distributors, and shopkeepers a thorough knowledge of textiles and the construction thereof. The schools are intended, not to supersede apprenticeship in the factory, but to convey knowledge which is not to be obtained save in exceptional factories. As a place in which to learn weaving, the factory is allowed to possess considerable advantages over any school. It is worked for profit—idleness is not allowed—everything is done under the spur of competition, and the necessities of business forbid anything conjectural, antiquated, or needlessly refined. On the other hand, the instruction given in the factory is merely instruction in routine. There is no time to explain the reason of anything, and labour is so minutely subdivided that every hand is limited to the incessant repetition of a single process. In England especially this subdivision has been carried to a degree which forbids the general knowledge of textiles to be obtained in any one factory, we might almost say in any one town.

Again, there are things not taught in any factory, and hardly to be acquired by the man who is earning his daily bread, which may, nevertheless, be of vital importance to the man of business whose personal aim it is not to execute more and more swiftly some constantly repeated operation, but to find out what the world wants and how that want can best be met. . . . Fashions can be set or they can be followed, and the student will find in his industrious experience how capricious and changeable they are; but experience will also teach him that whoever can satisfy the prevailing taste is sure of customers, and excellence in this respect stands on the same level with good wearing quality and low price. Moreover, this is the variable element, the quality with which calculation and experience of factory management have least to do, the one in which force and versatility carry all before them.

As is the case in other branches of industry—in pottery and porcelain, glass furniture and metal-work—where the higher qualities of design and artistic workmanship have developed trade and brought wealth to the producers, so in textile industry it is the design that sells the cloth. The quality of the fabric may be hard to tell, but every customer forms his own estimate of the pattern printed upon it or woven into it. The wool-comber, the spinner, the weaver may each do his part faultlessly, but if the design is unsatisfactory or inappropriate, or the colour or finishing of the piece ineffective, it will be cast aside by the purchaser as inferior the moment it is displayed on the shop counter against more effective, even though intrinsically less valuable work. False work, it is true, will not be permanently tolerated, even under the disguise of fair seeming; but it is folly in a manufacturer to neglect excellence in that department of his work where it tells most and costs least.—*Report*, vol. i. pp. 120-121.

The weaving schools of the Continent aim at giving a general acquaintance with various kinds of machinery and with a number of processes seldom carried on altogether, but they aim still more at giving familiarity with the arts of design. Some students have a natural gift for mechanism; others for art; but the mechanist learns a little art, and the artist comes to know something about machinery. Among these schools the German ones are pre-eminent; and, in Germany, those of Mulhausen, Crefeld, and Chemnitz take the foremost place.

As they are necessarily much alike, a brief description of the school at Crefeld may convey an idea of all the rest.

Students are admitted to the school at the age of fourteen if they can pass the entrance examination. The scale of fees is graduated for Prussians, for other Germans, and for foreigners. But the payments are low, a first year's course costing a Prussian only 6*l*., and a second year's course only 9*l*., with an extra fee of 5*l*. for the use of a private studio. There are scholarships which enable the poor student to take the benefit of the school without paying anything. The complete course of instruction extends over two years, but shorter courses may be arranged with the director. The course is divided into two sections—the theoretical and the practical: the first including a thorough study of drawing; the second including instruction on the loom. Drawing and painting are taught from copies and models, and from natural plants and flowers, with adaptations to printing and other branches of the textile industry. Due prominence is given to geometrical drawing and the drawing of machines, particularly of those parts of the loom which affect the pattern in the woven fabric. There are also lectures on textile fibres, on the elements of weaving, and on machinery. Fabrics are decomposed and explained, looms are arranged for weaving plain goods or goods with simple designs, and technical calculations and bookkeeping are carefully taught. In the second year lectures are given on the principles which govern the ornamentation of woven or printed fabrics, and the art teaching is continued until the student is able to invent and apply original designs. He is then admitted into one of the studios, where, under the guidance of qualified designers, he is encouraged to give play to his own imagination. At the same time he continues his studies in the decomposition of patterns, and in the composing and calculation of designed materials. He attends lectures on the construction, erection, and action of the looms and other machines used in weaving. He unmounts the power-loom piece by piece, and builds it up again. He works at the forge, and learns the use of the machine and hand-tools in the workshop; he cuts the cards in accordance with his own designs on the paper prepared by his own hands; he fixes the cards in the jacquard machine; and at length becomes thoroughly practised in weaving the most complex patterns, both in hand and power looms.

The weaving school of Crefeld is particularly remarkable for its museum of textile fabrics and patterns, perhaps the finest of the class in Europe. Besides cases of raw material and screens of modern silk and other textile designs, there is the Krauth collection of historical patterns, containing a wonderful variety of valuable specimens. The patterns are so arranged as to assist reference by students and designers. Upwards of 5,000 specimens are kept in glazed frames, which protect them from dust, yet can readily be removed when necessary. Others are arranged in cabinets in their due order from the tenth century to the present time. The school library contains more than 1,200 volumes of well-chosen books on art and the manufacture of textiles. The patent records are supplied by the Government, and the periodical literature includes the fashion papers from Paris and elsewhere. A large sum has been set aside for the purchase of books, and the library on certain days is open, not to teachers or students from the school only, but to the general public as well.

The dyeing and finishing department of the school is equally complete. Its aim is twofold: to give to those who wish to devote themselves to chemistry an education both in the science and in its practical applications, and to instruct dyers, bleachers, calico printers, and finishers in the manufacture of dyes and mordants, in the methods of examining and testing the value of dyes and other chemicals, and, lastly, to afford them the means of applying their knowledge to the practice of dyeing, bleaching, printing, and finishing. The buildings include, besides class-rooms, two chemical laboratories, a dyeing laboratory, and a dyeing and finishing house, furnished with new and complete machinery. Collections of specimens and a library are attached to the school. The course, extending over two years, includes the fullest instruction in machinery, drawing, textile fibres, physics, and, above all, chemistry.

Manufacturers are the best judges of the training given in a school of manufactures, and the leading citizens of Crefeld entertain the highest opinion of these schools. They informed the Commissioners that employers are always eager to secure young men who have been pupils there, and that old pupils can turn their knowledge to very good account. To the schools these gentlemen ascribed the extraordinary growth of their silk industry. When asked why the weaving school should pay so much attention to the manufacture of other materials—such as jute, wool, and cotton—they replied that they were anxious to introduce new manufactures as a fresh resource in bad times, and that in any case students who are to become designers or distributors of textile fabrics gain by making themselves familiar with every textile material.

In the Bradford Technical College and in the textile department of the Yorkshire College at Leeds we have schools which may fairly be compared with the weaving schools of Germany. But a general survey will show at once how few and how ill-provided are our special technical schools. Our general technical schools, although somewhat stronger, are still inadequate. In many of our manufacturing towns the citizens are now making vigorous efforts to amend this state of things. The City and Guilds Institute has undertaken to supply London with intermediate technical schools, and in the Finsbury Technical College has given a good model for imitation. It is to be feared, however, that English people do not understand the greatness of the task before them. None but thoroughly good technical schools are worth setting up in a country where practical skill is even now plentiful. In order to set up and maintain a good technical school we must have a well-considered plan and a copious and regular revenue. The best technical schools of France and Germany are at once grand in scale and elaborately wrought in the parts. Every detail has been worked out; every appliance has been provided; whilst a generous ideal has inspired the whole. But these schools have been in many instances founded, and are in all cases assisted, by the State, or by municipal bodies, and have, no less than the primary schools and the universities, their place in a vast scheme of national culture. There is some danger lest voluntary effort, unaided and undirected by any national agency, may issue in a crowd of incomplete and ill-organised schools. Another danger is that voluntary effort may not find a steady and abundant revenue to carry on the work of the schools when founded.

English people are methodic enough in business, but they are not methodic in education. When they become excited about their intellectual condition, they subscribe a large sum, erect a large building, concoct a programme of lectures, and think the matter ended. In truth the matter is only begun. For a seat of learning a fine edifice, although most desirable, is not the only thing needful. In the present state of knowledge a teaching institution cannot be efficient unless it have a staff so numerous as to allow of a minute subdivision of labour, and unless every member of the staff be really master of his own small province. But in England the demand for experts in applied science to assist in various manufactures is so great, and the salaries offered to them are so high, that they will always be tempted to quit the lecture-room for the factory. If they are to sit long in the professorial chair, it must be reasonably well cushioned. The staff of a technical school must be numerous, and it must be well paid; and to this end an ample endowment is necessary. The indispensable equipment of such schools, the apparatus, the museums, and the libraries in cost are second only to the staff. In short, a good technical school is an expensive thing.

For these reasons the assistance of the community will be wanted to finish the work which individuals have begun. It has been suggested that the School Boards should be empowered to found apprenticeship schools. The local authorities who may hereafter be judged fit to establish intermediate schools for general instruction should also be empowered to establish technical schools of a corresponding rank. Town councils should at once receive the power of making grants to technical schools within their jurisdiction. We have seen how constantly this power is exercised by municipal bodies on the Continent. At a later day, perhaps, the State may assume the business of inspecting and assisting technical schools. In the meantime the London companies would do nobly in enabling the City and Guilds Institute to increase the number and amount of its subsidies to colleges which are giving sound technical instruction. To strengthen the schools we have is even more urgent than to found new ones.

In founding intermediate technical schools we shall not

have much help from endowments under the control of the Charity Commissioners. Some of these endowments may be applicable to the provision of apprenticeship schools, but the bulk of them is wanted for schools of a general character. It is an illusion to think that we can have the charge of our technical education defrayed out of the bounty of our ancestors. We must take the burthen upon ourselves, and, after all, it is we, and not our ancestors, who will reap the advantage.

III. Schools of industrial art form a class distinct from all the schools heretofore discussed. It is difficult, and perhaps useless to draw a line between pure and applied art. It is difficult even to say which is better worth teaching, with a view to technical results. In this country the Science and Art Department began with trying to teach the application of art to manufactures, but now chiefly teaches pure art, and, through its art teaching, exercises a happy influence on our industries. The French have taken extraordinary pains to spread the knowledge of pure art, and find that industrial art takes care of itself. In their art schools the instruction is conformed to the principle that if only you can do enough for art, you are sure to do enough for industry; that if you can cultivate the workman's sense of beauty and power of rendering the beautiful, you will have done the best for his work and for the wealth of the community.

Drawing is taught from the purely artistic point of view, as this method is thought to be the only one by which the artistic power of the pupils can be encouraged and developed.—*Report*, vol. i. p. 35.

The French schools of art, supported by the State and the municipal bodies, are open free of charge; the buildings are spacious, well arranged, and well lighted; casts and models are lavishly supplied; the masters are skilful and enthusiastic; and the classes are crowded with eager pupils. The course of instruction is extensive. Thus the programme of the École Nationale des Arts Décoratifs includes mathematics, architectural construction, freehand drawing and ornament, modelling, drawing from the antique, drawing from life, the history of ornament and decoration.

The School of Fine Arts at Toulouse is well known as one in which a knowledge of drawing is rapidly acquired. The plan of teaching is as follows:—Classes of seven sit round a black-board, on which the monitor makes a sketch, which is copied on slates by the lads forming the class. There is a special class for monitors—seven or eight in number. From this room the boys pass into the next class, in which they begin to draw on sugar-paper with charcoal. Here they draw solid forms (what we should call model drawing), only in lieu of doing freehand work they are supplied with rulers, and encouraged to rule all the straight lines. The aim in this class is not so much to teach drawing as to teach a correct appreciation of form. The pupils begin with squares, cubes, prisms, and solid rectilineal figures, advancing afterwards to spherical forms and architectural details. When proficient in these exercises they learn copying from the flat, and then pass into the ornament room, where they make careful studies from lithographed copies of ornament; but some go to the model drawing room, and make shaded studies from solids. They can then commence drawing from the cast, and after a course of fragments, hands, and feet, they turn to the antique. Here the classes are divided, those intending to become painters and those studying as sculptors having each a separate course.

Elementary classes meet from six to eight o'clock on winter evenings, and from six to eight o'clock on summer mornings. These are attended chiefly by apprentices, and contain upwards of 1,000 pupils. Classes in mechanical drawing and projection are well attended. A good library is attached to the school.

In the Belgian art schools the boys begin by drawing geometrical forms with chalk on black-boards, which surround the walls of the room. When they can use the chalk with readiness they pass on to drawing similar forms with charcoal on sugar-paper. From outline drawing they advance to shading from the cast, and in the third year to drawing from the life. This method produces rapidity and boldness of work rather than precision. The Commissioners thought the quality of the drawing thus taught eminently suitable to artisans. The habit of rapid practice imparts such power of drawing as they require in a far shorter time than would suffice under the system adopted in English schools of art. Which of the two systems is better adapted to the needs of the artist may be a more doubtful question.

The industrial art schools of Germany differ from the art schools of France in laying more stress upon the application of art to manufactures. The schools of Dresden and Vienna are good examples of the class. That of Dresden has revived old and established new industries. Its work is to be found in every large shop in the city, and extends to every branch of industrial art. It contains no workshops, but the designs made by the pupils are sold to manufacturers. It is divided into the departments of designing, architecture, decorative painting, ornament, figure drawing, art modelling, and decorative painting from the figure. Besides the work done in the studios, there are lectures on such subjects as anatomy and the history of art. The school library contains 2,000 printed books and 16,000 mounted patterns and examples, together with 11,000 examples of embroidery and lace. It is open to the public, and is visited every year by thousands of persons. The school museum contains 140,000 patterns of textile fabrics of all kinds and of all ages. The director, at the time of the visit of the Commissioners, had studied in the University, in the Polytechnic School, and in the Berlin Academy of Arts. He was also a professional designer in metal-work, porcelain, furniture, wall papers, and textiles. He held that schools of this class should simply teach design, without making the objects designed. In the Vienna school a different plan is adopted. There carving, metal chasing, and working in brass and bronze are largely practised. The work done in wood-carving surpassed anything of the kind which can be seen in English schools, and all the workers were qualified to raise the standard of taste and execution in the workshops which they might enter.

Many of the students attending the industrial art schools maintain themselves by working elsewhere a certain number of hours daily, and selling what they make. These students are generally the most successful, because they have begun to attend the school after two or three years spent in seeking a livelihood have taught them their deficiencies, and inspired them with a wish to improve themselves. In South Germany the Fortbildung, or continuation schools, also serve as nurseries to the industrial art schools, and in them are produced excellent examples of modelling, carving, and smith's work. Thus in Germany, as in France, there is a wide diffusion of artistic taste and skill. Although the application of art to industry receives more attention in the German than in the French schools, yet the experts in both countries are thoroughly agreed upon the principles of artistic education. The German professors declare, with the French, that pure art is the groundwork of all good design, and that a thorough discipline in drawing is the key to an understanding of art.

If the student has any talent or art-feeling within him, his power of drawing will enable him to give it expression; but without thought and imagination there can be no originality in design. Mere knowledge of drawing will not make a man a good artist any more than knowledge of language will make him a poet; but designer and poet are helpless without the knowledge of the language by which their art can be expressed to others.—*Report*, vol. i. p. 237

The Germans, like the French, attach more value than we do to rapidity in drawing. One professor, with whom the Commissioners conversed, thought that the free use of charcoal and the stump, as practised in France, encouraged originality, boldness, and dexterity at the expense of precision and finish; whilst the English methods, which laid so much stress on exact outline and careful shading, fostered accuracy, but also timidity. He disapproved of the incessant competitions instituted in the French schools of art, considering that, although they might stimulate the sluggish, they exhausted the finer intellects. 'Genius in young men,' he said, 'needs oftener to be restrained than to be pushed forward, and constant competitions encourage some of the most prominent students to rush by leaps and bounds to the higher realms of pictorial representation before they have mastered the elementary rules of drawing and colouring.' (*Report*, vol. i. p. 239.)

The Commissioners came to conclusions resembling those cited above. They say that in England we do not lay enough stress upon combining rapidity with accuracy of drawing, and they insist repeatedly upon the necessity to the designer of a discipline in pure art. To quote their own words,—

Not until the student is thoroughly master of the various materials and processes by which art is capable of expression, and of the influence of style upon the development of fine arts, can the student do any good by concerning himself with the varieties of design, and the application of the same to industry. It is at this later period of his training when the designer can be materially benefited by placing before him well-selected illustrations of what the best designers and art workers of previous periods have achieved ; and it is here where the influence of industrial museums, collections of patterns, and drawings and exhibitions of art workmanship may exert a most powerful influence for good over the young designer. If, at the same time, we can make his work valuable to him by the actual use of what he is doing for the manufacturer or art workman, and if we can show him, further, how much more valuable his work may become to him in the future, by holding out to him the hope of a profitable and honourable career, we shall present the most powerful stimulus to the creation of the future designer. . . . The dignity of the designer's work and the importance of the position he occupies are not sufficiently acknowledged in our own country. . . . If the value of his labours were only acknowledged, . . . the 'artist designer' would soon take his proper rank in the country.—*Report*, vol. i. p. 165.

One of the witnesses examined by the Commission, Mr. Rawle, pointed out the good that the Royal Academy might do by recognising the art of design. The City Livery Companies might with advantage spend their wealth more freely than they have yet done in encouraging designers of talent to produce the highest possible work.

The evidence given before the Commission by several English witnesses confirms and illustrates the doctrines above laid down. Sir Edward Baines said that our paid professional designers obtained the material for their designs by copying from each other. He complained, and Mr. William Morris echoed the complaint, that they lack originality; that they are poor in thought. And Mr. Morris, no follower of outlandish fashions, declared that the French, above all other people, are masters of style in the arts of design. 'By mastery of style I mean,' he said, 'a kind of faculty which enables a man to take certain elements of form and work them into a congruous whole which strikes the eye at once. In appreciation 'for beauty,' he continued, 'in love for beautiful lines and colours, the French cannot be said to be superior to the English; certainly they are not superior in matters of colour.' If we may put the thing in other words, the Englishman is perhaps the equal, possibly the superior, of the Frenchman in artistic sensibility; but in the logic of art, in the discipline of the creative faculty, he is far inferior to him. Now, a good system of teaching in pure art is just the influence needed to rescue our designers from the bondage of imitation on the one hand, and from the anarchy of their own artistic impulses on the other. Doubtless we have made considerable progress in the arts of design. We are no longer *par excellence* the makers of hideous things; but we are only beginning our career as artistic manufacturers.

It is said that a famous English firm obtained a prize at the Paris Exhibition of 1878 for a cabinet entirely wrought by foreign artists. A Frenchman had furnished the design, a German had cut the marqueterie, and a German, assisted by a Dane, had done the work of the cabinet-maker.

It is not solely upon the number and excellence of their public schools of art that our neighbours rely for the maintenance of their artistic industries. In almost every one of the large towns of France, Belgium, and Germany may be found a good picture-gallery and a museum, either industrial or antiquarian. These galleries and museums are of the utmost service to the local schools of art and industry. The value of a picture-gallery in connection with a school of art is obvious. But the industrial museums are equally valuable to the technical schools. Among all the institutions for technical training which have made Mulhausen famous, none is more prized by the citizens than the museum of textile fabrics.

Some went so far as to say that they could not see how the trade could in any degree prosper without it. To the designer it is a constant source of inspiration. The museum is to him what the well-stored library is to the literary man, or a collection of the best pictures to a painter.—*Report*, vol. i. p. 354.

The usefulness of similar museums at Crefeld and Dresden

has been noticed elsewhere in this summary. In France, especially, the good done by galleries and museums has been thoroughly understood. The municipal bodies and the State work together with private munificence to multiply and enrich them. The State assists with grants of money and of such objects as can be spared from the national collection. Reproductions of works of art are invariably supplied on any request by local authorities. The control and management of the museums and galleries is shared between the central authority, which appoints directors, and the local authority, which appoints a committee of management.

In England only a few large towns have exerted themselves to diffuse a knowledge of industrial art, whether by means of schools or of galleries. Generally speaking, all that has been done with this object has been done by the Science and Art Department. In furtherance of the work of artistic instruction the Commissioners recommended the following changes. (i.) The abolition of the limit imposed by the Free Libraries Acts on the expense which local bodies may incur for the establishment of galleries and museums of art. One would suppose that in this matter the ratepayers were very well able to defend their own purses. (ii.) The abolition of the maximum of 500l. for the grant which the Science and Art Department may make in aid of the erection of local schools of art and museums in connection with them. Not only is this maximum in itself absurdly small, but it does harm by giving the public a mistaken idea of the outlay needed to make these institutions useful. The conditions accompanying even such grants as can now be made are embarrassing, and ought to be revised. (iii.) That the Department should not insist upon the payment of fees by artisans attending the art classes. (iv.) That in the awards for industrial design the Department should attend more than it does now to the applicability of the design to the material in which it is to be executed; also that the Department should make special grants for the execution of designs under such safeguards as would defeat fraud. Although experts are not all agreed on this point, it seems right, both on artistic and on commercial principles, that the designer should be familiar with and master of the material in which his design is to be executed. (v.) That the Department, which now supplies reproductions of works of art at a reduced cost, and lends collections of the works themselves to provincial galleries and museums, should also grant to them original examples of a nature to advance the industries of the several districts in which they are situated. (vi.) The opening of museums and galleries on Sunday.

These reforms, however, will not have their full effect without the help of individual munificence. England is rich beyond all other countries in private collections of art, and if the fashion of giving were once confirmed, these would be so many reservoirs to feed our public galleries. There is no better or safer mode of bounty than to enrich the community with gifts of this sort. They tend not merely to improve technical skill, but to civilise the whole people, to give them a taste for humane pleasures and a perception of the beautiful, and so, by degrees, to soften and to brighten that dull, hard world which the nation, as a nation, still inhabits.

C. *Advanced Instruction.*

The highest grade of technical education, what we may call the University grade, differs widely in its circumstances from the lower grades. The object of the highest technical instruction is twofold : first, to supply the national industries with the needful staff of experts in applied science; and secondly, to supply competent teachers to intermediate technical schools. As the number of persons who can find employment as experts and teachers is comparatively small, technical high schools need not be many, as compared with technical schools of inferior rank ; but, as everything depends on the quality of those teachers and experts, the institutions in which they are trained cannot be too complete or too efficient. The technical education of the common workman should be brought to his door if it is to be of any use ; the technical education of the student who has means and leisure will be near enough if it is good enough. Therefore, in providing for advanced technical instruction, the essential thing is to have a high standard of what such instruction ought to be. To try to make instruction altogether practical, to be too impatient for results, to exclude the spirit of research and the love of science—this is the certain means to make it poor, shallow, unfruitful, and, in the strictest sense, useless. The technical high school will do no good unless it is liberally planned. The noblest type of such a school is to be found in the Polytechnics of Germany and Switzerland. A very brief description of one of the most celebrated—the Polytechnic of Zurich—will serve to show what our intelligent neighbours think necessary for a technical high school. We should remember that Switzerland in extent is equal to about half of Scotland, in population is little superior to Yorkshire, does not contain a single large city, and may be termed a poor country.

The Polytechnic is housed in a vast edifice, which forms one of the most conspicuous features of Zurich. It includes seven special schools—of architecture, of civil engineering, of mechanical engineering, of chemical technology, of agriculture and forestry, a normal school, and a school of philosophical and political science. But the magnitude of the foundation will best be understood from the subjoined list of the collections which have been provided for the use of the students :—

1. Several libraries belonging, some to the school, some to the canton, and some to the city of Zurich.

2. Various collections belonging to the engineering and architectural divisions, and consisting of models, instruments, &c.

3. A collection of plaster casts of architectural ornaments.

4. A collection of specimens of construction and of materials used in building.

5. A collection of antique vases.

6. A collection of engravings, about 24,000 in number.

7. A collection of geometrical instruments.

8. A collection of models of machinery.

9. A collection of tools and models attached to the division of applied mechanical technology.

10. A collection of models of raw and finished products attached to the section of chemical technology.

11. A collection of mathematical and geometrical models.

12. A collection of interesting specimens, tools, &c., relating to forestry.

13. A collection of models, implements, and produce in all departments of agriculture.

14. A collection of specimens relating to natural history,

zoology, botany, mineralogy, geology, palæontology, and entomology.

15. An archæological collection.

16. A workshop for moulding and casting in clay and plaster.

17. A workshop for metal-work.

18. Laboratories for instruction in theoretical and applied chemistry.

19. A special laboratory for agricultural chemistry.

20. A cabinet of physical apparatus and a physical laboratory.

21. An institute of vegetable physiology, comprising a room for microscopic researches, a physiological laboratory, botanical collections, and hothouses.

22. A botanical garden with a museum for the general and botanical collections.

The chemical laboratories having become too narrow for the crowd of students resorting to them, the Federal Council recently voted a sum of 50,000l. for their extension. The staff is immense, and at the time of the visit of the Commissioners consisted of forty-five professors and thirteen assistants, exclusive of the tutors and the curators of the museums. An establishment of this magnitude is necessarily expensive. Modest as are Swiss salaries and economic as is Swiss management, the expenses amount to fully 20,000l. a year, and of this sum not one-fifth is recouped by fees received from the students. The fees must be low indeed, since those paid by a student of chemistry, including his laboratory charges, do not exceed 12l. a year.

A student must be at least eighteen years of age on admission. The length of the course of instruction varies in the various departments of the Polytechnic, but on an average is about three years. The instruction is scientific almost to a fault; thus there is no manual instruction in mechanical work. To quote the words of the Commissioners,—

This renowned school has from its very commencement endeavoured to impart the greatest possible extent of scientific instruction in each of its departments, and its efforts have been to direct thought and research of the highest kind in their application to industrial pursuits, and thus to bring about the necessary mutual interchange of ideas between science and practice ; and it has been so far successful that students have come to it from all parts of the world. The Commissioners had the opportunity of judging of the advantages which it has bestowed, not only upon Switzerland, but also upon Germany, by the number of thoroughly trained scientific men who have been educated within its walls, and who are now holding important positions in various industrial establishments which the Commissioners have visited.—*Report*, vol. i. p. 191.

The German Polytechnics in all their essential features resemble the school at Zurich. The services which they have rendered to German industry are unquestionable. Professor Zeuner, rector of the Dresden Polytechnic, pointed out to the Commissioners that in all the chief industrial centres of Germany the Polytechnic students were filling the posts of managers and directors. To their superior education he ascribed much of the advance of Germany in mechanical industry, and said that whereas Germans formerly purchased locomotives from abroad they now use only those which they build themselves. Professor Helmholtz very clearly explained not only the general advantage but also the absolute economy of employing as heads of departments persons conversant with the theory of their work, able to anticipate results and to calculate beforehand the quantity and quality of material required. How could it be otherwise ? Here in England Professor Huxley has told us that industry under its present condition depends almost entirely on either ' the application of science or the development of mechanical processes of complexity, requiring a great deal of attention and intelligence to carry them out.' But this intelligence and attention most people can exercise only after long training. In those industries which depend on chemistry for their first principles the advantage of the education given in the Polytechnic Schools is most apparent. In England, says Mr. Haeffely, there are very few chemists in print-works, and generally the sampler is not a chemist ('Report,' vol. iii. p. 2). Yet as a knowledge of art forms the basis of instruction for the designer, so a knowledge of chemistry is the true groundwork for the student of dyeing. Chemical industries, we read in the Report, are assuming more and more a scientific character, and a chemical works is nothing more than a large laboratory in which the victory remains to those who have been most scientifically educated. Reasoning from these facts, the commercial heads of colour-works in Switzerland and Germany have been led to the necessity of placing trained scientific chemists at the head not only of the whole establishment, but also at the head of every department in which a special manufacture is going on.

The extent to which the most successful Continental manufactures employ educated talent may be illustrated from the account given by the Commissioners of the chemical works of Messrs. Bindschedler and Busch, at Basle.

In the first place (they say) the scientific director, Dr. Bindschedler, is a thoroughly educated chemist, cognizant of and able to make use of the discoveries emanating from the various scientific laboratories of the world. Under him are three scientific chemists, to each of whom is intrusted one of the three main departments into which the works are divided. Each of these head chemists, who have in this instance enjoyed a thorough training in the Zurich Polytechnic, has several assistant chemists placed under him, and all these are gentlemen who have had a theoretical education in either a German university or in a Polytechnic school.—*Report*, vol. i. p. 223.

No less than ten well-equipped experimental laboratories, perfectly distinct from the workshops, were available for the researches of these highly trained chemists, who could also refer to a complete scientific library. Who ever heard of English chemical works so provided?

The number of the Polytechnic schools of Germany is much in excess of the actual demand for technical instruction. In the early part of this century the Germans found themselves immeasurably inferior in practical knowledge to countries like England. They were obliged to learn in the schools, if anywhere, much that Englishmen could learn in the workshop. Again, a generous emulation moved the states of Germany to vie with one another in making liberal provision for every branch of learning. Lastly, the old universities, fearing lest the spirit of disinterested inquiry which had hitherto animated their studies might be depressed by the introduction of studies pursued entirely for practical ends, were unwilling to make provision for technical education, and so forced the authorities to found for that purpose independent Polytechnic schools. Some of these causes have ceased to operate in Germany, and none have much influence in England. Although Oxford and Cambridge will remain, and ought to remain, the seats of liberal learning, cherished for its own sake, many other institutions of university rank, such as the great colleges of the capital, of Manchester, and Liverpool, have departments of applied science, which, if the necessary funds were forthcoming, might be expanded into Polytechnic schools. The Central Institute at South Kensington might become a true Polytechnic. In short, we have the nuclei of as many technical high schools as we require.

It is true that advantages may be discovered in the total separation of universities from Polytechnic schools. The multiplication of seats of learning is a good thing so long as it does not lower the intellectual standard. The rivalry between institutions similar, yet diverse, may be a spur to improvement. The exclusion of technical studies from the university course may favour the disinterested love of knowledge. But the separation of Polytechnic schools from universities involves a considerable waste of money and of power. With the utmost economy we shall barely have power and money enough to put technical education on a good footing. Neither the Central Institution in London, nor the colleges in such cities as Liverpool and Birmingham, are rich enough to increase their staff and their appliances to that degree which is imperatively demanded by the present state of knowledge. The money which we can spare should be spent upon a few great schools, not frittered away among a crowd of petty ones. Besides, we are so differently situated from the Germans that their mode of giving advanced technical instruction is not to be copied by us in every detail. The following remarks by the Commissioners clearly show where we may with advantage depart from German precedents:—

We should not wish every proprietor or manager of industrial works to continue his theoretical studies till the age of twenty-two or twenty-three years in a Polytechnic school, and so lose the advantage of a practical instruction in our workshops (which are really the best technical schools in the world) during the years from eighteen or nineteen to twenty-one or twenty-two, when he is best able to profit by it.

In determining what is the best preparation for the industrial career of those who may expect to occupy the highest positions, it is necessary to differentiate between capitalists who will take the general, as distinguished from the technical, direction of large establishments, and those at the head of small undertakings, or the persons more specially charged with the technical details of either. For the education of the former ample time is available, and they have the choice between several of our modernised grammar schools, to be followed by attendance at the various colleges in which science teaching is made an essential feature, or the great public schools and universities; provided that in these latter science and modern languages should take a more prominent place.

Either of these methods may furnish an appropriate education for those persons to whom such general cultivation as will prepare them to deal with questions of administration is of greater value than an intimate acquaintance with technical details. It is different in regard to the smaller manufacturers and to the practical managers of works. In their case sound knowledge of scientific principles has to be combined with the practical training of the factory, and, therefore, the time which can be appropriated to the former—that is, to theoretical instruction—will generally be more limited.

How this combination is to be carried out will vary with the trade and with the circumstances of the individual. In those cases in which theoretical knowledge and scientific training are of pre-eminent importance, as in the case of the manufacture of fine chemicals, or in that of the metallurgical chemist or the electrical engineer, the higher technical education may with advantage be extended to the age of twenty-one or twenty-two. In the case, however, of those who are to be, for example, managers of chemical works in which complex machinery is used, or managers of rolling mills, or mechanical engineers, where early and prolonged workshop training is all-important, the theoretical training should be completed at not later than nineteen years of age, when the works must be entered and the scientific education carried further by private study, or by such other means as do not interfere with the practical work of their callings.—*Report*, vol. i. pp. 514–516.

NOTE ON TECHNICAL INSTRUCTION FOR WOMEN.

The Commissioners found schools for the industrial and professional training of girls in most of the large towns in the countries visited by them. These schools closely resembled each other. They are intended chiefly for the daughters of small shopkeepers and well-to-do artisans. In most of them the education given in the primary school is continued and supplemented by instruction in one foreign language and in drawing. Drawing is particularly well taught in these schools. At the same time the pupils are taught one or more trades. The technical instruction varies with the habits and industries of the various countries. In almost all the schools needlework and dressmaking are subjects of the first importance. In many of the French schools the girls learn bookkeeping, the elements of law, and commercial correspondence. In the German and Austrian schools the technical teaching is almost wholly restricted to plain sewing, embroidery, dressmaking, millinery, laundry work, and cooking. In Belgium, Holland, and Italy it includes the making of artificial flowers, the designing of lace, painting on fans, glass, or porcelain, typography, telegraphy, and pharmacy. Many of the pupils pay substantial fees, but some hold exhibitions from the primary schools. Inquiry showed that the education given in these schools was thoroughly practical, and enabled many young women to find suitable employment without having to leave their homes.

The Royal School of Art Embroidery at Vienna is entirely technical. Girls seeking admission must be at least fourteen years of age, and must have completed their education at the primary school. They must be able to draw, and must have a thorough knowledge of plain needlework. The course of instruction extends over five years. All the pupils are taught freehand drawing. They have to prepare written accounts of the lectures given by the professors. They are taught every kind of fancy needlework and designing for needlework, and at the end of each year they work samplers, to show their proficiency. Foreign students have to pay fees, but natives are admitted free of charge. Many of the girls become teachers in Austria and in other countries. The directress, at the time of the visit of the Commissioners, was a lady whose books on the subject of embroidery are regarded as standard works. The Commissioners thought the instruction given here the highest which they had found given in any school of the same class.

The Embroidery School of Vienna is a special school devoted to the cultivation of one art. But technical schools for women, somewhat more general in character, might with advantage be established in our large towns. In such schools the morning hours would be devoted to the study of languages, drawing, and elementary science, and the afternoons would be set aside for practical instruction in some industry. At present the art schools afford almost the only means which women have of learning a craft whereby to support themselves; but the art schools are overcrowded, and few women are meant by nature to be artists. If it is urgent to open up new pursuits for men, how much more urgent is it to open up new pursuits for women! Above all, women should have every means of becoming skilled in industries which can be combined with domestic life.

III. Technical Instruction in Agriculture.

Grave difficulties beset the improvement of agricultural education. Agriculture is practised by men who believe much in tradition and little in science. Country people, living apart from one another, are less capable of concerted voluntary action than are the inhabitants of cities. The administration of our rural districts is certainly not framed so as to supply the lack of spontaneous energy. Just now these districts are somewhat impoverished and particularly averse to paying new rates. All these considerations limit the range of practical proposals for giving that technical instruction which has become more than ever necessary to the prosperity of English agriculture.

Having quite enough to do in other branches of the inquiry into technical education, the Commissioners assigned the agricultural branch to their Sub-Commissioner, the late Mr. Jenkins, Secretary to the Royal Agricultural Society of England. Mr. Jenkins drew up a report, which will be found in the second volume of the Report of the Commission, and which gives a full view of the methods of agricultural education adopted in France, Germany, Denmark, Holland, and Belgium, as well as in the United Kingdom. In this respect all these countries differ extremely from one another. The agriculture, and therefore the agricultural education of every country, varies with the varying physical and economical conditions, so that foreign examples are to be used more cautiously in this than in any other department of our inquiry. Here it will be enough to note what has already been done in the United Kingdom to further agricultural instruction, and what recommendations for its advancement have been made by Mr. Jenkins and adopted by the Commissioners.

What has already been done may be briefly summed up. In England the State has recognised instruction in the principles of agriculture as instruction in elementary science, which may be taken up as a class subject in elementary schools. It has established an agricultural department in the Normal School of Science, has appointed a professor of agriculture, who lectures at South Kensington, and has provided for the formation of an agricultural class in any place which may desire to have one. In Scotland the agricultural instruction given in elementary schools is much the same as in England. The State pays a small stipend to the Professor of Agriculture in the University of Edinburgh. In Ireland the authorities have done more than in England or in Scotland. The principles of agriculture are taught in the elementary schools; but they are better taught, because the National Schools Board has a model farm at Glasnevin, near Dublin, where teachers in elementary schools receive practical instruction in agriculture; and many of the schools under the Board have school gardens or small farms, where the teachers can illustrate their agricultural lessons and accustom the pupils to agricultural work. The Munster Dairy School is also a Government institution. Other agricultural schools were formerly maintained by the State, but were sacrificed to what many consider a mistaken policy.

Something has been done, too, by agricultural associations and by private enterprise. The agricultural colleges at Cirencester and Downton give an excellent training to those who can afford to pay heavy fees. The Royal Agricultural Society of England, and similar societies in England and elsewhere, hold examinations and give prizes to the candidates who distinguish themselves. By means of their journals, by exhibitions of live stock and agricultural produce, and by various other expedients, these societies do much to extend the farmer's professional knowledge and to sustain his professional enthusiasm. The experimental farm at Rothamstead, founded and endowed by Sir John Lawes, is a unique and magnificent laboratory of agricultural research. But, after taking account of all these agencies, it may be said that the technical education of the ordinary farmer—English, Scotch, or Irish—is almost wholly empirical, and his technical skill the result of extreme subdivision of labour.

The recommendations made by Mr. Jenkins for the improvement of technical instruction in agriculture may be summarised under the heads of primary, intermediate, and advanced instruction. Primary instruction in agriculture is for the farm labourer, farm bailiff, or small farmer. To some extent this instruction could be given in the public elementary schools of country parishes. Agriculture should be made one of the compulsory subjects in rural schools. Each school should be provided with a garden proportioned to the number of scholars, and in this garden they should be employed for a certain time every day. Together with this practice they would have a series of elementary lessons on the principles of agriculture. Children in the first three standards would have lessons on the common objects of rural life, the familiar animals and plants of the country. In the higher standards they would study these in particular reference to agriculture. They would also study the construction of farm implements and simple agricultural machinery, and of simple mechanical and physical apparatus, such as the lever, pulley, wheel and axle, spirit level, barometer, and thermometer. This obligatory course would take the place of the optional course in the principles of agriculture which is now comprised under the title of elementary science. On the above scheme every child going to a country school would obtain some insight into the principles of agriculture, and the common labourer would cease to be merely a living tool.

But for the clever lads of the labouring class who might

hope to rise higher, and for the sons of the small farmer, a further training would be necessary. For these Mr. Jenkins proposed a new system of instruction, suggested by the French farm schools. He stated his plan as follows :—

In each county there should be selected a good farm, the tenant of which would agree under certain terms to take agricultural apprentices for a term of, say, two or three years, according to the age at which the apprenticeship commenced. On most grounds I should prefer an agricultural district to a county as the definition of the area, but as the county is the only local unit in country districts which calls forth local energy, it is necessary to select it for my present purpose. It would be a great advantage if to each farm there could be attached a teacher capable of continuing the general education of the apprentices by lessons given in the mornings and evenings, but the remainder of whose time might be otherwise employed, according to local circumstances—for instance, as rate-collector, bookkeeper, &c.—or he might also be teacher during the remainder of the day at some neighbouring school. He should be capable of teaching the elements of chemistry, land-surveying, book-keeping in a simple way, and the elementary principles of agriculture. Most of this technical instruction could be given during the winter evenings, and the apprentices should be entitled to pass the examinations of the Science and Art Department in the same way as the pupils of science classes, if they desired to do so, and to earn for themselves and their instructors all the distinctions and rewards that are given to pupils and teachers in elementary schools and science classes.

I am not inclined to follow the French system in requiring that all the farm labour should be performed by the apprentices; on the contrary, in my opinion it would be better to limit their number to a manageable one, according to the size of the farm, say from three to six in each year. This number, with an apprenticeship of three years, would make a maximum of from nine to eighteen on the farm at any one time; and of course the older apprentices would, or at least should, be worth more as workmen than the ordinary farm labourers.

The apprentices should be selected from those who distinguish themselves most in an examination held annually in connection with that of the Science and Art Department; and to a great extent, or perhaps entirely, the same papers might suffice for both examinations. . . . If the number of elementary school scholarships and of science and art scholarships were increased with a view of encouraging such farm schools, by making a certain number of the scholarships tenable at them, they would be more likely to be established and to work successfully. . . . During their stay at the farm school the apprentices should be compelled to pass an annual examination in practical as well as theoretical subjects, and prizes might be given for proficiency; but in the event of any of the apprentices being found deficient in knowledge up to a certain point, their apprenticeship should cease. At the termination of their apprenticeship they should receive a certificate of proficiency according to merit.

In a somewhat similar manner girls not less than sixteen years of age might be sent to learn dairying and household work at selected dairy farms, such as those which abound in Germany and Denmark.

I would suggest that a period of three months should be the minimum, but that a complete season of from, say, the middle of March to the middle of November would be much better.

My impression is that a sufficient number of good farmers would be found to take farm apprentices and dairy apprentices from public elementary schools in their own locality or county upon terms that would fairly reimburse them for two accessory reasons: —(1) They would be contributing to remove the present inefficiency of the farm labourers and dairymaids in their districts; and (2) they would be likely to receive as pupils sons of wealthy people, at highly remunerative terms, in consequence of their farms being recognised as 'County Farm Schools.'—*Report*, vol. ii. pp. 316-318.

In consequence of the recognition of agriculture by the Science and Art Department, many agricultural classes have been established in various parts of the United Kingdom. These classes resemble in their organisation the classes in science and art so often mentioned in this summary. They are usually held in market towns and in the evenings. Mr. Jenkins was of opinion that 'very few indeed of these teachers can give instruction in objective agriculture. They may have learnt the words of the language, and they can teach them, but they do not know their signification; in fact, they cannot translate them.' But he allowed that 'some of the teachers are thoroughly well-qualified men, and do really good work.' ('Report,' vol. ii. p. 231.)

The education of the teachers themselves must determine the usefulness of their teaching, and their education cannot be complete until it includes a regular course of practical work on a farm, for which apparently provision has not yet been made. If the farm schools suggested by Mr. Jenkins were in operation they would afford practical instruction to those who wished to teach agriculture under the department, and the apprentices at the farm schools could get scientific instruction by going to the lectures of the teachers. In this way the lower and intermediate instruction of farmers would attain a fulness hitherto unknown. But so long as a course of practical lessons is not included in the qualification of a lecturer on agriculture he will be of little use, and will inspire less confidence. The agricultural course of the schools of science at South Kensington might also be made more strictly professional than it is at present; but of this we shall have to speak a little later.

We next come to intermediate instruction in agriculture suitable for the ordinary tenant farmer, farm steward, or land agent. The obstacles to the spread of this instruction arise partly from the nature of agricultural education itself, but still more from the bad state of secondary education, and the absence of any energetic administrative power in the counties. Those who are to receive intermediate instruction in agriculture ought to receive also a good general education. Whether they can do this at present depends on the accidental distribution of efficient schools. In most districts such schools are scarce, and the education of the tenant farmer is exceedingly defective. Anybody who knows the rural parts of England can recall cases of men who farm, say, three hundred acres each, and in general culture are little, if at all, superior to an intelligent artisan. The education of the middle class in the country, even more than in towns, will never be put on a thoroughly sound footing without help from local authorities, such as do not yet exist in the counties. Given good middle-class schools, we have yet to find the means of imparting agricultural together with general instruction. For men must begin to farm early in life if they are to like farming or to become able farmers. Mr. Jenkins suggested that in each of the chief middle-class schools in rural districts there should be established a farming department, with a farm of perhaps one hundred acres attached. On this farm all the principal kinds of agricultural produce would be raised, and the boys would in turn share in all the branches of work. Everything should be conducted in a practical manner, and a skilled director of the farm would be necessary.

It is admitted that there would be some trouble in finding the means needed to carry out this scheme. The school-farm ought to pay its expenses and yield a profit, otherwise it would not be a place in which to train practical farmers. But the first outlay upon it would be considerable.

If we suppose that the school-farm has an area of one hundred acres, it would be desirable to provide under all the circumstances a working capital of 20*l*. per acre, or say 2,000*l*. In some cases it would be necessary to spend money in either a farm-steading or a house for a farm manager, who should be the working bailiff; but it is impossible to give any estimate on this head. Extravagance, however, should be distinctly prohibited, and a complete set of new farm buildings should not be allowed to cost more than 10*l*. per acre. Additional annual expenditure would be required for the salaries of the agricultural teacher and the farm bailiff, and for the maintenance of the experimental field (for purposes of demonstration only) and the botanic garden. An allowance of 500*l*. per annum would be amply sufficient for these purposes, and would leave a margin to be spent in gradually increasing the means of instruction, such as natural history collections.

Scholarships and exhibitions would, of course, diminish the amount of money available out of the profits of the farm towards the payment of the items just mentioned. After a few years' experience, and by keeping a reserve fund, any rewards drawn from that source might be rendered tolerably equal.—*Report*, vol. ii. p. 314.

Mr. Jenkins suggested that the county in which such a school was situated might raise by subscription the capital sum necessary for its equipment, if the Government would contribute to the building fund such a grant as it now makes for the erection of a school of science. Subscribers of not less than a certain sum might be rewarded with the privilege of nominating a pupil to be received for half the usual fees. The exhibitions granted by the Crown in the existing science schools might be made tenable at a farming school, and the Crown might annually grant a scholarship tenable at the Normal School of Science, or at the Agricultural College of Cirencester or Downton, to the best pupil in each of the farming schools.

Agricultural education of the most advanced kind is more flourishing than primary or intermediate agricultural education, because the class which wants it can afford to pay a heavy price for it. The agricultural colleges of Cirencester and Downton are able to meet all their expenses, and are doing their work well. They are attended chiefly by the sons of landowners and of tenants of the largest farms. They charge fees, indeed, much beyond the capacity of the ordinary farmer's purse. But experience has shown that the ordinary farmer, even when scholarships are available to meet the expense, distrusts a technical training continued to so late a time in life. He prefers to put his sons to work before they have reached the age of twenty-one or twenty-two years. His judgment is probably justified in the majority of cases. For the minority, for the boys of unusual talent, and for the fathers of unusual ambition, the suggested Queen's Scholarships would provide. There would be no use in taxing the public to multiply scholarships or reduce fees at the agricultural colleges merely for the benefit of the sons of rich men.

For a supply of teachers of agriculture we should be able to look less to the agricultural colleges than to the agricultural department of the School of Science at South Kensington. Mr. Jenkins found several faults in the course of instruction given there. He thinks it unduly prolonged, and would reduce it to three years; he thinks it too much burthened with non-professional subjects, and would omit some of these, imposing an entrance examination to test the general knowledge possessed by candidates for admission; and, finally, he thinks that it is not practical enough, that it embraces too many lectures and too few demonstrations.

No scheme of technical instruction in agriculture would be complete unless it made provision for teaching forestry. Great Britain and Ireland contain large tracts of desolate land which might be planted with valuable timber. Some of the commonest trees are almost worthless, and might be replaced with more useful species. Our older colonies already feel the bad effects of the reckless destruction of forests. The Governments of India and Cyprus have dedicated a branch of the public service to the preservation and management of the forests. Every enlightened country of the Continent has one or more schools of forestry; but the whole subject of forestry, as it concerns the United Kingdom, is now under the consideration of a Select Committee of the House of Commons, and it seems better not to anticipate the conclusions which they will be able to found upon the fullest evidence.

IV. CONCLUSION.

We have now taken a rapid survey of the whole field of technical education. It only remains to sum up, as briefly as possible, the results of this survey.

In the first place, technical education, although a most important branch, is only one branch of national education. If national education is bad, technical education cannot be good. Neither the workman, nor the foreman, nor the designer, nor the employer can profit by a technical training unless he has first been trained to use his mind and to feel pleasure in using it. Technical training merely directs into the channels of the various industries that activity of intellect which is called forth by a good general training in literature, science, or art. The first step, therefore, in establishing a complete system of technical education is to supply as far as possible all deficiencies in our system of general education; and more especially to perfect our elementary and intermediate schools.

In the second place, schools established to give special technical instruction must be carefully suited to the wants of the particular trades for which they are intended. They must give really useful instruction, and give it in such places, at such times, and generally in such a manner as to be available to all who would like to profit by it. If the instruction is to be really useful, it must be made as thorough and scientific as possible. The indifferent technical school will soon be found out, despised, and deserted. Our manufacturers and agriculturists already know too much to take lessons of bad teachers. If we cover the country with third-rate technical schools, we shall find, too late, that we have spent our money and our pains merely in strengthening that distrust of theory which is already too strong in the half-educated Englishman. We shall have wasted the season of enthusiasm and destroyed the hopes of technical education. At the same time the technical schools must accommodate themselves to the circumstances of industrial life. Especially the primary technical school must be accessible, cheap, and practical, or it will not attract the common workman, with his small surplus of time, money, and energy. The higher technical school is not bound by such strict conditions; yet it must constantly keep in view the needs of industry. It must so contrive its courses of science and art that they shall not clash with the empirical training which can be had only in the factory or the workshop. Extremely difficult is the reconciliation of theoretical with practical instruction; but upon this reconciliation the whole usefulness of a technical school depends. And it must be remembered that utility, as distinct from culture, is the aim of every technical school.

Thirdly, we must remember that a good technical school cannot be a good commercial speculation. Its buildings, its equipment, its teaching staff, all are costly, and their cost cannot be recouped out of fees paid by scholars, for high fees would exclude those who must form the bulk of the scholars at all but a few technical schools. Not only must the expense of establishing a technical school be defrayed either out of voluntary subscriptions, or out of rates and taxes, but the expense of maintaining it must, in a considerable degree, be defrayed from the same sources. The income derived from fees must be supplemented with a further income more permanent and trustworthy. The wise founders of old time did not exhaust their bounty in building; they also provided for the sustenance of the schools and colleges which they founded; and each school or college, having proved its worth, contrived subsequently to supply what might at first have been wanting to the size or splendour of its home. Modern founders, in their anxiety to leave handsome monuments, too often forget to provide a fund for maintenance, and leave an institution to feel the full severity of a struggle which cripples its usefulness, or even shortens its life. As the flow of subscriptions sinks or swells with the national prosperity, and with the passing fancies of the public mind, a technical school should always have an endowment, and if it has no endowment, it should, on fulfilling reasonable conditions, receive a subsidy from local or imperial funds.

Lastly, our technical schools must be brought into relation with one another and with schools of other descriptions. If they are left without co-ordination, some of the work will be done twice over, and much of the work will not be done at all. This co-ordination is almost impossible unless we establish a centre of knowledge and of power in reference to technical, such as we have already established in reference to elementary, education. Voluntary effort can do much, and to it we must chiefly trust. But if voluntary effort cannot guarantee to all the technical schools in the kingdom a revenue adequate to their needs, still less can voluntary effort assign to each of them its right place and function in a scheme of technical training adequate to the necessities of the greatest industrial society in Europe. Soon or late the Government will be forced to inspect and to assist technical schools. It is possible so to contrive this inspection and assistance as not to dry up the stream of private liberality. The experience of other countries, and of our own, the public spirit shown by rich men in France and Germany, the magnificent gifts made to such institutions as the museum at South Kensington or the National Gallery, all tend to show that private munificence can be led to flow copiously in the channels provided by public authority. It is natural that this should be so. The desire of connecting their names with great and durable institutions, of the assurance that their gifts will be well employed, encourage men to acts of liberality which they would not perform for a merely transient object, or under a depressing uncertainty as to whether they could effect any good at all.

INDUSTRIAL ART IN SCHOOLS.[1]

BY CHARLES G. LELAND, OF PHILADELPHIA.

LETTER.

DEPARTMENT OF THE INTERIOR,
BUREAU OF EDUCATION,
Washington, D.C., November 20, 1882.

SIR,—I have the honour to forward herewith the manuscript of an article prepared by Charles Godfrey Leland, Esq., of Philadelphia, on the subject of industrial art in schools. Mr. Leland's paper is a presentation of the matter from his standpoint, and the result of his own work and experience. No one can fail to see how valuable it is as a contribution to the solution of existing problems in education, art, and industry.

I recommend its publication as a circular of information, and am, sir, very respectfully, your obedient servant,

JOHN EATON, *Commissioner.*

The Hon. the SECRETARY OF THE INTERIOR.

Publication approved.

H. M. TELLER, *Secretary.*

I. INTRODUCTION.

Order of Development of Decorative and Industrial Art.

CONSTRUCTIVENESS, or the faculty of making things which are useful or ornamental, is in man innate or instinctive. It might be said that to produce useful objects is the result of the struggle for life; but the tendency to create that which is simply artistic results from no such urgent need, yet it is found wherever the former exists. In the rudest prehistoric times, in the earliest stone age, men and women made ornaments, though they were only strings of the commonest shells or beads of dried clay. Before the mammoth and cave bear had disappeared primeval men etched with great skill and taste their likenesses on their own bones. Great stress may be laid on the fact that, as the flower precedes the fruit, decorative art is developed in a race

[1] *Circulars of Information of the Bureau of Education,* No. IV., 1882.

before it attains proficiency in the practical. Before men had good axes or knives, ploughs or saws, they made jewellery and embroidery far superior in many respects to anything now produced anywhere. We can imitate the shield described by Homer, but the artist does not live who could design anything so elegant and original.

This universal truth, that man develops the ornamental during the infancy of every race before the useful, is illustrated in every individual. The child who cannot as yet make a shoe or file metals or master a trade can, however, learn to design decorative outline patterns, mould beautiful pottery, set mosaics, carve panels, work sheet-leather and *repousser* or emboss sheet brass. He or she can cut and apply stencils, model *papier-mâché*, or *carton-pierre* (a mixture of composition and paper pulp), inlay in wood, and make a great variety of elegant objects. The child corresponds to the primitive man. It is not improbable that the brain of the boy of twelve of this age, if it could be measured, would be found to be about the same as that of the early man of thirty. It has been definitely ascertained that the brains of the Parisian of the thirteenth century, a period when Gothic art in all its luxuriance adorned every object, were much smaller than they now are.

Educational Significance of this Order.

The deduction from this is that, as the child is capable of executing works of simple or easy decorative art before it can produce much that is useful, we should consider this fact in education. Of late years, almost simultaneously, the men who are interested in education have asked one another, 'How is it that we have taught the young nothing but reading, writing, and similar arts? We have given what we call culture to youth, and they leave school as little fitted to make a living as on the day they entered it.' It was very natural indeed that this complaint should rise from the growing republicanism of the age, and it was quite as natural that those who inspired it should demand that children should be taught to make a living while learning to read, write, and cipher. Of course by 'making a living' working at a *trade* was understood, and the first effort in consequence was to teach trades. And this for boys under fourteen years of age has not been a success. If it had really been possible for little boys and girls to make shoes, file iron and brass, and set type, capital would have long ago employed them; as it is, the fact is patent that to thus employ them is cruelty. It is not really right that children should ever be employed at uncongenial pursuits.

But as the Hebrews said of old that when the tale of bricks is doubled Moses comes, so the question rose as to what children could make at the time when there was simultaneously spreading over the civilised world a demand for decorative and hand-made art. The vast developments of capital, wealth, and science during the present century have naturally led to luxury and culture. With them scholarship and criticism are teaching wealth how to employ itself. Culture has also awakened humanity or benevolence. And it is gradually or rapidly being realised that children can while at school profitably practise decorative arts. It is also quite as true that this practice, far from interfering with the 'regular studies,' actually aids and stimulates them. While the minor arts, guided by a slight knowledge of decorative design, are so easy as to be regarded by all children as a recreation, they are at the same time of practical value in training the eye and hand and awakening quickness of perception. There have come under my observation a great number of instances in which children who have been regarded as dull in everything have shown great aptness and ingenuity in designing, modelling, or carving. When this skill is awakened, there comes with it far greater cleverness in those studies or pursuits in which the pupil was previously slow. I believe it to be a great truth, as yet too little studied, that sluggish minds may be made active, even by merely mechanical exercises. This holds good as regards the practice of the minor arts by children. It is somewhat remarkable that while every one is quick to observe mental ability or activity when transmitted from progenitors, very few notice the innumerable instances in which it is developed by education or circumstances. It is not a matter of theory, but of fact and observation, that all children who practise decorative arts are thereby improved both mentally and morally. The consciousness of being able to make something well which will sell gives them proper pride and confidence in their ability to master other studies. It also conduces to quiet habits and content. Every mother knows the value of a box of tools or of a small printing-press, of paints, and clay. When the use of these is properly taught in an artistic manner, children take unusual interest in them, as I have had ample opportunity to observe in the Public Industrial Art School of Philadelphia, which I have directed since its beginning. A girl of twelve loves modelling none the less for being taught how to make a vase which may be worth ten dollars.

A much larger proportion of all the elegant art work of India, Persia, Egypt, or indeed of the whole East, is made by mere children than we of the West would imagine. Much of the most elaborate wood-carving of Italy, the Tyrol, Bavaria, and Switzerland is cut by little fingers. Art pottery in Spain employs very young girls and boys. Of late years it has been definitely ascertained that very little children in the kindergarten organised on the plan of Fröbel are capable of developing much more artistic ability than has been supposed; and this, far from straining the mind, strengthens it. If a child can learn to sew, read, sing, draw, and model in the kindergarten, it can surely pursue higher branches, both literary and manual, in higher schools. The system on which this industrial art work should be taught is as follows: It does not merely consist of certain definite branches, such as modelling or carving according to patterns; *it is the learning how to design the patterns, and then working them out in any material*, such as wood, clay, brass, embroidery stuffs, or stencils. There are fifty or a hundred such minor arts, and anybody who can draw or design can with very little practice in a few days execute them fairly in any substance which will retain impressions. It is a remarkable law of nature or of humanity that all the minor arts, or such branches of industry as are allied to ornament, are very easy, and can generally be so far mastered in a day by anybody who can draw as to enable the pupil to produce a perfectly encouraging result. But industrial art, to be taught in schools, need not and should not be limited to ornamental work. This is to be at first followed simply because it is the *only* work easy enough for children and girls. Carpenter's work, or joinery, in its rudiments, or in fact any branch of practical industry, may be taken up as soon as the pupil is fitted for it. Industrial art in schools covers the ground or fills the time intervening between the kindergarten and the industrial school, but it blends with and includes the latter. It is characteristic in this that the system, as I conceive it, is capable of being introduced into every public or private school in the country, or into any institution where there is a preceptor who has some knowledge of drawing, with sense enough to apply it according to certain elementary handbooks of art. To aid all such teachers I have prepared a series of cheap artwork manuals.[1] These consist of instructions in decorative design, ceramic or porcelain painting, tapestry or dye-painting, outline and filled-in embroidery, decorative oil painting, wood-carving, *repoussé* or sheet brass-work, leather-work, *papier-mâché*, modelling in clay, with underglaze faïence decoration, and stencilling. The illustrations, working size, of one book are generally applicable to all. As I know of no other cheap manuals of the kind in any language which can be used for instruction, I have been compelled to prepare these as an absolutely necessary aid to those who cannot obtain teachers.

Outline Drawing and Design as a Preparation for Industrial Art Work.

Before setting forth the practical details of industrial art work for schools I would say something as to the method of drawing on which it is all based. This consists of making the pupil design original freehand patterns as soon as he or she can draw a clear, light line with accuracy and confidence. The boy or girl should be taught to draw such a line, like a spider's web or hair, on rather smooth paper, with a sharp, long, *hard* pencil. There should be no re-drawing on the line, no stumping, rubbing, or scratching, or sketching in breaks. As soon as this can be done let the pupil copy any simple leaf or ornament accurately, and then repeat it, let us say, twelve or twenty times in a circle, but in varying positions and of various sizes, so as to make a garland. After this, various kinds of finials or ornaments, such as the spots on a pack of cards, buds, flowers, leaves,

---

[1] Mailed for 35 cents each, by the Art Interchange Co., 140 Nassau Street, New York.

trefoils, fleurs-de-lis, &c., with stems added, may be made into circles, singly, doubled, or alternated. The pupil should then be taught the principles of construction lines. He is shown how to change a circle into a spiral, and that a spiral or volute consists approximatively of semicircles. Then he may learn that any shoot or branching or spiral line thrown off anywhere from either side of a circle, or spiral, or other curving figure so as to form a long $\jmath$ or l, or gradually departing curve, forms invariably the skeleton of an elegant design, and that it is not possible that it can be anything but graceful. This is an invariable law, and on it all outline decorative design as to curves is based. The next step is to double these lines, either as parallels or to form gradually diminishing 'vines' or cords, and then ornament them. Ornamenting is chiefly effected by applying *finials* or end ornaments, such as flowers, card spots, &c., and *crochets*, or side ornaments, which are like thorns on a rose twig. He then learns to double or quadruple the whole design. These principles of the $\jmath$ offshoot are next applied to the wave line, made of combined semicircles for borders. After a little practice in 'throwing off' freehand spirals or curves, and in examining a few examples of the decorative art of different ages, even young children begin to design with taste and skill, and when they once begin their progress is rapid. It may be observed that in all this there is no *picture* making, no shading, no very black lines. The first designs should all be large. Anything like the literal imitation of small leaves and petty flowers or any use of heavy lines should be avoided. As a rule, nothing should be drawn which cannot be perceived by the naked eye at the distance of fifteen feet. It is a rule, almost without exception, that all children in original design instinctively make pretty figures. They will draw scores of diminutive buds and leaves on a page. Just so in the infancy of a race; it perfects the pettiness of illuminating manuscripts before designing grandly. Now, it is always easy for one who can draw 'large' to come down to petty patterns, but it is impossible for the petty worker to rise to great execution.

To learn to make designs the pupils may freely use not only compasses and rule, but circles, curves, and ornaments cut from tin or cardboard, to be used as stencils. The youngest soon learn how to repeat and combine these so as to form borders or centre ornaments. The art of invention is not only rapidly developed by this short-hand method of drawing, but there is also developed with it a greater interest and confidence —the feeling, in fact, of creativeness or being really an artist. Now, if with these merely mechanical aids we combine constant practice in freehand drawing from the shoulder, it will be found that the pupil soon abandons the former and relies on the latter. No one swims long with bladders after he can dispense with them. This method is, therefore, a union of technological and freehand drawing applied to that merely outline decorative design which has a place between the two.

No person not familiar with the practice can have any idea of the extraordinary rapidity with which children learn to draw and design when they are confined to simple outline patterns for decorative work under the stimulus of invention. It is because there is no shading, or ' effects,' or ' picturesques' mingled with their drawing to bewilder their brains that they advance so quickly. As soon as they have a few lines and finials by heart, and know how to set the latter together to make circles, &c., they begin to design and combine boldly. The extreme degree of freehand sweep and the bold dash which result from making branching curves give a character to this system of drawing which is not found in any other with which I am acquainted. As the pupil is step by step familiarised with a great variety of curves and ornaments he finds that to combine and vary them becomes easier and easier. As a rule, with very rare exceptions, or in my experience with almost none, the child from twelve to fourteen years of age who can draw a clean, light, freehand line can be taught in a few weeks, at the utmost in a few months, to design beautiful original patterns. By this I mean patterns worth executing in art or patterns worth money. When this is acquired all is acquired. Either technological or artistic drawing may then be learned in half the time usually demanded for their mastery.

First Instruction in Colour.

When the pupil can make a good design and is desirous of advancing to simple decorative painting, he is taught to fill in the ground with India ink or any flat colour, and from this proceeds to varied monochrome or to large illumination. According to the old methods, by which everything was taught at once, such as drawing and shading, outline and blending, the mere beginner painted flowers in all tones and hues. I believe, with Turner, that it is through monochrome or single colours alone that a true colourist can be made. If we take two children and teach one to draw and shade together in the old style, and then to 'paint flowers' or to mix colours from the first, and then train another through freehand, outline, and monochrome to blending, it will be found that the latter will, at the end of the year, be far in advance of the former in every respect. I have tested both methods, and found the superiority of what may be called the single method is incredible. Simple decorative art is the best road to high art; and it has this advantage, that those who stop by the way at any stage have at least learned something by which money can be made.

Utility of Outline Design in other Directions.

If the pupil does not take up colour, and prefers, let us say, needlework, we find even here that a knowledge of outline design is more practically useful than would at first appear. The world always declares that the first thing that all girls should learn is plain sewing. But good plain sewing is a really difficult art. Experience has fully shown that crewel work and outline embroidery are very much easier. The child who begins with easy work may be led to hard work in half the time in which the latter, by itself, can be learned. This rule constitutes the beginning and the end of the whole system of industrial art. Now, the girl who can invent and draw her patterns always 'outlines' and 'crewels' much better than the bungler who has to rely on begged or bought designs. Few would believe at what an early age little girls who try can make their patterns. It does not take a child long to learn that with a teacup, a cent, and a pencil, she can draw a semicircle stem with from one to three grapes at the end, or that the stem may be made double or with two lines. It is no harder for her to learn to arrange these sprigs in a circle or in a straight border. With a very little practice in such stencilling she learns to draw. Those who object to such a method as mechanical have never tried the experiment of urging pupils to trace or use the compasses, rule, and stencils. If they will do so, and teach them at the same time to draw freehand lines, they will find that boys and girls soon become impatient of using what are still in most schools surreptitious and forbidden aids. Perhaps if man were given all he wants in this world he would want much less than he does.

It is the same if the pupil prefers modelling in clay. Those who begin by drawing well shape well. Their inventiveness has been awakened. Nothing conduces to inventiveness so much as design. I incline to believe that any man who can invent a machine could have been an artist, and that every true artist is only an inventor on another road. It is not theorising when I say that the pupil who can design, immediately shows his superiority in modelling in clay. All children in modelling follow a leader or go in a crowd. If they are set to making petty balls and blossoms and miniature fruit, and similar silly and mean work, they will keep on making mean things. It is a mistake even in the kindergarten to give children *petty* patterns. In the modelling class, if one gets a new idea, such as making a cat following a mouse, on a vase, or a giant frog, all the rest will take to cats, mice, or frogs. If one make something great which is admired, they must all do the same. And after the mere rudiments of manipulation are mastered, it is better that the pupils should work on a large scale in great variety of subjects than be kept to petty devices. It is the fault of all current systems of drawing that they limit the youthful mind to *small* inventions. The boy or girl who can design has in a way learned to invent, to seek for original devices, and what is learned in the lead pencil expands in the clay.

II. PRACTICAL TEACHING.

Material required.

I will suppose that the reader is desirous of introducing industrial art into an ordinary school. He has, I assume, carefully read what I have so far written on design, and the ease with which children acquire it if properly taught. Drawing is therefore the first step. For this will be required, of course, paper. Good, *smooth*, thin, hard drawing-paper is the best for this purpose, but there is sold all over the country, at about two cents for a very large sheet, a kind of firm, rather smooth wrapping paper with a good body, which is quite as good for ordinary work. It is generally used for design by many artists. It should be smooth, but not so glossy but that an H or hard pencil will make a good mark on it. Hard and medium pencils, with fine sand-paper for sharpening points, compasses, india-rubber in separate pieces—not at the ends of pencils—and a foot rule are of course requisite. Pupils should never draw with short pencils. Strange as it may seem, some like to do so, and will even cut their pencils in half. Short pieces may be utilised in tin holders, but long pencils are best. A collection of circles and curves of hard rubber, wood, or tin (*e.g.* Devoe's curves) will be found useful. Drawing-boards are not essential when there is a good, smooth, flat table; a black-board is, however.

Designing.

Design is the key to all arts. It is established that in nine trades out of ten a knowledge of it is of use, and in about eight of these it generally leads to foremanship. A very slight familiarity with modelling is also of great practical value. What drawing-design is to modelling, such is modelling to all arts where form is to be inspired with taste. Both can be learned by girls, or by all children, of almost any age. There are still in the world many people who do not see the 'practical advantage' of knowing how to read and write. Those who cannot see the real use of drawing-design and of modelling in education are quite as blind or narrow-minded. And those who would make 'mother wit' the main dependence of a boy are apt to forget what a vast proportion there are of orphans in this relation, and that when mother wit is wanting, what an admirable substitute is provided by step-mother education.

It may be borne in mind that the principal can learn to design, model, and carve with the aid of a manual, and teach while learning. If his designs or patterns are on a large scale and simple, they will be all the more elegant and saleable. Petty work, such as cannot be seen across a room, is generally worthless. To revert to design, I would here observe that one reason why beginners are so prone to cover a pattern with petty leaves and mean details is because they rest all the weight of their body on the *hand* while drawing. In this position there is not more than an inch of sweep for the point of the pencil, and the whole arm must be moved to enlarge this compass. Resting on the wrist gives a sweep of perhaps two or three inches, though not to all. When only the arm hardly touches the table the wrist sweep is again doubled. But those who draw freehand from the shoulder can with confidence cover a space of three feet diameter. Turner, the great painter, could do this, as he always painted without a maulstick, and every child can learn to do it. It not only gives greater freedom of execution, but much more accuracy.

Use of Copies.

If the teacher is *capable*, children may be taught design from the black-board alone, without drawings or patterns. None of the worn-out lithographs such as generally constitute 'copies' should ever be set before students. After a boy or girl can once draw lines decently, there is no occasion to copy anything. If 'copies' or pictures are then given out, it should be for *motives* or suggestions. They may be doubled or varied or used to supply finials or ornaments. Pupils should be encouraged to change and combine figures, devices, or decorations. They should be taught to seek them in carpets or wall papers, book covers, and the coverings of furniture. They will soon discover that whenever there is in these a connected *design*, and not a mere strewing or collocation of loose objects, it is extremely easy to understand and equal it. Nineteen-twentieths of all the most expensive carpets and wall papers sold are inferior in design to what nineteen children out of twenty could produce in a few months if properly trained. The general principles laid down in the 'Manual of Decorative Design' will be found sufficient for any teacher who can draw at all to instruct any class.

Early Choice of Subjects.

It may be here observed that the whole secret of learning to draw consists of making an easy beginning in the simplest rudiments, and in resolutely persevering. There is no 'gift' or 'talent' necessary. A lady once declared to me that there would be no use of attempting to teach her how to draw, that she had tried and failed. 'And what did you try to draw?' I inquired. 'I tried to draw a *horse*,' was the reply. Her next remark was to the effect that she supposed that 'a horse or a man' constituted as simple a figure as could be imagined. When educated people are so ignorant, it is not strange that the art of drawing even simple patterns is supposed to require a 'gift.'

As soon as the children produce anything well done, it should be duly praised. When any design is executed let the pupil copy it on a full scale on a sheet of superior paper, then fill in the background with india ink and hang it up on the wall, where it may serve as a model. The clever ones should be induced to teach or aid the less advanced. Among the young, the most disagreeable and hopeless scholars are the conceited 'geniuses' who have been 'discovered' or picked up, generally by some one on the look-out for wonders. They are the least inclined to follow a regular method of instruction, and aim from the beginning at making 'pictures' and astonishing their admiring friends. All first efforts should be destroyed. It cannot be too earnestly instilled into the minds of the young that what is to be observed in school is not to make works of art, but to learn how to make them. There is nothing so inartistic as impatience. Those who would execute a masterpiece at the beginning seldom have one to show at the end.

Needlework.

The class of girls in needlework may begin with outline embroidery or filled-in work or crewel as taught by manuals. There is a very easy and effective kind of work made by stencilling or painting flowers in flat or dead colour on brown holland, light canvas, or any similar stuff. The colours may be either dye-stuffs or water-colours. When the flowers or other patterns are painted they may be surrounded with an outline in corresponding colour of woollen or silk needlework. This is very easy work, yet rich and effective. The beneficial result of making even little girls in this class draw their own patterns will show itself from the first in all. With very little management, all that is made in this class can in most places be sold at a profit; if not on the spot, by sending it to 'depositories' or art stores in the cities. From ten to fifty dollars' worth of materials will suffice to establish an ordinary school class in needlework.

Modelling in Clay.

The next branch of industrial art study is modelling. If a teacher can draw or design even a little, he or she may, with the aid of a manual, confidently undertake to conduct such a class successfully. Clay fit for the purpose is to be obtained in most places at from three to five cents a pound. It should be kept in a waterproof cask or box. A very large box with a lid is best, as it serves not only to hold the clay, but also for a depository for the work, which must be kept damp from day to day. With this certain tools are requisite, the forms of which are given in the 'Art Work Manual for Modelling.' A set costs from 50 to 75 cents. Any boy with the ordinary American gift for whittling can reproduce them in pine wood. The fingers are, however, the principal tools. Some artists produce very good work with such adventitious aid as old spoons and any chance piece of stick cut into the form which the need of the moment may suggest. A pair of carpenter's compasses are, however, indispensable. As mud wasps occasionally make raids on sculptors for material, so in our school the youthful modellers now and then appropriate the tools of the wood carvers for certain mysterious purposes, a bent gouge being a favourite implement wherewith to make scales on fishes.

Modelling is drawing in clay. Any child who can copy an old shoe with a pencil can make it from a plastic material. More than this, it is easier to model anything than to draw it. A little boy can make a mud pie much better than he can copy it on paper. An old shoe, or a plaster cast of a rabbit, life size, forms a perfect model for imitation. When jugs, jars, or vases of green or wet clay can be obtained from a pottery it is easy for the children, after a few days' practice, to ornament them with flowers, lizards, fishes, crabs, leaves, or other figures. When the jars cannot be obtained they may be made by hand; thus cylindrical cups are easily formed around a broad pipe of pasteboard. Baskets of clay are often made in beautiful forms. A

U

corrugated ground is produced by breaking a stick in two, and pricking the clay with its jagged end. When finished and dried articles may be sent to a pottery and fired. The process of colouring and glazing such work is not more difficult than rough water colouring. It is fully described in the 'Manual of Modelling.' All the requisite materials for it may be had by express on sending an order to any dealer in artists' materials in any city.

Tangible Results of Industrial Training.

The practical results of a combined knowledge of decorative design and modelling are these :—The pupil learns to use the eyes and fingers in a way which will render any work easier. The boy or girl who can draw and model even tolerably well can easily find a situation wherever casting or any other kind of plastic work is executed. There is a great demand for boys with such knowledge. I could, without exception, find paid places in a great variety of manufactories for all the pupils in the Public Industrial School who have had about twenty lessons in design and modelling.

It may be well in this place to consider one or two of the popular objections to industrial art in schools. One is of those who, looking at vases with flowers or frogs, admit that they may be all very pretty, but that they cannot see in such 'fancy work' any trustworthy means for getting a living. Of another class are those who examine the work critically, ask its market value, and then inquire if it could not be made more cheaply by machinery, and, if so, whether it is worth while to set children to making it. Since this page was begun a distinguished reformer, whose name is known to every reader of a newspaper, and who professed great interest in art in schools, began with me by saying, 'I wish to see some of your children's work. I want to know its market value, and how much money it will bring. You see I am a *practical* person.' I did not see it, for it seems to me to be most senseless and unpractical to expect goods of average market value from mere children just beginning to learn. There are people 'deeply interested in education' who inquire what is the current shop value of the work of a child in its second or even first lesson. It is perfectly true that in the hands of competent teachers and directors the average art industry school may be always made to meet its expenses; yet it is almost as unreasonable to reckon on this as to expect that reading and writing will 'pay' from the alphabet onwards. In the words of William Gulager, of Philadelphia, 'whatever is worth teaching is worth paying for.' Meanwhile it is worth remembering that wherever ornamental castings in metal of any kind are manufactured, or wood, plaster, terra-cotta, stone, or any substance whatever is made to assume shape beyond size, there the workman who can design and model even but a little is wanted.

Wood Carving.

I consider that, as a general rule, the three branches of design, embroidery, and modelling are the best to introduce into an ordinary school. Yet in some places wood carving may be preferred by pupils or parents to modelling, as I have known it to be the case in England; or it may in time be added to the three branches already described. For wood carving a very strong common table and about two dollars' worth of good tools and fifty cents' worth of wood to each pupil may be called an outfit. The steps in wood carving from mere drawing to cutting are very gradual. It is to be desired that children in schools should be confined to 'flat cutting,' which is easy and profitable, and not be led at once, as they are in many schools, to ambitious and difficult sculpture 'in the round.'

With *design, embroidery, modelling,* and *wood carving* a school may be said to be fairly established as to industrial art. They may all be learned in the rudiments by book. When well established in these rudiments pupils can advance themselves to the higher branches. What I have described may be made a part of the course in every village or private school. When *design* is acquired, *every* art is acquired for those who want it. When these four branches are familiar to teacher or pupil all other varieties of the minor arts are really trifles, so far as acquisition is concerned.

Stencilling.

The next branch may be stencilling. The advantages of this art are but little understood. By means of it every whitewashed wall in the country might be made to look much better than it would when covered with ordinary wall paper, which paper, by the way, has been proved to be in innumerable cases when damp a fruitful cause of malaria. A well-stencilled wall is artistic, since only a good designer can draw the pattern, and it requires artistic taste to combine the stencils in more than one colour. This would give profitable employment to thousands in every State. It consists of nothing but drawing designs, cutting them out of cardboard or sheet metal, and then painting the patterns thus cut with a broad brush and coloured washes or paint on walls or other surfaces. The art is as yet in its infancy, and the vast majority of all the stencils sold are of a very commonplace, old-fashioned character. The expense requisite for stencilling would be about 50 cents a square yard for best cardboard; brushes, from 30 cents to 75 each; washes, best quality, 25 cents a gallon; paint at the ordinary prices.

Papier-mâché.

Papier-mâché is a very cheap art, little known and capable of wide application. It is closely allied to modelling in clay and casting. By means of it all flat surfaces can be decorated with permanent reliefs as durable as wood. Every kind of merely ornamental architectural moulding can be made of pressed and moulded paper. It is also worked by hand like clay. It is capable of being combined with paste, glue, clay, chalk, leather in fragments, pulp, peat, according to many recipes which change it to as many different textures. The number of practically useful as well as ornamental objects made from these combinations is really incredible. I know of one man who, by manufacturing a very simple object indeed from *papier-mâché*, has within a few years made a fortune. There is no person who, able to design and somewhat familiar with modelling in clay, could not make saleable objects in this material. It opens a wide field to inventiveness, and can be practised by girls and boys at home as well as made on a large scale in factories.

Sheet Leather-work.

In common with stencil and *papier-mâché*, sheet leather-work is very little understood or practised. It consists of pieces of leather soaked in alum water or plain water for a few hours, on which patterns are then drawn by means of a toothed wheel pricking through a design drawn on paper. This pattern is outlined with a small hand-wheel or tooling instrument, and the background put down and roughened with a common stamp or punch. When dry the pattern may be painted or stained with black or any other dye. Wet leather is capable of as much modification as clay or *papier-mâché*. Not only can sheets or skins be utilised in its manifold applications, but also all kinds of bookbinders' and shoemakers' waste. It can be applied to any surface, such as chairs, tables, or cabinets.

Ceramic Painting.

Of ceramic or porcelain painting little need be said if it meant no more than covering plaques or saucer plates with feeble pictures of flowers and dogs' heads, as it generally does; but there is a vigorous style of purely *decorative* tile painting in monochrome, or single colours, which is quite unknown to most painters, and which will yet become popular and possibly extinguish the current debilitated imitations of ivory, drawing-paper, and canvas pictures. The tile, as a wall ornament, should as a rule be decorated in single colours, simply and boldly designed, so as to be clearly visible at a distance, in common with the architectural details of a house. Were this kind of tile painting commoner the art would be more legitimate than it now is, and be more respected not only by those who understand art, but by the ignorant. Single-colour china or stoneware painting may be begun in stencil and carried on by hand. Those who have gone on from design to filling in the ground with colour will find it very easy. There is no certain sale or regular demand for such fancy work as is generally found on the plaques and tiles of art depositories and church fairs, but a single-colour tile painter who can work rapidly from good designs and also make them can always find a market. Therefore this form of industrial art may be introduced into schools, though it is not to be desired that it should become a leading branch of industry in them.

The teacher should beware of letting pupils choose too freely what they will do. Left to themselves, all the silly ones, and not a few of the wiser, would elect 'to paint,' probably to paint pretty little posies in water-colour, oil, or china, which would be the positive end of all practical or useful art industry with them. If you would keep a girl from becoming an artist, set her at flower-painting. There is, it is true, a natural appetite for colour and flowers as there is for sugar, but this is no reason why people should be fed on it. It should only be gratified after being well nurtured on design and monochrome.

Repoussé Work.

Embossing sheet metal, especially brass, though popular as an amusement for amateurs, is less generally *useful* than any of the branches already described. It requires a finished knowledge of design and a skill in tracing which few possess, if really good work is to be done. By means of it sheet metal is hammered into low relief by working it always *cold* on a piece of board, or into much higher relief and more varied form by beating it on a bed of composition made of pitch, plaster of Paris, and brick dust, and annealing it. The tools used are punches, usually costing from 20 to 30 cents each. They are generally either *tracers* for outlining patterns, or *mats* for grounding. The sheet brass costs from 30 to 35 cents a pound in small quantities. The only full description of the art, both in cold hammering and by annealing, is, I believe, given in the 'Manual of Repoussé Work.' Annealing consists in warming the work from time to time as it becomes hardened from hammering. It is easily done with a heater and tube from a gaslight. It is all-important in *repoussé* that the pupil, before attempting to work patterns, should learn to make lines, curves, &c., very accurately with the tracer. Unless this is done no good work will ever result. This work is, however, admirably useful as a preparation for all who intend at some future time to work in metal. Familiarity with the hammer, the punch, and stamps leads to a really practical knowledge of the properties of metal and how to turn them to advantage. There is, too, a growing demand for many hand-made objects of beaten brass. Facings for fireplaces, finger-plates for doors, bellows, panels for cabinets, picture or mirror frames, and a hundred other objects may be easily made by women and children. But let it be remembered that neither sheet brass nor any other kind of work is worth taking up unless it is preceded by a knowledge of design-drawing and perfect skill in the use of the tracer. Without such preparation it at once degenerates, as china painting has done, into a frivolous fancy work. This work can also be elegantly executed in sheet iron, tin, pewter, copper, or silver.

Painting.

Painting in oil or water colours, for the majority, requires a special teacher. Yet when the inevitable design-drawing is really mastered, monochrome or single colour presents no difficulty whatever to a person of ordinary intelligence, even without a master. And after monochrome, I see no reason why, with a good manual, any one cannot gradually and carefully mix colours and experiment and test and copy his way without any real difficulty into skill. Those who write a letter to an editor to know what colour would result from mixing blue with yellow would perhaps be too impatient to travel the only true road, which, seeming long, is yet the shortest. Painting, though the most popular branch among all pupils, because producing such pretty results, is the last to be thought of in an ordinary school. In proportion to the time, trouble, and expense which it involves, it is of less practical use than any of the minor arts. Yet in one branch it is easy and commendable. I refer to mural or purely decorative painting of walls and ceilings. Here flowers have their place and may be appropriately introduced. In a large experimental industrial art school, painting will of course form a regular part of the branches.

Artists' Supplies.

In most cities there are dealers in artists' materials who will supply or obtain anything needful. Where these cannot be had, every bookseller will get for the applicant the art manuals or similar works, and the publishers of these will always send to order what is wanted or answer a letter containing a postage stamp. I presume that the editor of any newspaper will be able to give the address of any advertising agent in New York or Philadelphia or other large city, who will obtain what is wanted or hand the order to a general agent. The latter will always, being allowed a discount, obtain the article as cheaply for the consumer as he himself could do. Finally, the directors or teachers of the art schools or ladies' art clubs or associations of any of our cities would reply to any questions from any persons far inland. I myself have always made it a point to do so in the interest of education, and will always give information or counsel most willingly to all who wish to learn an art or to introduce industrial pursuits into schools, and who in addressing me will inclose a stamp for return of postage.

Importance of Freehand.

It is much easier to learn to draw well than to write well, and there is no child that would not do both admirably if it were obliged from the first hour to use *freehand*; that is to say, to control the pen or pencil from the shoulder, allowing the arm to rest on the table just enough to prevent fatigue. The whole difficulty of drawing lies not, as is popularly and very ignorantly supposed, in composing and inventing figures, but in drawing simple lines. Now, let the teacher in every school, however humble, bear in mind this great truth, that if a child acquire true freehand in writing it can not only *draw* well, but do almost anything well which requires perfect control of the hand. This wonderful faculty enables the possessor to almost at once feel, as it were, the chief difficulty of wood carving—the light artistic touch—and to overcome it. So is it with all other arts. With this power they can all be literally mastered. The younger the pupil who acquires it, the sooner in life will he make it his own, and the greater will be his manual skill in all things when older grown. There are very few teachers who fully realise this, few parents who ever think of it; yet it is the mainspring of all manual art. For the sake of this it would be worth while to make industrial art a part of the education of all children, the younger the better. Therefore all who propose to teach or learn art in any form should seriously consider *freehand* as the true key to all its practice. It is a great stimulant to quickness of perception.

Larger Schools.

I have, in what is previously written, considered the expediency of industrial art as a branch of education, and shown how it may be introduced to village or private schools. I have of course only considered the pupils; but it is worth remarking that the teachers themselves, 'learning while instructing,' will also become accomplished, and in many instances fit themselves for a more congenial career as artists or teachers of art. No one can doubt that if every teacher in America could practise one or more strictly industrial decorative arts of a more practical nature than are now taught in schools, there would be an immense impetus given to our national culture and industry. There was very little really *solid* in old-fashioned drawing, water-colour, theorems, wax flowers, and china flower plaques, but there is a great deal of real value in freehand design, and in executing it in wood, metal, leather, and all other suitable substances. Not only does the teacher find in decorative art a means of making more money, but he is also provided with what to all is an agreeable change from other duties; for, while teaching, the instructor, in common with the pupils, can produce something saleable or valuable.

The Introduction of Art Training.

Where it is proposed to introduce industrial art work to public schools in large cities or to whole communities, there will be either much opposition or great indifference to the innovation on the part of those who do not understand it. The best way to begin in such cases is to establish on a small scale a single primary school of from twenty to thirty pupils, to be taught design, embroidery and plain sewing, modelling in clay, and wood carving. This school may be supported by private contributions and the aid of ladies and gentlemen who will give time and teaching for nothing, as several have done in Philadelphia, or it may be entirely based on appropriations from school boards, or the latter source may be eked out by the former. When the school is established and well under way, all that is necessary to convince any rational man of its utility will be to have him inspect it while in session. If managed with any ability it will speak for itself. The sight of the girls and boys proving to the most prejudiced their ability to make a living on leaving school, is all that is needed to make converts. The walls of the school may be decorated with specimens of work, but I do not urge the appeal to these as the sole proof of the expediency of teaching children to use their hands. As a rule without exception, it is the unreasoning and ignorant visitor who is amazed at plaques and panels made by children, and who cries at every indication of what is or should be only *ordinary* talent, 'How wonderful! Is not that child a genius? Has she not extraordinary talent?' The children themselves soon learn to laugh at this false estimate of their skill. They know that they can all do these things with practice. And, as I have previously said, the ignorant examiner, looking only at the *results* and considering only market values, immediately misunderstands the entire system. Thus newspapers have unthinkingly compared the results of the work done by little children who had had, many of them, only a dozen lessons, or at most twenty, and that once a week, with that effected by grown-up young women who had been for years employed all day, and every day, in higher art schools. Yet even these children showed, in proportion to their age and opportunities, superiority in every respect to all rivals.

Material required.

In an ordinary experimental school we first need a room. The upper story of a city school, when not in use, is perfectly adapted to the purpose. It should of course be well lighted. Tables made of two-inch plank, placed on very strong, firm trestles, are requisite, particularly if wood carving and brass-work are contemplated. There must be abundant shelving for many purposes. The pupils will every one require a place whereon to put half-finished work. There must of course be chairs and a black-board. An adjacent small store-room or large closet will be a great convenience. If this be wanting a large plain wooden cabinet must be provided.

It may happen that the director or principal of an experimental school is capable of teaching not only drawing, but modelling. In like manner the lady teacher of embroidery may be qualified to teach something else. In the smaller schools of course one teacher must supervise everything. In the smallest it will soon be found necessary to convert the most advanced pupils into assistants. Economies of teaching may be carried out in many ways. But where it can be done the director should have no direct teaching. There should be one instructor for every branch. There should consequently be teachers for drawing, carving, and modelling in clay. But in different localities and in large schools well supported many branches may be taught. I could easily enumerate fifty, large and small, all worth learning and all very easy to learn if the pupil can design. Thus *leather-work* may be divided into several branches, all elegant and profitable. There is sewn leather, in which fragments of bookbinders' and shoemakers' waste are cut into shape and sewed together, as well as the two great divisions of sheet leather stamped and leather moulded into shapes. In Russia, Turkey, and Persia there are whole villages or large communes devoted to sewn leather-work, and if really artistic patterns were supplied there would be many thousands of people in America doing the same.

With regard to what seems to be the only great and real difficulty in popularising art and industrial art education, something may here be most appropriately said. This difficulty is that of getting patterns to guide taste. I long since suggested in published lectures that this might be met by either private charity or municipal or Government aid. Sheets of patterns for every branch of the minor arts, costing not more than two cents a sheet, would be of incalculable value to every industry in which taste is required. From art works already published, from our museums, and from those abroad, inexhaustible material could be taken. It should all be drawn from specimens illustrating and expressing some marked era of art. Very little should be made or drawn to order for these sheets, not even by the best artists. What is wanted is instruction and inspiration for artists, not from men, but from eras of culture. When the demand makes itself felt our Government will doubtless supply it. It has been met in England in an inadequate way by publishing illustrated pamphlet summaries of the works in the South Kensington Museum. But what is wanted is simply large sheets with large outline designs of different kinds of art industry work. Let me illustrate this by a single instance. In many parts of America, boards, even of oak, walnut, or more valuable woods, are cheap enough, and men who can manage saws and planes are not wanting. These people are often without furniture, and pay extravagant prices for the flimsy, worthless, ugly, glued together, and varnished trash of the factories. Now, there is a type and style of very elegant solid furniture, such as was made in South Germany for centuries, which would cost no more than the glued and veneered trash. It is made by simply sawing, boring, and pinning or bolting planks or boards together. Any man of ordinary intelligence having the design for a table or chair of this kind before him can take the measurements and make it. A series of such designs at a low price would be very welcome and very useful all through the West.

As I shall explain in another place, there are several useful industries which would soon be practised in thousands of families were cheap illustrations devoted to them disseminated everywhere. Such pictures would form a very important aid to industry in schools. I have done what I could to help in this respect by giving in the series of art manuals, which were written for education, large working patterns, those in any one of the works being adaptable to another. Thus a design for sheet brass may also be used for flat carving. It is to be regretted that in works of art half the engravings are executed not with a view to making them practically useful to workmen, but to give a general picturesque effect. There is a great deal of expensive shading, but the details are scumbled. This is the case even in many of the illustrations of the South Kensington works.

I will here recapitulate the possible or probable requirements of an experimental school on a large scale for a city:

A large room, well lighted.
From 30 to 50 feet of common pine shelving.
One gas-burner to six pupils.
Water, soap, and towels.
One closet or cabinet (pine).
One waterproof barrel or large box, for clay.
Clay, from 30 to 100 pounds.

Modelling tools, one set.
Carpenter's compasses.
Chest of carpenter's tools.
Drawing-boards.
Drawing-paper.
Pencils.
Cups or small tumblers.
India-rubber.
Tiles, for colours.
Foot rules.
Compasses.
Water-colours.
Paint-brushes.
Black-board.
Wood-carving tools for each pupil.
Wood, half inch to inch, at from 4 to 10 cents a foot.
One set of Art Work Manuals or other handbooks.
Whetstones or hones.
One grindstone.
One bucket or pail.
One fret-sawing apparatus.
Material for needlework for each pupil.
Leather, from 25 cents to $1 a skin, besides waste.
Tools for leather-work, each pupil.
Stencil-cutting, each pupil.
Brass-work, each pupil; tools, $1; brass, $1.
Flour paste or dextrine.
Plaster for moulds.

It will be seen that it is very difficult to adjust the prices for such a list, especially for all parts of the United States. For a small school or club on the humblest scale, drawing materials, two or three carving tools to each pupil, boards or wood (such as can be generally had for a trifle), waste newspapers, and common paste and clay for *papier-mâché*, with a little paint, bits of marble or stone of different kinds, and a hammer and iron bar for mosaic making, with rags for artistic rag carpet work, and manuals, will not, with management, cost in all more than from $20 to $30. A clever teacher with clever pupils could almost undertake to begin work on $10 and increase the stock of implements by sales. If the teacher can only design, all the rest will or may follow of itself.

How to select Work for Practice.

It is extremely difficult to determine, beyond design-drawing, modelling, embroidery, and wood carving, exactly what may or may not be taken up. There are places about factories where the material for rag carpeting is very cheap; in others it is dear. This, as I shall show, supplies material for a really elegant and practically useful art. In others mosaic stones or marble may be had for the taking, while in certain places such material is not to be had. I have seen a bed of finest clay, ranging from white to red, in Minnesota, several miles in extent, not very far from Duluth. In the East such clay costs from three to five cents a pound. It will be seen by this that the prices of the materials and implements for industrial art work are very variable; but there is no place in which some of them are not within the reach of the poorest. Sculpturing brick is a beautiful and profitable art, not difficult to learn, and bricks are to be had everywhere.

There is one rule by which all such schools may be safely guided. Making money immediately should not be the main object of any branch of education, but where schools are very poor a sufficient income to pay for tools and materials may be confidently relied on. Let the teacher, or those who are interested in the pupils, after they can design patterns, and not till then, consider what industries in their neighbourhood will pay. In the first place, a stencilled wall is really, if well executed, better than a papered one. Elegant stencilling costs little more than that which is ugly. It should be found in every house in the country. Just at present it seems to be confined to the Fifth Avenue or to the most expensive mansions. If brass or sheet metal work is taken up, fronts for fireplaces are easily made and can be sold, as also finger-plates for doors, sconces, and frames. Leather-work will supply baskets, chair seats, and coverings for the backs of chairs, table-covers, and albums. Of sewn leather, cushions or pillows are extensively made in Turkey, Russia, and Persia. These can be made from bookbinder's waste. Elegant coverings for furniture, rugs, and slippers are also made of this now wasted material, which may be used for a great variety of purposes. Let it always be remembered that if the teachers and pupils set themselves resolutely to make certain objects well, according to what authority recommends as good patterns, they can always find some agency in every town where their work can be sold. But if they only produce average church fair work of the common flower plaque and dog's-head school, it will not sell. The writer is in the constant receipt of letters from people in the country asking him where their small art work can be sold, or even requesting him to kindly exert himself to sell it for them. Now, there is always a market for anything worth having, but the only way to sell it is to find out by inquiry some honest agent or merchant in a city or town who will deal in art work, and trust to him. The ladies' decorative art associations in our large cities all sell such work, with a discount in their favour of about ten per cent. It is to be advised that, in all cases where the pupils produce work of substantial merit, specimens adapted to house decoration —such as brass fronts and tiles for fireplaces, leather chair covers, and carved panels with squares of mosaic—be exhibited, not for sale, but as samples of work which will be executed to order.

I may here speak of a few minor arts which may be taken up according to opportunity. I cannot urge too strongly the fact that after design is learned every kind of material presents a subject for art work, and that every artist should be continually discovering new varieties of it. From modelling vases down to painting oyster-shells, or making wampum beads with a drill, or turning the under shell of a terrapin into an old ivory menu, there is but *one art*, and there is money to be made out of it all, or at least skill to be acquired with amusement from its practice.

Rag Carpets.—Sort the rag strings for carpeting according to colour, and let them be woven up singly. Thus you may have one which is black or brown or blue. Take preferably a black for a beginning, and work a pattern by running white tape with a bodkin through the threads. Sew this where needed. If Etruscan or Greek designs are followed, the result will be a rug or *portière* or hanging, cheap indeed, but if properly made, elegant enough for the drawing-room of a duchess. The simpler the colours the better, but a variety may be employed according to the subject. It is not generally understood that weaving is by no means a very difficult art, and that light and cheap looms can be made for ladies. In the East at the present day the most exquisite weaving is done without looms, the threads being simply arranged between pins and drawn along, the pattern being worked or drawn in by hand.

Painted Embroidery.—This is made by painting or stencilling patterns in water-colour or dyes on any suitable stuff. The flowers or arabesques are then simply outlined in woollen or silk. A manual of this work, as well as one of rag carpet embroidery and other arts mentioned, is in course of preparation.

Mosaic.—The stone cubes for this work are sold in New York, but at a very high price. They may be made with a little practice by anybody with a square hammer and an iron bar from almost any kind of marble or stone. They are from a fourth of an inch to a half-inch square, set so as to form patterns in cement; they make not only a durable and elegant pavement, but also squares which may be used to cover walls or as panels in cabinets. For summer, mosaic floors are preferable to wood. They are specially suited to bath-rooms. Cubes of earthenware, though far inferior to stone, may, however, be used for mosaic. They are easily made in moulds, and may be baked or fired even by amateurs at a trifling expense.

Sculptured Brick.—Any brick and mortar wall may be sculptured. It is a question whether after the relief is executed the mortar should be stained red to match with the bricks, or whether all should be left in primitive material. Brick sculpture may be very elegantly executed on a small scale, from a single brick up to half a dozen. There is really no artistic reason why these should not be set in red mortar or cement. A single sculptured square set under each window of a house, or between the stories on the front, will change the whole façade and greatly improve it.

Applicability and Value of Art Training.

It is a curious matter to reflect what may be done for an ordinary country house by a family who will devote their evenings to its improvement, with a few tools and cheap materials. In the first place, good planed plank or boards can, by pattern and measurement, be converted by most men or boys into solid and even elegant furniture. It will cost less when finished than is usually paid for machine-made varnished and veneered rubbish. I have before me as I write two chairs, each 250 years old, as good as new. The chair back fits by a socket into the seat, and is bolted beneath; the legs are simply stuck through holes, as in a three-legged stool, into the seat. The backs are carved, and the result is a very beautiful yet convenient piece of furniture. Tables, settees, and all kinds of furniture may be made on this plan. The floor of the cottage may be set in mosaic, at the expense of time, an iron bar, a hammer, and stone of different colours; or it may be inlaid in wood and covered with rag carpets in Etruscan or Greek pattern—all home-made. The walls may be covered with stencilled designs, or ornamented with carved panels at intervals, or strips or panels of stamped leather in old Spanish patterns, touched with gold. The doors may be hung with rag carpet *portières*, or cheap materials, such as crash towelling, dye-painted and outlined with embroidery. The ceiling may be stencilled or adorned with *papier-mâché* mouldings.

There are many people who say, as many have said to me, 'What is the use or sense of inducing a backwoods-dweller in a log cabin or shanty to adorn his house in a manner which he can neither understand nor enjoy?' There are others who continually cry that educating girls up to æsthetic tastes unfits them for 'mechanics' wives.' This has been the old cry in one form or another in all ages. It was heard everywhere a century ago, as it may still be heard occasionally from a few 'aristocrats,' that reading and writing are the ruin of 'the lower orders.' There is a gentleman in Philadelphia who has always maintained that our civil war, which he regarded simply as a needless nuisance because it inconvenienced him, 'all came from educating the common people so that they could read the newspapers.' Industrial art is rapidly becoming, in education and in life, as essential as reading or writing. Thousands who are absorbed in politics, whisky, or business, are as yet ignorant of this; even some editors seem to ignore it; but the women, the clergy, and the teachers are already generally aware of it. But all the people in America do not live in backwoods-shanties,

x

and where they do, they are not on that account to be universally set down as incapable of appreciating homes made beautiful. There are millions of people in America, not so badly off, whose homes, in which much money has been spent, are not really creditable, good-looking, or comfortable. They would all have tasteful or artistic and cheap adornment if they could get it. The money which they pay for their present ornamentations represents just so much labour. Now, this labour would be better bestowed on making for themselves what they want, or, in other words, in keeping the profits which at present simply go to enrich the manufacturers of machinery-made and very trashy and ugly objects. The problem of political economy lies in the greatest possible distribution of wealth and industry.

There is another argument in favour of industrial art education. It is the enormous and rapidly growing demand for hand-made objects. As education and culture progress, people begin to find out that in jewellery as in pictures, or even in fire-irons, a thing to be truly artistic must be hand-made. It is not as yet generally understood that machinery, though it may manufacture pretty things, cannot make anything *artistic*. There are no such things as artistic works made in any way except by hand. Only the vulgar and ignorant confuse or confound that which is beautiful with what is artistic. The merchant is guilty of an illiterate blunder who advertises as 'artistic' goods turned out by the million from moulds. It is more correct to speak of a pair of well-made and handsome trousers as artistic than of a chromo-lithograph as such. This demand for hand-made art will ere long give employment to that very large class whom it is at present difficult to fit to anything. The day is not distant when the public will be so well educated as to distinguish clearly between hand-made and machinery-made in everything pertaining to ornament. When that time comes we shall be a nation not only of artists, but of mutual purchasers of art work. Meanwhile let it be distinctly understood that art does not consist entirely in prettiness. Its best characteristic is the impression of individual character. This disappears in the machine. In fact, the more perfect machine work is, the less is it artistic. The faultlessly finished piece of silver-work, such as no mere smith could ever rival, shows indeed the result of ingenuity, but not of art. A Soudan bracelet made with a stone and a nail is far more artistic than a Connecticut mill-manufactured dollar bangle, yet the latter is infinitely the more 'finished' of the two.

As for the argument that girls are unfitted for becoming mechanics' wives by a knowledge of art, it is like the hackneyed cry against the piano, and against all kinds of education or culture for the poor. The best arbiters in this question would be the young mechanics themselves, especially those who have been at art schools. Much as has been said against the piano, the mechanic himself is generally the first to make his wife a present of one, and I doubt if he would object to arts which are practised at home and which bring money in. There is much cheap ridicule of dados, and what is misrepresented as being the staple of all decorative art work; but the truth is—and it is to be desired that all newspaper wits would admit it—that the fancy work of the last generation is gradually assuming a substantial and valuable form. The 'china craze,' as it is called, was at any rate better than potichomanie or wax-fruit work. The arts of which I have spoken deal with something more 'practical' than plaques.

Art Instruction in its Relations to the Trades.

I cannot set forth too strongly the fact that decorative art is to be taught to children and girls simply because it is better adapted to their age or nature than a trade or mechanical pursuits, and that whenever it is possible the pupils should be put into practical work. Thus, when boys or even girls manifest an aptness or a fitness for it, they may be taught simple carpentry or joinery, turning, or any of the trades, if there be an opportunity to do so and they can learn. It requires many thousands of dollars to establish an industrial school, but industrial art may be taught from the infant school or kindergarten upward. Let it, however, be borne in mind that industrial art, especially as regards boys, is really only a training for a trade, and that, far from giving them a distaste for useful work, it only whets the appetite.

I was one of the first, if not the first, to point out in a lecture a fact which has since been re-echoed by others, that the decay of the apprentice system must very soon lead to industrial education in schools. Machinery is making men into machines at such a rate that humanity is becoming seriously alarmed at the inevitable result. The old apprentice had a chance to rise, since he learned a whole trade; the modern workman, who is kept at making the sixtieth part of a shoe, and at nothing else, by a master whom he never sees, is becoming a mere serf to capital. Even the industrial school with its 'practical' work can do nothing against this onward and terrible march of utilitaria. It is in the teaching of art and of the superiority of handwork in all that constitutes taste that the remedy will be found. By-and-by, when culture shall have advanced—as it will—there will be an adjustment of interests. Machinery will supply mere physical comforts. Man, and not machinery, will minister to taste and refinement.

According to the method and means which I have indicated, industrial art work may be acquired and taught by any one who will first of all learn simple decorative design. From this point I consider that the several minor arts, also described in the works already referred to, may be easily comprehended, mastered, and taught. But, in fact, the one who can design and model has the capacity to master the rudiments of any of these arts, since they all constitute substantially one art. I have also shown how the system of instruction may be extended to large preparatory schools in cities.

Admission to the Philadelphia School.

A word may here be said as to the method or system by which the pupils are taken into the Philadelphia School. Every teacher in the public schools selects one or two scholars. These are divided into two classes, one attending on Tuesdays from three to five, the other on Thursdays at the same hours. When the pupils can make a fair original design they are advanced to another class, either to paint, model, carve, or learn embroidery. The pupils are, without exception, fond of their work, and would willingly come oftener if possible. In some cases, as a reward, proficients are permitted to attend twice a week. In a few weeks all who advance beyond design produce work which has a market value.

III. GENERAL OBSERVATIONS.

Equality of the Sexes in Artistic Capacity.

It may interest the reader to know that in design-drawing there is no difference as regards merit or capacity between the sexes. In *brass-work* boys excel, not because it requires more strength, for it does not, and the gentlest worker who makes least exertion does best; but because women and girls will not take so much pains to learn to work a line well with a tracer before proceeding to make what they are confident will be saleable and beautiful productions. In wood carving the sexes are more nearly equal, with an advantage, however, in favour of the male. In modelling the equality is almost re-established. Teachers who have had much experience in Europe all declare that American girls or grown women, while clever, are the most difficult to teach, owing to their impatience. As a rule, when not under restraint, they have not the patience to learn to design, but are eager to take up at once one or several arts, hoping to beg, buy, or borrow patterns, as luck may provide. Those who do proceed by the right road of drawing learn rapidly and do well.

Misapprehension of 'Art' an Obstacle to Industrial Education.

The most serious obstacle with which industrial art has to contend is the extravagant and inflated ideas which are popularly attached to the word *art*. It has been so long identified with pictures and statues that in every newspaper, under the heading of 'The Fine Arts,' nothing but news of pictures and statues is expected. Now, as not one person in scores can accurately distinguish a good picture from a bad one, and as the kind of art knowledge which is current sets itself forth in a vast vocabulary of cant, it is not remarkable that 'art' has become a terror. There are men in high places who profess to be authorities, who declare that 'art' is something for only the very few to rightly understand, and that it requires a special inspiration and much education to appreciate it. When every one, rich or poor, shall know what design is, though it be only simply decorative, and has become familiar with a tastefully ornamented house, however humble, then art in its highest, purest, and noblest sense will have no mystery for any one. It is most unfortunately true that, while taste, learning, and culture are spreading rapidly, there has been, so far, no rational or common-sensible effort to really teach the poor and ignorant anything of the kind. There is a great deal of writing about the ennobling tendencies of art, but there have been as yet very few efforts to really go down to the basis and make a proper beginning. The dilettanti and cognoscenti, and of late years the æsthetes, have all preached in their time and way the glory of Raphael or Michael Angelo, and how desirable it would be to bring a knowledge of them down to the people. But they have never tried bringing the people up to Raphael. Now, Raphael and Michael Angelo sprang from the people in an age when every object was made with decorative art. And when this shall be the case with us we shall have Raphaels again, and not till then. There never was a real art in the world that did not spring from the people, that was not fully shared in by the people, and that did not belong to the people. If there were to-day as much knowledge of and fondness for design as there seems to have been among the prehistoric savages of Europe, we should in a few years raise our manufactures of every kind to pre-eminence, and with them improve ourselves personally, morally, and socially.[1]

There is a great coming revival of culture and of art, but it will not be with us until we teach its principles to every child in every school. There is an instinct in mankind for decoration, for colour, for manifestations of what is beautiful. It has been starved out temporarily by the practical developments of science

[1] Mr. William Morris, the eminent poet and artist, speaks to the same effect in his recent address at the opening of a fine art and industrial exhibition at Manchester, England: 'In truth, these decorative arts, when they are genuine, real from the root up, have one claim to be considered serious matters which even the greater works do in a way lack, and this claim is that they are the direct expression of the thoughts and aspirations of the mass of the people; and I assert that the higher class of artist, the individual artist—he whose work is, as it were, a work in itself—cannot live healthily and happily without the lower kind of art—if we must call it lower—the kind which we may think of as co-operative art, and which, when it is genuine, gives your great man, be he never so great, the peaceful and beautiful surroundings and the sympathetic audience which he justly thinks he has a right to.'

or by the useful. This was well; but while comfort should be paramount there is no need of suppressing taste. Those who talk about the sunflower mania and 'art craze' as something temporary, and who mistake the æsthetes for the main army yet to come, are like the ambassadors sent by an African king to visit London, and who at the first small Arab village thought themselves at the end of their journey. As yet the *people* have not moved. A writer in a Cincinnati journal, I know not who, has wisely said that 'because some people have blue jugs and one gentleman an art gallery, therefore we are a great artistic people. But where are the works of our united citizens? What have the masses of our people done?'

What the masses of our people can do will be first shown when every one of them shall have been taught, first decorative design, and then one or more minor arts. This design will be simple, and deal only with outline and mere ornament at first. This is the only easy and proper preparation for more advanced drawing, be it practical or technological, or for prospective picture making. Hitherto all elementary drawing has been misdirected, either in copying shaded pictures or, what is little better, in stiff and formal 'systems.' When all can design, and all know something about decorative art, the mystery will depart, and the world feel less awed before old masters and modern Gothic churches; neither will it believe that a pile of building is necessarily beautiful because it cost fifteen million dollars.

Moral Effects of Art Instruction.

I cannot urge too earnestly or too often on clergymen as on parents, the fact that an interesting industry is conducive to moral culture. Boys who are really absorbed in some kind of industrious amusement are kept out of much mischief. The world, unfortunately, while it observes those who are always in mischief, takes no note of those who are kept out of it. How much the more, therefore, is art industry in schools to be commended, since it not only keeps children busy as an amusement, but aids them practically as to future callings! Year by year sees the old bugbear fading away, the demon of our childhood, which taught that as all medicines to be effective must needs be nauseous, so all school study must needs be wearisome and painful. I am sure that industrial art will go far to make children love school. In England rural clergymen and their wives soon saw into this, and Mrs. Jebb, of Ellesmere, was the first to establish village art schools. But if it be advisable from moral grounds to teach children some way to employ their leisure pleasantly, what shall we say of the immense number of the older grown who rush into vice, impelled by the sheer *ennui* of idleness? Here is an immense number of girls knowing nothing but a little plain sewing, or, in the higher grades, a little pianoplaying. They cannot all get places in shops or factories, and it they do, many of them break down. When a rainy day comes there is suffering indeed. At such a time almost any fancy work, however trifling, often intervenes to save them from ruin. There are now many thousands of young women in America who owe the real comfort, or what constitutes the enjoyment, of life to the teaching or making what is in itself almost worthless, to feeble cards and washy plaques and wretched drawing and daubing; yet it saves them. How much better would it be if they understood design and the decorative arts, which are not more difficult, and which are far more certain to command a market!

There is another class of young people, mostly female, who, having taken the first step in vice, linger awhile before the second, and then are rapidly and utterly degraded. If we look through the ranks of the uneducated, half-educated, or even so-called educated young women, how many are there who have any resources to fill up their leisure? Is it a wonder that they gossip, and thereby develop the sociable evil, who makes even more mischief than her humbler sister, the social evil? I do not think that among the best educated there is one in ten who has any handwork or resource, artistic or literary, in which she really delights. It is the same with the men. Hence 'politics,' gossip, and the most frivolous waste of time. The clergy know this, and they would welcome any remedy for it. When I recently published in the 'Messenger' an appeal to them to aid in introducing art into schools on moral grounds, I began at once to receive, as I still do, letters from clergymen all over the country in reference to the subject. It is a fact that when a girl once masters an art she generally remains true to it and makes the most of it.

Its practice gives a certain sense of superiority and of self-reliance which goes far to strengthen morals in the truest sense of the word.

Industrial Art as an Economic Factor.

There is not one person living, having the usual command of brain and hands, who cannot learn to design well in simply decorative drawing in a few weeks, or, in extremest cases, in a few months, if he or she will try to acquire it. There is not one person who can execute simple design who cannot also master one or more minor arts. And finally, there is no youth of either sex who understands one minor art who cannot make a living by it or by teaching it. By mastering an art I do not mean the ability to feebly copy a wreath of flowers on a china plate, or to indifferently hammer on a brass plaque a borrowed pattern. As it is within the power of all to learn design, so it is quite as easy to perfect themselves in these arts, without a master. All that they require is will and industrious application. This is not mere theory. It has been proved in millions of instances. The history of whole countries, nations, and eras has proved it. I will give the examples.

In the East from remote times, during the days of Greece and Rome, and through the European Middle Ages, the conditions of life were such that but for hand-made minor art the number of paupers would have been literally overpowering. Nothing produces idlers and beggars so much as aristocracy or an extravagant and wealthy court and nobility, and society was then entirely aristocratic. Yet there were fewer paupers then than there are now, if by paupers we mean the entirely dependent. To-day in the United States they wear good clothes and seem well off, but they depend on somebody. There have been states of society in which the producer was more cruelly taxed, but none in which he supported so many. It is very creditable to the average mechanic of the United States that he spends twice or thrice as much on his family as does his British brother, but it is very discreditable to his family that they take so much. Now, if there was such a demand for hand-made decoration in this country as there was, let us say, in Europe five hundred years ago; if every home, however small, were properly adorned, all in the country who are willing to work would find employment. It is a curious reflection that even in the time of Elizabeth the 'sitting-room' of Anne Hathaway's cottage was far more beautiful than any drawing-room in modern Philadelphia, for it was entirely lined with old carved oak. This was the home of people who were then called poor. The demand for handmade decoration is coming very rapidly. When it comes, when people learn the truth that a thing is not artistic *because* it is beautiful, there will be a vast field thrown open not only to the poor, but to the poor who are neither very clever nor strong. In any case it is always worth while to have some art which one can always teach for money, or by which one can live. How many poor young people with spare time, spending all they earn for living, would be really happy when holidays approach if they had a few dollars more! And how certainly they could depend on earning them if they could embroider, model, and ornament, or colour and glaze vases, carve panels, or work in leather! It is hardly possible to suppose that any one who could do all this need be very poor. Yet all these arts, and many more, are actually within the reach of all who choose to master them.

I have shown that the expenses of designing and modelling amount to so little that they may be introduced to the poorest country school. I find that embroidery is often made to cost more than it should. The wool for crewel, at five cents a skein, crash, or common grey stuff of several kinds, costs very little. Scraps of velvet, cloth, and ribbon, for appliqué work, are expensive or the contrary, as people are careful in collecting. A class may be well taught in design, chiefly with the black-board alone; beyond this, good wrapping or shop paper and lead pencils at a cent apiece are not hard to obtain. No rule can be laid down as to selling work. The pupil should not try to sell anything until it is really well made. Unfortunately the delight of the amateur at his own work is always such that his first or at least second or third attempt always seems to him to be very valuable, and there are always ignorant friends who are of the same opinion. What has degraded china painting is the enormous production of it by women who knew nothing of design, and who were accordingly destitute of the energy and character which spring from originality.

Objections considered.

I have found that a great deal of the opposition or indifference to art industry in schools comes from men who, because they are themselves ignorant, do not like to have the whole world trained to what they are too idle or stupid to master. Others argue that as their children are not intended for pursuits into which art knowledge enters, therefore no children need or ought to learn anything of the kind. In the face of these and many other equally wise objections, such as are generally urged at meetings where the subject is discussed, the facts remain that art industry can be taught without infringing on other branches of education; that children while at school can learn to design and model so well in a few months with one weekly lesson as to readily obtain a place as under-designers in factories; and that, thirdly, they can even produce wares which will sell. They can at the same time acquire more culture and intelligence than the objectors to the system can appreciate, but which is appreciated by all persons who are themselves really well informed or intelligent. On this point I speak with knowledge from experience. I have observed that my pupils, from the time they ceased to be mere copyists, began to observe many things to which they were previously indifferent, and manifested the awakening of a much higher intelligence.

But there is a final argument which cannot be resisted; it is that there is a tremendous demand among the manufacturers of Europe and of this country for decorative artists and artisans. It was thought in England that the great art-schools of South Kensington and Manchester and such places would afford a supply, but it has been as a drop in the bucket. The industrial schools have been as inadequate. For it is not only a supply of artistic goods that is needed, but also a taste for them, a manufactory and a market as well as a greater demand, and to meet this double want there must be extensive radical art education among the people. The highest statesmen in Europe know this, and the saying of the Prince of Wales, cited in a late article in the 'Nineteenth Century,' that 'learning and earning should go together,' indicates the solution of a great problem by a brief rhyme. True, there are millions who do not see this. The year before gas was introduced into Philadelphia, all her most influential citizens signed a protest against lighting the city in any such abominable way. The light which gas costs is trifling compared to the enlightenment which would result from the reform in education of which I speak, yet there are still many in that very city who ridicule the idea of industrial art in schools.

From time to time the world comes to a period when it discovers all at once, like a hungry somnambulist awaking in a room full of smoking charcoal, that it is both starving and strangling. It cries now that in education we are starving for fresh knowledge, and are being stifled with old methods. People are beginning to think there must be some shorter and more practical cut to drawing than all the old road, with its blocks, perspective, diagrams, and geometry, ever indicated. These are all good in their way, but there is no practical easy introduction to the art. There is a growing belief that all study may be made easier. There may be no 'royal road' to mathematics, but that is no reason why the way to everything should be over corduroy planks and breakneck rocks. There must be work to win art or learning, but work need not be offensive.

There is a final plea to be offered for the introduction of industrial art into all schools. It is that by making *hand-work* a part of every child's education we shall destroy the vulgar prejudice against work as being itself vulgar. This we greatly need, for there is no country in the world where manual work is practically in so little respect, or where there are so many trying to get above it, as in this American republic. We have had those who proclaimed that work is only fit for negroes or mudsills. As it is, the native born citizen all too eagerly flies to any occupation in which, by wearing a black coat all day and keeping his hands soft, he makes one move nearer to being 'a gentleman.' It is only in my native land that I ever heard a man gravely boast, as a proof of his social superiority, that he had never done 'a day's work' in his life. While there are a few superior to this snobbishness, there are still millions who are practically enslaved by it. It arises from the fact that work—hand-work—is not as yet sufficiently identified with education and culture. Now, industrial art in schools, based on design and associated with studies, will go very far to make manual labour 'respectable' in the eyes of those professing democrats who pant for aristocracy as the hart for the water-brooks. The minor arts are as much associated as the fine arts with all that pertains to the very cream of culture. To know them at all is to know in time the names and works of Benvenuto Cellini, Albrecht Dürer—in a word, of all the great men whose names and works cast the highest splendour on splendid ages. The boy or girl who has gone even but a little way into industrial art visits the great museums and collections of this country or of Europe with a hundred times more real knowledge and appreciation of their magnificence than can the amateur who has only *read*, though it be 'never so wisely.' No boy or girl learns to design, model and carve, inlay and embroider, without in time reading with keenest interest Owen Jones, Labarthe, Fergusson, Whewell, and Dresser, with many more such writers. And with such practical knowledge and reading every object of taste and almost every book reveal beauties and awaken associations such as the many envy and the few possess; for the one who has worked in industrial art understands and feels decoration and beauty as no mere reader can. I once read through all that I could get on wood engraving, but two days' work at a block taught me more than a library on the subject could have done. For of all learning since books were invented there was never aught like experience, and of all experience there is none like one's own.

It should be remembered that industrial art may not only be taught in schools, but also form the subject or principle of a club, a society, or a private class, or be practised by a family or an individual. There should be indeed a ladies' industrial art association in every village. It will promote culture; it will or should lead to much reading of history and its social developments, and it will be a source of pecuniary profit.

It is to be supposed that in most instances these private societies will aid the local schools by teaching and by joint sales. Where even two or three unite for such a purpose they will find that mutual aid and consultation are quite equivalent to a teacher. Last, not least, I can assure them that the work is fascinating or agreeable to a degree which none can realise who has not attempted it. When asked what was most remarkable in the ladies' art club of which I am president, I replied, 'The love of the students for their work.'

EDUCATION, EMIGRATION, AND COLONISATION.

To make colonisation by the State a success, two things are necessary. First, it must at least form part of a system that will benefit not merely a few thousands of individuals, but the vast masses of the people of this country; and second, it must ensure the sending out of emigrants who will be of value to the colonies themselves, and not of those whose chief qualification is that they are unable to gain a livelihood in the mother country.

As to the first, it is plain that with such numbers of working men now unable to get employment, and with a population increasing at a rate not far short of 1,000 a day, any plan which would provide for the settlement, on farms, of one-twentieth of this number, while it would be valuable as a help, would never overtake this increase.

As to the second, if a colonist is to succeed in farming, he must be trained with at least some view to cultivating the soil, and to the self-help called for by an isolated position.

These are ends that are not to be attained in a day, or without cost; but I believe they may be reached in a few years by making certain changes in our machinery of education, which it is the object of this paper to explain, and which would not only meet the needs of the colonies, and greatly strengthen their connection with us, but would also remove some hardships in our present system of Board Schools, and make them more popular and more useful to the working classes than they now are.

The system of compulsory education initiated by William Edward Forster was in its day a step of incalculable importance; but we cannot stand still upon it, if the British Islands are to remain in the future what they have been in the past—a principal centre of commerce and industry, and a chief source of colonisation for other parts of the world.

The truth is that as a nation we are in the position in which almost every one of our manufacturers has been at some time during the last few years—that of finding that the advance of the times has compelled him to change his machinery for newer kinds, unless he would be shut out of competition or fall into an altogether inferior position.

It is true that steps are now being taken for the furtherance of technical education. The value of such training is unquestionable, since, without it, we are not likely to keep our ground in some directions against foreign competition. But this scheme deals with far too small a number of workmen—probably only some 12,000 or 14,000; while anything that is to keep pace with the increasing population must reach at least five-and-twenty times as many. It is impossible to make the whole nation skilled artisans; but it is perfectly practicable to make the entire population 'handy' men and women, and therefore more ready to become either skilled artisans or better workers in any other direction, no matter what.

The chief complaint against the present system is the length of time during which parents, who are ill able to afford it, are obliged to keep their children at school, thus preventing boys or girls from earning wages until they are thirteen or fourteen years of age. Of course the reply to this is that it is done in the interest of the children themselves; that is, some portion of the comfort of the family is sacrificed in the present in order to secure a larger measure of well-being to its younger members later on. If, however, the same end could be attained with a smaller present sacrifice of the child's wage-earning time, it would remove a real hardship, and greatly lessen the dislike that many have for the Board School system.

I believe that a far more useful education for the majority could be given if the subjects taught in the earliest stage of the compulsory system were confined to what are called the three R's—reading, writing, and arithmetic. Directly a child could pass in these, no matter what his age might be, his parents should have the option either of letting him continue in the day school, exactly as at present, or of his ceasing to attend the day school on condition of his going to an evening class for one hour six nights a week. While this would not interfere with the present arrangement, unless at the wish of the parents, it would, where the parents preferred it, release a boy who had mastered the means of self-education from being compelled to spend his mornings and afternoons over the desk, when he would be better employed in the fields, or in such work in a town as is suited to his age, and so by his earnings enable his father and mother to feed and clothe him more comfortably. This aims at no alteration in the Factory Acts; for fourteen years is quite young enough for a child to begin working among complicated machinery, and to be subjected to the rigid and monotonous life it entails.

The whole change turns upon the evening classes, which I would suggest being constituted as follows :—

On every alternate night—that is, three nights a week, the teaching to go on upon lines very similar to those of the present day schools. The other three nights to be devoted to handicraft training, *not* with the aim of teaching boys a trade, but certain simple things connected with a trade.

In large towns this might be done on the Board School premises; in small towns and in the country, in a carpenter's or wheelwright's shop, under the guidance of a journeyman of one or other of these trades. He would teach the boys under him simply the use of the saw and the chisel and auger, and the way to sharpen and set them. When a lad could make a tenon and mortise, and could dovetail and dowel, and fish a beam, all perfectly true and square, and could sharpen his tools properly, he should receive a certificate, to which I will return presently. It will be observed that I purposely omit the use of the plane; first, because so far as my boy is concerned, planing is an ornamental accomplishment, which he can acquire afterwards on his own account, if he is going to be a carpenter; while as a workman in any other line, or as a farm labourer, the occasional use of the saw and chisel is a hundred times more likely to fall to his lot than that of the plane; and next, because the lessons, whether in the school-room itself or anywhere else, would cause much less litter and much smaller risk of fire if no shavings were made.

A simple mode of examination would suffice. In the first place, let the journeyman or teacher in charge of each group of boys be furnished with a time-sheet, with their names and numbers, every lad writing his own initials, with the time of his coming to the class. On a given day the teacher sends in to the School Board two specimens of each of the subjects fitted by each boy, these specimens marked with a pencilled number corresponding to that he bears on the time-sheet. Only those boys who have been punctual in their attendance should have their work examined, failure in this point being in all cases treated as disqualifying for advancement.

The members of the Board themselves, unless they were sadly incapable, would be able to decide whether the pieces were well or badly done; or any joiner or coachbuilder or cabinet-maker would do it in an hour or two for a very large number of competitors.

Every lad who passed this test should receive a printed certificate, signed on behalf of the School Board; this, for simplicity, I will call his note of woodwork. The boy, on gaining it, to have the choice of which class he will next enter. Let us suppose he takes *iron*. He goes on the handicraft-class night to a forge or smithy, appointed by the Board, and is there taught to upset and weld iron of a given size, and to forge and cut the thread in a bolt and nut, the sides of which he is to file perfectly square and true.[1] For the examination, his pieces are stamped with his number by the smith, and sent in with the time-sheet, as already described, judged by some member of the Board, or any firm of engineers in the town, and the best ones passed. The successful lad now receives his iron-note, and, at his own desire, passes on, we will suppose, to the machine class. This is held in a shed, where he is taught to take to pieces, clean, and put together again two steam-engines, by different makers, and any other two machines approved by the School Board, say, in a country village, two agricultural implements. In this class

[1] Filing flat is a test of considerable skill. In talking over the item of welding with a Birmingham engineer of great experience, he suggested that it would add greatly to the value of the teaching, for a colonist, to include in it the welding and tempering of steel, so much needed in tools and agricultural implements. A further and special 'note' for steel would meet this.

Y

the examination might either be made by some mechanic appointed by the Board, or before a committee of the local or county Agricultural Society.

The fourth class might take the arrangement and lashing of poles for scaffolding, bridging streams, hut-building, derrick poles for lifting weights, and so on, including the making of knots. Men of the Royal Engineers, or any A.B. seamen, would make good teachers in this class.

The fifth class would be usefully devoted to basket-making, straw-hurdle work, &c. I do not, of course, suggest restricting the handicraft classes to these five kinds. It is enough if they roughly indicate the lines on which a change of great practical value might be made in the existing system of school teaching.

I now return to the three evenings per week which alternate with the handicraft classes. These would be in the main what the day school itself is; but they should include occasional ambulance lectures with practical lessons, and during the summer months, in all places where there are facilities for it, the boys should be taught swimming. Once a fortnight, or once a month, simple lectures should be given, with help of the blackboard, on the proper management of the animals with which we are most frequently brought into contact, especially in the country or in the colonies.[1]

The main subject taught should, however, be *geography*, to which one evening should be allotted weekly. Instead of beginning with a book I would take the blackboard or slate and let the boys learn to draw a local plan; say, in a town school, the lie of some of the principal streets and squares, with the public buildings, or, in a country school, making a sketch of some

[1] I would not, for instance, have any lad so ignorant as two of our well-known authors. Charles Dickens and his biographer Foster once drove some miles to see a friend, who happened on their arrival to be absent from home. As his man was also away, they tried to put up the horse themselves, but found their whole strength unequal to dragging off his collar. At last, after a suggestion by one of them that the animal's head must have got bigger since they had started, they asked the servant if she could help them. The girl came, called Dickens and his friend a pair of fools, turned the collar upside down and got it off. If Charles Dickens had become a state-aided colonist, it is painful to think of the fate that would have awaited his horses, never having their collars taken off, when once on, until they died in harness!

EDUCATION, EMIGRATION, AND COLONISATION

portion of the parish, with a farm or two, and their fields and roads.[1] Rising from this to the outlines of general geography, I would only use these so far as they are needful as a basis for teaching the geography of the British Colonies. Into this subject I would throw the chief force of the instruction, inasmuch as it would be the most important one for numbers of the scholars, helping to determine the whole future of their lives. The greatest care should therefore be bestowed on the text-books used in the teaching. They should be compiled under Government supervision, and revised at least every five years by the authorities of the colonies of which they treat. In this compilation and revision everything should be considered from the point of view of an intending emigrant: the nature and scope of the farming; the rates of wages in various trades; the demand for labour; the cost of living and amount of taxation, &c., as well as the time and expense of the passage from Great Britain. The effect of this teaching would be to familiarise the entire population of this country with the subject of emigration, and to substitute for the vague and often utterly erroneous notions associated with the names of Canada, Australia, New Zealand, or the Cape, an intelligent knowledge of what these countries are and of what they have to offer a new comer. The colony would no longer be to the masses of these isles a land that is very far off, but a home, not so very distant, in which they would find more comfort and greater prosperity than here.

The way in which I would bring the school training to lead practically to emigration, and through emigration to colonisation, is this. Each of the certificates or notes for wood, for iron, for machinery, &c., should carry with it a certain *borrowing value* in case the lad who had won it should decide on going to a British colony—say, for example, 30s., 40s., and 60s. respectively. Suppose a youth holding three of these notes applies to the Emigration Office, and asks to be sent to Manitoba. He

[1] Professor Huxley says boys ought to learn to draw, if it were only a pint pot. True: but the power gained in making the straight lines and curves that show the position of a street or of a house in the street, and which grows into the power to make a map of the British Isles, also carries with it the potentiality of indicating pint pots, and of planning and designing of every kind. We start with the most simple and most useful drawing, and work up, through pint pots, if need be, to Portland vases.

is told that the passage will be, say, 8*l*. 10*s*., and that he can at once have 6*l*. 10*s*. of this advanced to him if he will find the remaining 40*s*. At the same time he is informed that, as labour is more scarce in Assiniboia, a number of farmers there have notified their willingness to advance the balance needed over and above the Government grant to any lads holding three notes. He goes accordingly, finding on his arrival assured work and good wages. Meanwhile his certificates are retained in London as security for the repayment of the loan, plus six per cent. interest.[1] In twelve or eighteen months, or two years, he clears himself, and the endorsement on his notes that he has repaid now entitles him to precedence in getting one of the state-aided farms, each note being good for a grant of 20 acres. He has to wait, it may be, another year before his turn comes, and then with the experience gained and the further wages saved in the interval, he steps into a farm of 60 acres, of which in ten years more he will have paid off the purchase-money, with interest, and become the freeholder. I say with interest: for one good turn deserves another: and every man who has risen by the national help to a state of comfort and independence ought in this form to contribute to the National Emigration and Colonisation Fund, and so help others, and other generations, to rise as he has risen.[2]

But suppose a boy does not wish to emigrate: of what use would his certificates be to him? Of this use: that wherever and whenever he sought for work, whether as an apprentice or

[1] Six per cent. is a very reasonable interest in Western farms. Hundreds of thousands of pounds have been borrowed on Farm Mortgages in Iowa, &c., at six per cent. and even higher, and punctually repaid.

[2] I should also endeavour to come to an arrangement with each colony to make the production of handicraft notes from Great Britain the condition of naturalisation in such colony, inasmuch as it would be an effectual guarantee against pauper immigration.

The forms should be non-transferable, except in case of death, or by special permission of the local authority, to meet exceptional circumstances, until after five years' actual occupation by the grantee. Five years in any one situation, subject to clear record as to sentence from any court, whether for debt, misdemeanour, or crime, might fitly entitle the note-holder to the further privilege of free citizenship of the whole Empire (as suggested by Goldwin Smith); so that a Canadian, showing six months' residence in Bristol or Birmingham, could claim to be put on the Register; and the same with a Glasgow or a Leeds or a Derby man in Melbourne or New Westminster or Natal. This would be Imperialisation with a simple safeguard.

otherwise, he would be taken on in preference to any number of boys who could bring no such guarantees of their industry and ability. The idle boy, or the incompetent one, would by a process of natural selection find his exact level; the lads with no certificates would break stones on the road or sweep the streets, in the spare time between their professional duties of breaking one another's heads and picking pockets; those with one certificate would fill lower places than those with two; while the twos would come below the threes—and so on.

In the same way that I would make the possession of the handicraft notes the means of getting a farm in Canada or Australia, I would reward exceptional ability by giving any holder of four notes, who asked for it, a free scholarship for technical education of high grade. This would fit the cleverest boys into the places for which they are best adapted. And as the system got fully into work, after a given date no one should be eligible for a place in the police force, or for any other official employment unless he could show at least *two* notes. Under any system of education whatever, after ample notice—say, after the year 1900—it would surely be reasonable that no man should be allowed to record his vote at any election of any kind unless he could read and write.

I have said little about country schools, because, as over two-thirds of our population, unfortunately, live in towns, the education in towns is the more urgent question. But in rural districts, also, common sense should show that the training should be devoted chiefly to the work which boys will have to do to gain a livelihood; and the more this is kept in view the better will they be fitted, not only for life in a colony, but for farm life in England. In addition, therefore, to handicraft classes in a country or village school, there should be lessons, during the long light evenings, in hedging, rick-thatching, planting, pruning and grafting of fruit trees; the management of bees, poultry, and so on; while at agricultural meetings the competitions in ploughing, &c. might be largely extended, and every prize won at them followed by the grant of a handicraft note similar in character to those already described, though, in some cases, representing a smaller value.

A certain degree of elasticity should be allowed to meet the wants of exceptional districts, say, such as the inclusion of sheep management in Radnorshire and of quarrymen's work in Carnarvonshire; of net-making in fishing villages, and so on.

The chances are that, when once the plan had got into working order, the demand from Australia for lads holding 'shepherd notes' (certifying skill in shearing) would be always in excess of the supply, and that the Australian farmers would offer a special bounty on such notes, or at least advance liberally towards passage-money for the holders.

As speed is of course an important element in work, I would propose a moderate test applicable to nearly every kind of competition. Suppose, for example, a class of 50 boys are set to dig half a perch of ground each. They are placed in three or four rows, and start at a signal. As soon as each lad has finished his piece, he steps back from the rank, the teacher or trainer keeping count until 25 have fallen back, when the names are called over; and, subject to the work not being 'scamped,' these 25 would be passed and the others rejected, because they are below the average, which is represented by the latest boy of the first five-and-twenty. Of course the rejected ones might pass at a future match, unless they are physically weak or lazy.

I have said nothing about the training of girls, because my space will not admit of it; but the same broad principle will apply to them—that they ought to be taught to use their hands deftly in the work most likely to fall to their lot in daily life. It is of some consequence to a girl to be able to spell 'potatoes;' it is of fifty times more consequence that she should know how to boil them. It does not very much matter whether she knows where Russia is; she is not likely to go there: but it does matter very much whether she can light a fire without using half an apronful of sticks and half a box of matches, and taking half an hour to make it burn; or whether she can clean a room as it ought to be cleaned. An evening school in the summer, and an afternoon class in winter would enable girls in rural districts to earn wages at farm work, and still get an infinitely better education than under the present system of teaching them things that are of some use, but *not of the most use*, to them, and of leaving them grossly and ruinously ignorant of the A B C of housework.

To sum up: the plan I propose leaves it purely a voluntary

matter for every parent whether his child should go on with his schooling exactly as he does at present; or whether he should exchange part of that schooling for a class of work that will be more useful to him, and at the same time enable him to earn wages sooner. While somewhat less compulsory than the present system, it gives more stimulus to self-help, and offers a course which, to the infinite majority of boys, would be far more interesting, and therefore more heartily co-operated with.[1] It would train thoroughly for Emigration and for Colonisation the great mass of those whom Emigration would most help, and it would ensure a continual and healthy stream of Emigration of our own people to our own colonies: not driven away from us in the despair of poverty, but bound to the mother country by ties closer than any of which we have hitherto had experience; and therefore tending towards that federation of the colonies

---

[1] As to cost, it would be nearly, but probably not quite, self-supporting; because a small percentage of the boys, who turn out badly, would not redeem their 'notes.' But we must not forget what the cost of the *present system* is likely to be—'of letting things take their chance'—which means standing still, with our eyes open, and letting the house take fire from top to bottom before getting the engines to work on it. A Manchester manufacturer once told a visitor that he was losing a penny a day by every spindle he was running. 'Then why don't you stop?' was the natural remark. '*Because by stopping I should lose threehalfpence instead of a penny!*' he replied.

It is a question, not of *whether* the State shall aid, but of *which* it shall aid—hopeless pauperism or self-reliant industry; crime or thrift.

The migration of those who are deserving, and yet who can only get partial employ, to other parts of the Empire, means, not only more room and better chances of employ to those who are left behind, but the creation of a vast body of new customers for our manufactures—so that wages must rise. —I say, MIGRATION; for should anything similar to this scheme be adopted, this word might fitly be used in speaking of removal to any part of Greater Britain; and EMIGRATION, in reference to foreign lands.

By releasing children from the day school, say, on an average of one year sooner than at present (continuing at evening schools, if needful, three or even four years longer), some 1,000,000 more than at present would be free to earn wages. The less of factory life for them the better; and without factory work the earnings would be lower—but even an average of 1s. 9d. per week would give over 4½ millions per year extra earnings among the working classes. In addition to this must be taken into account the enormous increase in the skill of the whole industrial population, which must result from the improved training, and which means *increase in power of earning wages*. Besides this, interesting occupation would lead to some diminution of low and debasing amusements, and therefore of crime, and the cost of repressing it.

with the British Islands which may be the alternative to their ceasing to form part of the Empire.

Since this scheme was drafted the admirable letters have appeared in the 'Times' on Education, by Samuel Smith, which in some points put the case better than I have done, though not on the same lines.

JOHN BELLOWS.

Gloucester: November 28, 1887.

EDUCATION IN GERMANY.

TO THE EDITOR OF THE 'TIMES.'

SIR,—I should be glad if you could find space in your columns for some remarks on the state of education in Germany. I have just completed a short tour in this country mainly to inquire into its educational system, especially with reference to primary and technical schools. England has at last roused herself to the necessity for technical education.

The Bill, which was unhappily crowded out last session, will be reproduced next year, and, I trust, expanded to larger dimensions. It will contain, I hope, a clause for the establishment of evening continuation schools, for which object I gave notice of an amendment last session. My trip to Germany has been chiefly taken to learn what is doing here in this direction, and what is the drift of educated German opinion. With your permission I will briefly summarise my impressions. I premise by observing that each State of the German Empire manages its own education, and that the laws and regulations differ somewhat, so that general statements referring to all Germany cannot be made without qualifications. I will not weary your readers, however, by going into details respecting each State, but place broadly before them the general features of German education.

The salient fact which strikes all observers is the universality of good education in this country. There is no such thing as an uneducated class; there are no such things, speaking broadly, as neglected and uncared-for children. All classes of the community are better educated than the corresponding ones in our country; and this applies quite as much to primary as to secondary education. Nothing struck me more than the general intelligence of the humbler working classes. Waiters, porters, guides, &c., have a knowledge of history, geography, and other subjects far beyond that possessed by corresponding classes in England; and the reason is not far to seek. The whole population has long been passed through a thorough and comprehensive system of instruction, obligatory by law, and far more extended than is given in our elementary schools. I went through several of these schools and observed the method of teaching, which was simply admirable. The children are not crammed, but are taught to reason from the earliest stages. The first object of the teacher is to make his pupils comprehend the meaning of everything they learn, and to carry them from stage to stage so as to keep up an eager interest.

I saw no signs of weariness or apathy among either teachers or scholars. The teaching was all *vivâ voce*, the teacher always standing beside the blackboard and illustrating his subject by object lessons. The instruction was through the eye and the hand as well as the ear, and question and answer succeeded so sharply as to keep the whole class on the *qui vive*. The teachers are, as a body, much better trained than in England, and seem to be enthusiasts in their calling, and the school holds a far higher position in the social economy of the country than it does with us. What I am saying here applies equally to Switzerland as to Germany, and for educational progress Zurich will compare with any part of this empire. The main advantage, however, that primary education has in Germany over England lies in the regularity of attendance and the longer period of school life. There is none of the difficulty of getting children to school that exists in England; the laws are very rigid, and permit no frivolous excuses; and, what is even more important, the people entirely acquiesce in the laws, and are inclined rather to increase than to relax their rigour. It is well known that in London and all our great cities a large part of the population seek to avoid school attendance by every means in their power, and consequently the attendance is most irregular. There is very little of this in Germany; at least, I have not found it so. Then in our country a great portion of our children are withdrawn altogether from school, after passing the fourth or fifth standard, at the age of eleven or twelve, whereas in Germany almost every attendance is compulsory until fourteen for boys, though in some places girls are allowed to leave at thirteen.

This last point is the one I wish to emphasise. The great defect—I might almost call it the fatal defect—of our system is that it stops just at the time when real education should begin. It allows a child to leave school at an age when its learning is soon forgotten and its discipline effaced. It is hardly too much to say that the two years' additional training the German child receives in the elementary school doubles its chance in life as compared with the English child.

But this is not all. The Germans are rapidly developing a system of evening continuation classes, which carry on education for two or three years longer. In Saxony the boys who leave the primary school, if they do not go to the higher schools, must attend for three years longer—say until they are seventeen —continuation classes for at least five hours per week. But teaching is provided for them, and they are encouraged to attend twelve hours per week. So complete is this system that even the waiters at the hotels up to the age of seventeen attend afternoon classes, and are taught one or two foreign languages. I take Saxony as one of the most advanced states; but the law is much the same in Würtemburg and Baden, and the system is found to work so well that it is in contemplation to extend it to all the states in the German Empire, and Austria will probably follow suit. This is confidently expected to happen in the course of 1888. I may state, as an undoubted fact, that in Germany and Switzerland, and I believe in some other Continental countries, the opinion is ripening into a conviction that the education, even of the poorest class, should be continued, in some form or another, to the age of sixteen or seventeen. They find by experience that wherever this is adopted it gives an enormous advantage to the people in the competition of life, and, above all, trains them to habits of industry and mental application. I believe it is owing to this system of thorough education that Germany has almost extinguished the pauper and semi-pauper class, which is the bane and disgrace of our country.

Wherever I have gone I have inquired how they deal with the ragged and squalid class of children, and I have been told in every city I visited—in Zurich, Stuttgart, Nuremburg, Chemnitz, Dresden, and Berlin—that such a class practically does not exist. I do not mean that there is not poverty and plenty of it in Germany. Wages are much lower than in England, and many have a hard struggle to live. But there does not seem to exist to any extent that mass of sunken degraded beings who with us cast their children upon the streets, or throw them on the rates, or leave them to charity. Some half a million of children in the United Kingdom are dependent, more or less, on the alms or the rates of the community, and probably another half-million are miserably underfed and underclad. Nothing to correspond with this exists in Germany. The poorest people here would be ashamed to treat their children as multitudes do with us. Indeed, I have not seen since I left home a single case of a ragged or begging child. I repeat that the great cause of this, both in Germany and Switzerland, is the far greater care they have taken of the education of the children for at least two or three generations, whereas we have only taken the matter up seriously since 1870, when Mr. Forster's great Act was passed.

Let us contrast the general condition of our London children, for instance, at the age of fifteen or sixteen, with that of the same class in Berlin or Dresden or Chemnitz. With us nine-tenths of the children have long since left school, and a too large proportion of them are receiving no training but the coarse and brutalising education of the streets. Most of them retain little of what they have learnt at school, except the power to read the 'penny dreadful,' which stuffs their minds with everything a child should not know. They are to a very large extent adepts in profane and obscene language, and are frequenters of the public-house, the 'penny gaff,' and such like amusements: a great many of them are learning no useful trade or calling, but are drifting helplessly into the class of wretched, ill-paid, casual labourers. Very many of them marry before they are twenty, and are soon the parents of a numerous progeny, half starved and stunted both in body and mind. Compare, or rather contrast this with Germany. At fifteen or sixteen a great part of the children are still under excellent instruction.

Exceedingly few are to be found roaming about the streets. They are prohibited, at least in some parts of Germany, from entering the public-houses (except with their parents) until the age of seventeen, and I am told are everywhere prohibited from smoking until sixteen. In fact, there are, both by law and public sentiment, barriers placed against the corruption of the young which do not exist in England.

No country has ever suffered more from the abuse of the idea of individual liberty than England has done. Owing to this overstrained idea we did not get compulsory education until long after the advanced nations of the Continent, and still we are far behind them in the care we take of our children. It is intolerable that this state of things should continue longer. Democratic government everywhere insists upon good education, and expects each citizen to fulfil his duties to the State.

Public opinion in our country will certainly insist, and that before long, that we shall not be for ever disgraced with a residuum of the most drunken, demoralised, and utterly incapable population to be found in any modern state. It will insist that some time be spared for the solution of this vital question from the wrangles of party politics and the party recriminations of party leaders. When one sees what a poor country like Germany has done to raise its people in spite of the conscription and three years' compulsory military service, in spite of frequent and exhausting wars, from which our island home has been free, one has grave doubts whether our system of party government is not a failure.

Certainly we waste on barren conflicts and wordy strife far more time than other nations do in the conduct of their affairs. They direct their energies with business-like precision to supply the exact needs of the people; we fritter away our enormous political energy in fruitless party contests, which every year degrade Parliament lower and lower, and make it less and less fit for the practical work of governing the nation.

One thing seems certain : unless we can give more attention to the vital questions which concern the welfare of the masses, our country must go down in the scale of nations. No honest observer can doubt that in many respects the Germans are already ahead of us, and they are making far more rapid progress than we are. They are applying technical science to every department of industry in a way that Englishmen have little idea of. Their polytechnics and their practical technical schools are far ahead of anything we possess in England, the leaders of industry are far better trained, the workmen are better educated and far more temperate and thrifty than ours are. Wherever the Germans and English are coming into competition upon equal terms, the Germans are beating us. This is not because the Germans have greater natural power. I believe the British race is the more vigorous naturally. But they are organised, disciplined, and trained far better than we are. They bring science to bear upon every department of the national life; whereas we, up till lately, resented all State interference, and so exaggerated the doctrines of freedom as almost to glory in our abuses.

There is much more that I might say if space permitted, but it will not do to trespass further on your indulgence. I will only add in conclusion that England must wake up, and that immediately, to the necessity of a far more thorough and practical system of education, else she will lose the great place she has hitherto held in the world's history.—I am, sir, yours faithfully,

SAMUEL SMITH.

Berlin: Oct. 4.

EVENING SCHOOLS UNDER HEALTHY CONDITIONS.

BY THE REV. J. B. PATON, D.D.

EDUCATIONAL Agencies have been formed and are being widely established in the country which, speaking generally, are adapted to our youth from sixteen to eighteen years of age and upwards. I refer particularly to the University Extension and South Kensington classes. Thus the educational ladder has been let down from above to this level. Meanwhile this ladder has been set up from below, so that our children mount on it till they are thirteen years old (the age at which the great proportion of our children leave the elementary schools, having passed the standard that gives exemption from school); or, if they are half-timers, till they are fourteen years old. Now, there is a terrible gap here between the years of thirteen and sixteen or seventeen, which it is of the utmost moment to fill up. It will be seen that I have in my mind, in speaking thus, the great mass of the children of our industrial classes, and not the comparatively few who attend the higher-grade elementary schools, or other secondary schools, which connect at once with the South Kensington and popular University classes, and other educational agencies. And speaking of that great mass, it may be said that, so far as regards the intellectual, technical, and humane interests which education promotes, they pass from the school to the streets, where these interests are trodden underfoot; they fall into a gulf, where, so far as regards the higher good which education may bring to life, they are almost irretrievably lost;—so few are able, by enormous exertions in later years, to creep up from the abyss into which they had fallen. That gulf must be bridged over.

I read in a very powerful letter, which appeared in a Manchester paper last September, these words: 'A foreman in a large mill informs me that he makes it a point to ascertain how far the boys and girls employed about him are keeping up their school knowledge. He finds that only about 4 per cent. are making any progress, these go to night schools; the others, 96 per cent., are relapsing into their primitive ignorance, &c.' This calculation, so far as my inquiries have gone, represents fairly, I think, the average in our large towns; and I cannot speak of country districts. Dr. Percival sent questions to all the head masters of elementary schools in Bristol last year, asking them how many boys and girls had left their school, after passing the fifth standard, or any higher standard, between January 1st, 1883, and January 1st, 1884, and how many of these continued their education by attending night schools and otherwise. The following figures sum up the answers: 776 boys and 409 girls left school after passing the fifth or higher standard, and of these 67 boys and 58 girls were continuing their education somehow, more or less. Many of these girls, however, were pupil teachers, so that the proportion continuing their education (even of this higher order of scholars who had passed the fifth or higher standard) was not more than 1 in 10 or 11. But if we consider the number of children leaving in the lower standards, probably the proportion even in Bristol, which is a highly favoured town, will be very little higher than the proportion of children working in the Manchester mill. And the Educational Returns for last year startle us with the lamentable fact that the number of our night schools and the scholars attending them are rapidly decreasing. During the year the number of schools had fallen from 932 to 847, and the number of scholars qualified by attendance for examination from 32,937 to 28,588. Doubtless this decrease is partly explained by the change in the character of night schools. They are not needed so much now to teach the first elements to youths and adults, who had little or no schooling in their childhood. They must now be 'continuation' schools, to continue the instruction of children who have left the day school, so as to conserve and increase the knowledge they learnt there, and to help them in applying that knowledge to the manifold uses of life. Still the statistics show that there is a falling off alike in the older and younger scholars, and thus show that while the old need and use of the night school are passing away, the new and higher use of the night school, as a continuation school, is not yet in vogue.

Now what a contrast to this state of things we find on the Continent, especially in Germany, Switzerland, Belgium, and Holland. In Germany, *e.g.*, where the law enforces attendance at the day school till the child is fourteen years of age, it also enforces attendance, two evenings a week, two hours an evening, in the 'Fortbildungs-Schule,' or continuation school, till the scholar is sixteen years of age. And in some towns this is not held to be enough. In Chemnitz, *e.g.*, a town of Saxony with a population of 92,000 inhabitants, the Handwerker-Verein, or Workmen's Union, have an evening continuation school, with a far completer programme of subjects and classes than the State continuation school, and it was attended last year by 2,066 scholars—a fact which speaks volumes, and is full at once of warning and exhortation to us.

For, think what is implied in the statement I have made. First we build up at immense expense a colossal system of primary education, and then see and allow the results of it to be very largely wasted and lost. Teachers speak dismally of the havoc of the fruit of their labour in the first two years after school is left. The Manchester correspondent, whom I have already quoted, says justly : 'The garden which by daily culture has been brought into such an admirable and promising condition is given over to utter neglect; the money, the time, the labour bestowed upon it are lost. We cease to educate at the most important, most plastic, most receptive period of life.' Secondly, we have, I said, let down a ladder to the people for their Higher Education, but at present for the great mass of them it is left dangling in the air out of their reach. One fact roused my attention to the urgency of this question nine years ago. I was told by an intelligent mechanic that he had joined the South Kensington class for mechanics with some twenty young men like himself, but he was the only one who had struggled through the winter and passed his examination at the close of the session ; all the rest had dropped out of the class, one by one, in sheer despair. They had lost the little knowledge once acquired by which they might have learnt more. And their mental faculties, coated with rust from long disuse, so creaked and groaned when set to work again, that the poor fellows gave up the too irksome toil. And so our noble schemes for the elevation of our working people are, to a large extent, abortive. Thirdly, technical education, if it is to avail this country so as to enable her to keep her place at the head of the industrial countries of the world, must reach the working classes and inform their handiwork with the deftness and skill which trained intelligence alone can give to labour. Much is being done to extend technical education, and the necessity is urgent; but at present these efforts reach only a very few of the labouring classes, for they demand knowledge and faculty on the part of the pupil, which our children, at thirteen, when they leave school, do not possess—and how much less at fifteen, after the lapse of two years towards (as our correspondent said) primitive ignorance ! But, lastly, education is not for labour only, but for life ; and the years between thirteen and seventeen are the critical and formative years for every human being. Then the physical energies of the body, as in a spring tide, thrill out into every limb and organ. Then the callow brood of instinctive desires, both intellectual and social, are agape, and young native faculties shoot out in rapid, random growth. Then, if ever, is the need of education to guide, restrain, inspire. In these years character is formed and destiny made, almost unalterably. And in these years first the need and use of knowledge begin to be seen, as it quickens and directs the mind for the wise enjoyment, the true understanding, and the right conduct of life. Yet it is just in these all-important years, during which other classes of society know that education is most needed and valuable, that the mass of our working children are robbed of its blessing. Here, then, I say, is the paramount problem of our time in relation to the education of the people.

And now that I may approach more nearly the subject of my paper, let us examine and state precisely the problem we have to solve. The large majority of children leave the elementary school at, or soon after, thirteen, or, if half-timers, at fourteen; they then begin to work for ten hours a day. Unfortunately great numbers of them leave school with little liking for it, or interest in the subjects they have learnt there. They are tired with their hard day's work, and revel in the freedom of the evening hours when work is done and they can frolic with companions. We have no compulsory law, as in Germany, to drag them, however reluctant, to school, and for the present let me say, by way of parenthesis, I hope we shall not have one. Yet these children have begun the business of their life, and, in a dim way, the sense of the realities of life comes upon them thus early. They begin to see that their success in their trade will depend upon their superior skill and their industry, and they also scent from afar some of the high pleasures and responsibilities that lie before them in that manhood or womanhood which glimmers wondrously through a golden haze in prospect. And their nature opens out with strange yearnings, and sometimes fierce impulses and activities, of the true meaning and measure of which they are ignorant. Now it is for these children, under these circumstances, we wish to provide some helpful education. It is added, in the subject given me, education *under healthy conditions*, which is almost, to my mind, tautological, for that alone is education which yields *health* as its fruit, *i.e.*, the vigorous, free, harmonious and happy use of all the faculties of our nature, which we rightly name health; and surely health cannot be attained save under healthy or health-giving conditions.

Now how can any true education be given to children—circumstanced as we have seen—in the evening hours of the day, which alone are available? Plainly, in the first instance, the education must be such as will attract, interest, and recreate tired children. It has to compete with the social gambollings of the street, or even with the gaudy, specious amusements which too early allure them. Then, in the second place, the education must touch and draw forth the opening nature of children of that age, so that the instinctive impulses and growing powers of their body and soul shall be rightly nourished and trained. And, lastly, the education must bear directly upon the work of their daily business, making it luminous with the light of intelligence, and making them, in the old sense of the word, cunning craftsmen therein; and also upon the pure enjoyments of life that are possible to them, and the noble duties of life that devolve on them.

It is in the light of these three principles that I suggest the following scheme of an evening school, which is educational throughout, but is two-sided, one side being recreative and the other instructive. Thus, looking at the one side of the evening school, the recreative, there should be (1) rhythmic or musical drill, *i.e.*, calisthenic exercises, and pleasant orderly movements, accompanied and inspired by music. The bodies of the children need the refreshment of play, and the minds want the stimulus of bright companionship. Let them have these in such exercises, —brighter and pleasanter than aught they can have in the street; whilst by means of them, at the same time, their bodies are trained to graceful movement, and the grace wrought upon rude bodies will work inwardly and subtly upon the rude minds and manners; and, in addition, the instinct of obedience and the love of order will grow as moral habits to ennoble their future life. There should be (2) much singing of good songs—good both in their music and in their words,—this, not only because of the inspiring influence of good music in itself, but because of the power it has to make whatever truth it wings on its pulsing harmonies to thrill and reverberate with a strange power in the hidden places of the soul where are the springs of life. And (3) there should be along with the recreation of harmonious movement and sound, the refreshing stimulus of light, by the constant use of the magic or projection lantern. Eyes wearied with long labour in the day cannot endure the fatigue of much book-work by night, but they are revived and charmed by the splendour of gay colour and brilliant light. This, which attracts them like moths to places of amusement, may be used to attract and refresh them in the evening school; and whilst attracting them, the magic lantern may also be made the most potent instrument of instruction, for we are only beginning to learn its powers and uses as an educational agent.

And looking at the other side of the evening school—the instructive—we must consider both the method and subjects of instruction.

1. If we think of the children and youths we teach we shall agree that the teaching (1) should be largely oral teaching, and such as will provoke the pupils to, or by, frequent questioning. The eye of the youth is weary—not the ear; and the vivacity of earnest colloquial instruction, reinforced by the use of the blackboard and rapid interplay of question and answer, operates like an electric current though a glass; (2) it should be, as far as possible, object teaching, so as to give it actuality, because dealing with things which children see and which belong to the world they live in; and (3) it should be freely illustrated with diagrams and pictures, or better still, simple experiments. All of us remember the wondering delight and new revelation of truth given to us when young by such experiments, and to the youths we deal with they mean and do far more than for such as my readers.

2. Now, as to the subjects of our instruction, let it be remembered that we can use the 'three R's' which the Government demand in the schools which they support, so that they may have an interest and give an education quite apart from the mere technical knowledge of reading, writing, and counting. The reading lessons can relate to the business of the boy himself, or of the town he lives in; to birds, beasts, trees and flowers of the country round about; or to the duties and joys of the life that is before him. Writing can be taught in the writing

of a letter, the description of a piece of work, the portraiture of a hero, the enforcement of a duty ; and arithmetic at every stage can get its examples from the life-work of the scholars, so as to fit them for it. In speaking of the two class subjects, I cannot but express my gratitude to the Government for having this year made drawing a class subject, so that the teaching of it will now be amply rewarded in the night schools. This I consider the greatest advance made of late years. On the Continent they insist everywhere on Drawing as the very foundation of technical instruction, because by it the eye and hand are trained to act in concert, and are respectively trained to the correct perception and production of form. Hitherto this essential element, the necessary beginning of all skilled handicraft, which also attracts a boy of the night-school age, whose life seems to be budding out in his finger-tips, so that he wants to be doing something with them, has been practically tabooed from our night school —a fatal mistake. Now it will be, I trust, universal and conspicuous. As to the other class, or specific, subject, which is allowed in the night school, girls will find that which interests them in itself, and will prepare their future life, in Domestic Economy, with its continuation of Elementary Lessons in Cookery ; and boys will probably find such a subject in some elementary science, whose principles are applied in the trade of their daily occupation, and which will be capable of delightful experimental illustration. One more subject, however, which Government does not at present encourage should find a place in a night school, because of the healthy relief it affords to other subjects, because of the pleasure it yields to boys of that age, and especially because of the relation it bears to further technical training in later years. I mean modelling, carving, or design in form and colour. The working lad of fourteen and fifteen is in, what I might not inaptly call, the Red Indian stage of mental development. His hands itch to cut and whittle out things of rude form, and his fancy is fascinated by garish peacock colours. Then let us take these eager instincts as they rise in his mind, and use them for our purpose to lure him to school and delight him in school, whilst we imbue and elevate these instincts with the true sense of beauty, and thus at once give him artistic skill in his trade, and a soul to enjoy the endless beauty which shines in the world around him.

An evening school, thus arranged as to subjects, and in which the more arduous teaching is thus mixed with recreative enjoyments, is an evening school under healthy conditions, and one that will solve the problem which is for me the pressing educational problem of the present, so far as the people are concerned.

Let me in a few words indicate how such schools can be secured and made successful. First, the Government has done much during the last three years, and especially in their last concession. There are, however, three things we must still solicit from them : (1) There should be a small, and it need be very small, grant for singing, and for modelling, carving, or designing. (2) It is preposterous to expect that with the weary children whom we teach in night schools we can hope to do as much in 60 attendances as is done in elementary schools with 400 attendances; yet this is practically demanded now when our night-school children must do the work of one standard in five subjects. The London School Board have, with reason, insisted and entreated that a half standard's work should alone be required in a winter's session at the night school; in other words, let the standards be divided for night schools. And (3) seeing that by the very conditions of night-school work we cannot cram the memory with book-lore, whilst we can and must quicken the intelligence in other ways, through the ear and by the eye, the examination should be conducted in view of this necessity of the case—should therefore be more elastic in its method and more observant of the general intelligence that is developed than of the multitude of facts accurately remembered. Or, if the examination must be thus precise—dooming an evening school, perforce, to heavy failures in it—let compensation be given by a merit grant, as in day schools, which shall be given for those qualities of good order, quickness of mind, and manifest interest of the children in their class subjects, which can and should be pre-eminent in the night school.

But if our night schools are to be effective and successful, it must be through the action of the School Boards, whose influence is immense in enlisting the right teachers for them, in encouraging children leaving school to continue in them, and in arousing the co-operation of all classes of the community to work for their success. In this good work the London and

Glasgow School Boards have set an example to be followed. The Nottingham School Board also has rendered good service, and in one respect has, I think, found the key to the solution of many difficulties connected with night schools. They have appointed seven working-men to be managers of each night school, and the thirty-five men, who have thus been appointed to our five schools, have so laboured during this year of their service that the numbers in attendance have been doubled, and next year will show far greater results. This is pre-eminently a working-man's question. It is only in the night school that his children can climb the educational ladder. Accordingly these working-men have appealed to clergymen, Sunday-school teachers, employers of labour, and to the leaders of trade-unions to use their influence to induce the children to go to these schools. And in ways which I cannot detail now they have added to the attractions of the school, and safeguarded its healthy conditions.

To these seven working-men we shall ask the School Board to add two lady managers in each school, who shall be associated with them, and who will take special charge of the girls' school and aid the working men in clerkly duties which are irksome to them. Then we have formed an association in Nottingham for the promotion of night schools in the town and county. This association is composed of two classes of members, (1) those contributing a little towards expenses which the Board cannot pay, and (2) those assisting in the teaching and recreation of the school. Some of the work done in the night school must be done by volunteers—or at least by those who are not remunerated by the Board, for the Board cannot pay for more than Government sanctions. Yet more must be done, as I have said, to give us Night Schools under Healthy Conditions.

PRINTED BY
SPOTTISWOODE AND CO., NEW-STREET SQUARE
LONDON

Second Edition. Crown 8vo. ONE SHILLING, boards; 5s. cloth.

SOCIAL ARROWS.

A SERIES OF ARTICLES REPRINTED FROM MAGAZINES AND NEWSPAPERS.

By the EARL OF MEATH
(Lord Brabazon).

CONTENTS.

OPEN SPACES.
1. Health and Physique of our City Populations.
2. A Plea for Public Playgrounds.
3. Open Spaces and the Cultivation of Flowers.
4. Open Spaces and Physical Education.

ASSOCIATIONS FOR THE BENEFIT OF YOUNG MEN, WOMEN, AND CHILDREN.
1. A Woman's Work.
2. Address to the Dublin Young Men's Christian Association.
3. The Welfare of Young Men.
4. The Ministering Children's League.
5. Gordon Division of the Ministering League.

OVER-POPULATION: ITS EVILS AND REMEDIES.
1. State-Directed Colonisation: its Necessity.
2. Great Cities and Social Reform.
3. Some Suggested Remedies for Over-Population and its Attendant Evils.

THE CAUSE OF THE OVER-WORKED SHOP-ASSISTANT.
1. The Shop Hours League.
2. The Early Closing Movement.
3. Sir John Lubbock's Shop Hours Regulation Bill and the Compulsory Closing of Shops.

SOME SOCIAL WANTS OF LONDON.
1. Public Wash-Houses, Laundries, and Swimming Baths.
2. Clubs for Young Men and Women.

THE DUTY OF THE CHURCH IN RESPECT TO RECREATION AND LITERATURE.

THE NEED OF NATIONAL INDUSTRIAL AND TECHNICAL TRAINING.

AN APPEAL TO MEN OF LEISURE.

AN APPEAL TO MEN OF WEALTH.

London: LONGMANS, GREEN, & CO.

www.ingramcontent.com/pod-product-compliance
Lightning Source LLC
Chambersburg PA
CBHW032357230426
43672CB00007B/729